Dance with Angels

A Journey of Grief and Healing

Exploring Religion, Science,

Spirituality, and

What happens after you die?

Warwick Dunnett

Published by Lighthouse Lane Books

LightHouseLaneBooks.com

Dance with Angels is a work of nonfiction. Some names and identifying details have been changed to protect the privacy of individuals.

Library of Congress Control Number: 2026901475

ISBN (Paperback): 979-8-9942899-0-7

ISBN (eBook): 979-8-9942899-1-4

ISBN (Special Edition Hardcover): 979-8-9942899-2-1

(Audiobook): At LighthouseLaneBooks.com (expected mid. 2026)

Cover design:

Jacqueline Dunnett

Dragan Bilic (dragan74@gmail.com)

Interior design:

Dragan Bilic

Special edition is printed in the UK.

Paperback is printed in the USA

First edition: 2026

Contents

The Smaller Faiths

Commonality

This book is dedicated to:

Harrison *Subvers!ve* Dunnett

1996-2016

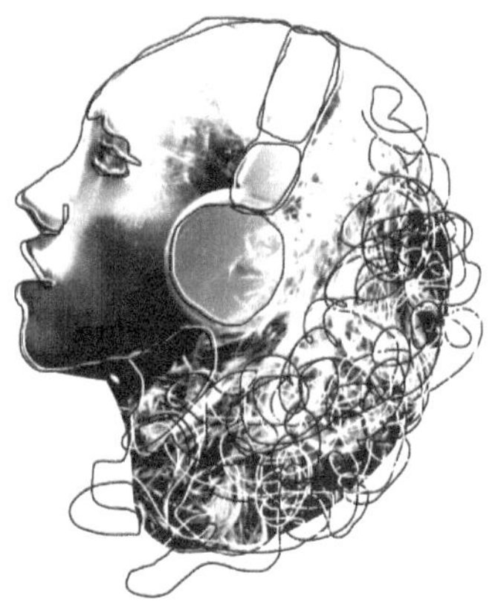

Singer, Songwriter, Poet

The title

Dance with Angels

was inspired by TobMac's beautiful song

21 Years.

Our Journey Forward After Loss

Thank you for taking this journey and purchasing *Dance with Angels*, a story of dealing with grief and discovery, to compare different beliefs and understand what happens after a loved one dies. In doing so, I hope you find a belief, as I did, that will help overcome some of your grief and suffering.

We all face the same destiny with death when we lose people we love and care for. Have you ever wondered what happens after we die or whether our loved ones are really in a better place? I wanted to know if we truly *Dance with Angels* after we die, or if we simply disappear. Is there no afterlife, no transfer of energy, and no reincarnation, or is there a destiny we can believe in with a degree of conviction?

Many people rely on a belief structure to help them with this dilemma without genuinely understanding the realities and truth behind what they grab onto. Others, like me and possibly you, want more information, answers, and proof before deciding on this lifelong mystery.

> *Losing my amazing 20-year-old son to preventable death caused by wrongdoing and insurance fraud left me devastated for years.*

After his death and the initial wave of emotions, unanswered questions, and disbelief subsided, I wanted to find a way to ease the pain and grief. I embarked on a search for a belief structure and a sense of community that could support me and give me some reason for living. However, I was also determined not to just grasp the most straightforward answer to help me through the darkness — a belief in God and a religious doctrine that tells me, *He went to heaven and is in a better place*. I needed more…

> *I wanted to solve the mystery of what happened to my lovely boy's energy, love, and spirit and come up with the most plausible explanation of what happens when our spirit and body part ways.*
>
> *I needed to find something that I could believe in. I have, and I hope you do as well.*

The News

Flying for a living can be a lonely game. Glamorous to some, yes. But to the seasoned pilot who's been around the world hundreds of times, the 17-odd days *on the road* each month away from your family seem to grow longer as your career folds itself into the fourth decade of disturbed sleep and hours of monotony interrupted by very brief periods of intense focus. Mainly, life as an international pilot involves many intervals of fatigue and loneliness in foreign lands, with layovers in hotel rooms far away from family and friends.

It was a freezing cold day on December 31st, 2016, when I arrived in Anchorage, Alaska, from a trip to China via Australia. For the first time in at least 15 years, I'd missed Christmas with my children. I was comforted that my son, Harrison, was safe in a Los Angeles rehab facility after three weeks of total sobriety. He had one more week before he would be attending his dream music school in LA.

My daughter, Jacqueline, was in Tahoe skiing with friends. Still, I wanted to get back to San Francisco as soon as possible, so after four hours of sleep in a hotel, I jumped on a midnight flight out of Anchorage to San Francisco via Seattle, arriving early on the morning of January 1st, 2017. Once again, I was fatigued and looking forward to getting home and sleeping in a familiar bed.

Only a few minutes from my house, sometime around 9 am, I stopped at a Starbucks for coffee and took a bathroom break. In that neon-lit bathroom surrounded by the stench of disinfectant and blinding light, *I, like many other people who suffer sudden loss, received a call that changed my life forever.* I'll never forget that room or the call. It was my ex-wife, Gail. Through her sobbing pain and gasps of air, I heard the words…

"Harrison is dead."

For the first few minutes after the terrible news of Harrison's death, I was overcome with total disbelief and confusion. All I could say was, "No." There was no rational thought. It was simply a refusal to believe. I asked questions, but the answers weren't sinking in. Again, the word "No" kept coming out of my mouth. A surreal "No," as if I'd disconnected from my life and was no longer a part of the scene around me.

You know this feeling if you've experienced the crippling shock of receiving an unexpected message that you've lost a child or somebody you deeply love. It's like the mind fogginess when you awaken from a dream. Confusion and an inability to figure out what's happening overwhelms your ability to think. As TobyMac says in the lyrics of *21 Years* says… "My heart was shattered in a thousand ways." The realisation of that sets in later, after the initial shock and denial hits you, but when I first heard the devastating news, my reaction was more physical and one that can better be described as a case of mental shock. Initially, all I could do was shake my head in confusion, cry, try to breathe, and utter "No" over and over.

Finally, I was able to say to Gail, who was still crying on the phone, "He's only 20, healthy, in love, happy, and safe. How can he be dead? It just isn't possible. There must be some mistake—a mistake! It can't be real. I want to see him and make sure it's Harrison. It can't be him!"

She, too, was overcome with confusion and pain. "They won't let us see him," she said.

I wanted to be with him so desperately, to hold him and make sure it was him they were talking about. It seemed so impossible to fathom.

As I was speaking to Gail, I noticed an incoming call from Jacqueline and declined it. "We can't tell her until we're sure," I thought. Neither of us could believe this was real, much less tell our daughter the news. I declined the call a second time. Then Jacqueline called back a third time.

"She must know," I said to Gail, "but how?" Taking a deep breath, I answered. I was scared to speak, but before I could even try, Jacqueline said, "It's not true, is it? Harrison's okay, right?"

Jacqueline had received a notification and a picture of her dead brother over a social media platform before we could even tell her.

Harrison's girlfriend from the rehab facility, whom he'd fallen so desperately in love with, had just posted a picture of Harrison, dead, with the byline, *My boyfriend has just died.*

Of course, I didn't go home. Jacqueline was our first concern. With insufficient sleep and exhausted, I immediately began the four-hour drive from that fateful Starbucks near Mill Valley to

Lake Tahoe to be with her and hold her. As much for myself as for her, I suppose. We needed to bear the terrible shock together.

I felt an urgency to fix this, do anything I could, and act, but all I could do was drive to be with my daughter. When you receive news of a terrible loss, you reach immediately for those closest to you. My need to be with my lovely daughter was so overwhelming that overcoming my exhaustion, shock, and pain wasn't an issue. After having had only four hours of sleep in the last 24 hours, having been up all the previous day and the night before, working and travelling to get home, I immediately started driving to Lake Tahoe to be with my poor daughter. We were both in shock!

Not long after lunchtime on January 1st, I pulled up to the motel where Jacqueline was staying in Tahoe and determined to hold it together for a while, at least long enough to let her know that there was a rock she could cling to.

Little did she know that her rock of a father was teetering on a cliff of despair. I got out of my car, and she came out of her room to greet me. We just held each other and cried.

It was over a month before they let us see Harrison's body because of the investigation into his death. Let me tell you, the morgue is nothing like you see in the movies—at least not the morgue in Orange County, where they investigate over a hundred deaths each week. I assume the bodies of loved ones are taken to the morgue and can't be claimed by their child, husband, or other loved one for logistical reasons until the coroner releases them, which can take weeks. It hurts deeply to be separated at such a terrible time.

Initially, all I wanted was to be with him. To see if this terrible dream was real. To tell him I love him and hold his hand. To be next to him one more time!

The Trauma of Sudden Loss

If you haven't experienced it yourself, the only way I can describe that initial, terrible feeling of sudden traumatic loss would be to ask you to imagine you are swimming in the ocean. Suddenly, a massive shark takes you. Your body is gone in a moment, and your mind can still think, but nothing else is left of you. You are confused and can't feel anything except a sense of devastating nothingness that surrounds you. That's the feeling I experienced for weeks.

After writing the paragraph above, I researched it, and it seems that feelings of unreality, guilt, helplessness, and meaninglessness are all very common responses to a sudden traumatic event. It goes without saying that there is also a terrific amount of crying, sadness, depression, and anger. Many more typical reactions, responses, and ways to help you cope are available at *medical.mit.edu*[1] *(see link in footnotes).* We have also created access to this information on our resources page at LighthouseLaneBooks.com/pages/resources

Cry for as long as you want. Try to go through it and not around it. That route will often be the fastest to recovery. I, for one, felt that my entire life was crushed. If you are reading this book, you may have experienced the same feeling. Indeed, when

---

1 MIT Health, "FAQ: Common Reactions to Traumatic Events," MIT Health, April 21, 2025, https://health.mit.edu/faqs/faqs-about-mental-health.

faced with loss, it is common to feel like your life is over. We lose total perspective and feel hopeless and lost.

> *Sadly, no matter how terrible and devastating the feeling of traumatic loss is, sooner or later, there will be times when you have to face the grief by yourself. However, it doesn't have to defeat you. I found that surrounding myself with community a belief, purpose, and compassion for myself and others really helps.*

Cold Encounter

When, after weeks of waiting, I finally saw Harrison again—this time in the funeral home. He lay on a gurney, a white sheet over his entire body except for his face and lovely flowing hair. His arms and hands were free of the shroud and lay folded peacefully across his chest. Another smaller cloth covered his forehead, which I suspect hid ugly scars from the coroner's examination.

Standing there, frozen in that cold and solemn room of the funeral home, I knew immediately that what I was looking at was not my son Harrison. This was just Harrison's body. Harrison's life force was so bright and full of energy... and that energy, spirit, soul, or whatever you want to call it, must have gone somewhere! Did it go back into the earth and the air around us, or to some higher plane—an ethereal location called heaven, or perhaps it had started on a beautiful journey and eventual rebirth into another living thing?

Over time after that cold encounter with the reality of death and seeing my sons lifeless body covered by a sheet, it became apparent to me that I needed to answer those questions to help overcome the depth of my own despair and start on some sort of road to recovery.

Determined not to grasp onto the most convenient answer without a fundamental belief structure to support it, I decided to investigate the various possibilities and try to come to a likely conclusion as to what happened to my beautiful boy after he left his body. I knew Harrison was not lying in front of me that day in the funeral home. It was not possible that so much love, energy, passion, enthusiasm, and creative energy had simply disappeared!

> *"Perhaps the fundamental beliefs of the main religions would help me get through this?" And if so... Which Religion or Scientific Belief, Should I Have Faith In, If Any?*

Are any spiritual beliefs more than just words and fables or ancient belief structures without proof? I had no plan or belief system when I started this journey. Hopefully, comparing the summaries of views on death by various religions that I researched to prepare this book will help you decide what resonates with you and provide some sense of support, as it did for me.

Three Possibilities

> *As part of my journey, I discovered there are only three possible outcomes following death: Either...*

1. *The soul or spirit of our loved one is in another realm and can see us and our pain.*

(If this is the case, ask yourself, would they want you to be in pain?)

2. *Our loved one's soul or spirit is in some other realm and cannot see us or how we long to hold them again.*

(If this is the situation, only you feel this suffering. The person you lost does not know how you feel. They are gone, and all the pain we feel will not bring them back, and you are only hurting yourself.)

3. *Or—the genuine possibility—our loved one has ceased to exist. There's no spirit world, no heaven, no reincarnation. However, the energy that was the person you loved is now part of the infinite energy around us.*

(Is this such a terrible option?)

It Doesn't Really Matter, Tim!

About three and a half years after my son died, I slowly started to put my life together again. Part of my process was listening to an educational or positive podcast every day to help me climb out of my darkness and live life with more purpose. On one of those podcasts, Deepak Chopra, during an interview with Oprah Winfrey, talked about dealing with trauma and past hardship, and what he said struck a chord. It goes something like this:

***The past is the past; the future hasn't happened yet, and for now, I choose joy.*[2]**

In an attempt to find that joy again, I moved to Sydney, Australia, and started dating a wonderful woman named Rici, who became my best friend. Although I didn't have a tremendous amount of money, I took 80% of it and purchased a small holiday rental unit that could generate a modest retirement income. With most of the remainder, I bought a little 16-year-old, 32-foot Halvorsen motor cruiser to spend time out on Sydney's beautiful harbour when the rental unit was occupied.

Buying a boat is not an investment strategy I would recommend, but…

After a loss, it makes sense to be kind to yourself.

I wanted to replenish my spirit, and being on the water has always done that for me. We are not all lucky enough to afford a little boat, but I suspect that any lake or stream around sunset will work just as well… without the stress of monthly bills that come with a boat!

During one excursion on a lovely Spring day on my boat, Rici and I picked up an old friend to join us for a few hours of cruising around beautiful Sydney Harbour. Our guest, Tim, was a knowledgeable and witty PR guy who knew everything about everybody in Sydney. During the conversation over the ensuing beer or two, Tim pointed out to Rici all the waterfront mansions around us in this costly section of Sydney that had

2 Deepak Chopra LLC, "Deepak Chopra- Official Website," 2025, https://www.deepakchopra.com/.

a story—how many millions this person had paid or how that person had spent $100 million on a bunch of adjoining blocks so he could knock down the houses and build a mega-mansion. As we travelled around the salubrious foreshore of Sydney's Eastern suburbs, Tim would point and say things like, "That place was purchased by the Chinese guy for $65 million and is abandoned." And so the stories of gratuitous wealth went on and on. It was fascinating that the two of them were so intrigued by tales of excessive opulence, and I wasn't. Eventually, I wondered why I had no interest in what they said, and then…*I suddenly realised their fascination with wealth repulsed me.*

The afternoon went on, and after an hour or two of listening to their adoration over modern-day excesses of the super-rich, we finally dropped Tim off and puttered my little blue boat through the choppy waves of lovely Sydney Harbour westward toward another wonderful crimson sunset…something that felt much more valuable to me than the waterside mansion my friends admired so much.

Later that night, when I was by myself, I thought about what had happened. During the interaction on the boat, a part of me just wanted to blurt out what I was actually thinking—to try and explain that, from my newly found perspective, none of what they found so compelling really mattered in the grand scheme of life. I didn't, but even if I had shared my thoughts, I don't think they would have really understood.

> *Very few people, if any, can truly understand the magnitude and impact of loss and the need to reevaluate what is truly important in life until they experience that loss for themselves.*

I had also been interested in all that stuff before Harrison died, but now, listening to them, I realised a door had closed inside me. The language of wealth and status, which I once understood, now sounded foreign. It wasn't their fault; it was my world that had changed. Rici and Tim had not done anything wrong, of course. This was all about my perception of their conversation. It was not because I didn't have all the money that those people in the mansions did. That I knew. Once, I may have aspired to those road signs of wealth and achievement, but I no longer did. It was also not because the stories were boring; they weren't. It was simply that…

None of that information was interesting because nothing matters after you have lost a child or someone who was a large part of you. Indeed, one thing I can tell you is that the size or position of your house or the amount of money or power you hold makes absolutely no difference in your new reality. Financial achievement is insignificant once you have enough to put a roof over your head, feed your loved ones, and enjoy some small luxuries like going out to a restaurant or being on a little boat or beach surrounded by the beautiful wealth of golden sands, a warm sea, children, family, and good friends.

My experience of losing Harrison had put life in perspective for me.

Beyond meeting our basic needs, nothing in life matters except connection, consciousness, and love.

Most material desires beyond our basic requirements are just a way to fill what Victor Frankl[3] describes in his well-known book, *Man's Search for Meaning,*[4] as our *existential void*, which, poorly paraphrased by me, is the space between where we currently are emotionally and spiritually and where we'd be if we reached our full potential as a human being. In this profoundly insightful book, which has sold over 12 million copies, Frankl eloquently explains… (Paraphrased)

> *Often, we strive for an excess of money, power, or sex to fill the gap between where we are and what we would be doing if we could follow and achieve our bliss, purpose, and meaning in life. He also draws the direct correlation between our happiness and if we have found meaning in what we do and how we live. When you have lost somebody who felt like they were a part of you and gave you significant meaning—what then?*

Later that same year, and partly because she sensed my deep, lingering sadness and a sorrow I could not heal, Rici, whom I loved deeply, moved on. She was fundamentally a good woman, but one of her parting gifts to me was to say (in a less than kind manner), "Do you know how hard it is to deal with someone sad and grieving? It isn't easy!"

---

3 Encyclopaedia Britannica Editors, "Viktor Frankl," March 22, 2025, https://www.britannica.com/biography/Viktor-Frankl.

4 Viktor E. Frankl, *Man's Search for Meaning* (Beacon Press, 2006), https://www.viktorfrankl.org/books_by_vf.html#English.

She was right, of course, but her statement made me realise that she lacked the empathy I needed in a partner. When we grieve, we do need to be surrounded by love and compassion. It is not selfish to want that. I am not a person to make a public display of my grief or sadness, and I never walk around trying to initiate conversations designed to solicit empathy. However, sometimes, when a beautiful sunset, a song, or simply a picture triggers your pain and brings some tears, you need to have the right people around you.

After my painful breakup with Rici, I was lucky enough to start dating a far more empathetic, beautiful, powerful, and charismatic overachiever called Amanda. Amanda (fortunately), when calm, reverted to a more hippie-like and very affectionate deep thinker. Her days were full of drive and high energy, but in one of her reflective quiet moments, she asked me why I was feeling guilty about enjoying life now that I had retired. After much thought, the truth of it emerged, and as I recall, my answer went something like this…

> *When you lose a child or somebody intensely close to you, the world does not make sense anymore; life's natural progression and order have been upturned. You start to question the meaning of life and want to know what happened to their beautiful soul. I can't fully explain it, but I just feel guilt for experiencing pleasure when they lost everything.*

I can attest to the fact that, as time goes by, you feel less of that guilt and eventually do allow yourself the opportunity to feel some pleasure, but it still really does feel like the world has been turned upside down for an extended period of time. It is just a natural part of the healing process.

One of the biggest questions you keep asking yourself after a tragic loss is—Why was my loved one taken while I was left behind? I was not sure why, but maybe it was so I could write this book?

The Process

When I finally had the emotional strength to go on this journey, I first decided to start with the prominent religion I knew best, Christianity. I then worked my way through the other major religions and then minor religions, scientific beliefs, and then the more spiritual beliefs of where we go after we die. Comparing them, I discovered what I loved, could grasp, and which facts and stories stood out to me as being believable or not. The process is set out in the following order.

Part 1 of this book summarises each of the more prominent religions so you can quickly get a sense of them and a feel for which, if any, sound reasonable and believable. There is also a chapter summarising the minor religions. None of the summaries are meant to provide an in-depth exposé, and you should be able to read each section in about 15 minutes. After doing so, I suggest taking some time to let the information sink in and see if any one of them resonates with you. Some of you will toss one particular religion aside initially, as I did, but beware; you may change your initial reaction as you look at the proof behind each one, move through each, and unravel some similarities between them.

Part 2: Investigates scientific theories surrounding life after death rather than religious ones.

Part 3: Approaches the questions of spirituality and the afterlife, my beliefs as they evolved through my research, the concepts of a soulful being, and life in general.

Part 4: Is more about recovery, looking inward, and reflecting on the journey of healing.

To get the most out of this book, I suggest you read all the sections—even those you immediately dismiss as irrelevant. If you do, I believe something will happen for you, as it did for me, which will start to provide some clarity. If you can, read each section, not just those that you feel discuss something plausible, and see if you find some exciting patterns emerging.

Hopefully, the common threads running through these belief structures will start to connect the pieces of a puzzle and eventually create an ah-ha moment for you, as they did for me. Initially, I intended to provide an overview of the different philosophies and religions, compare them practically, and see if there was any evidence that they were based on fact. Something else started to happen to me as I delved into the different belief choices offered to us ...

I gained insights and revelations from each book, article, and philosophy I researched. The combination of those small insights from each section does add up, but even gaining one thought or insight from a chapter in this book makes it worth reading. Even though I am highly critical and often display tones of sarcasm about some beliefs, they all have many positive influences that I try to recognise as well... I was also struck by one pervasive thread—the importance of community, and how that power usually overrides even the most preposterous stories and claims.

As in any book you read, some takeaways can be beneficial. That is what mainly happens when you can look at the various belief structures around religion, the afterlife, and death together in one summary. Some of those insights can be transformative when combined, even if you deem the individual belief structure implausible.

The summaries of the various religions themselves will seem overly simplistic to theologians, but my primary intention in this book is to present an outline of each religion as I understand it, not an expert summary. I will be the first to admit I am not objective. If a religion seems too far-fetched, I say so. If another resonated with me purely on an emotional level, I may have adopted a less critical stance. If so, I apologise. My intention in writing this book is to follow my heart, not always to be level-headed… although I do my best.

My primary focus was to understand if the historical creation of the particular belief or religion was credible enough to follow and also understand what each believes about the subject of death and an afterlife to see if I could feel comfortable enough to embrace any one belief and find the solace and support that I desperately needed.

Please do not feel you need to embrace one of the religions or concepts I mention to be whole as a person or experience recovery from loss; finding your own community and personal belief structure can often be enough. I also understand that at times during grief, it may feel more comfortable for you to choose not to be part of a community at all. For me—certainly in the first few years after my loss—being happy and fitting in with the crowd when so much had been taken away caused a lot of stress. Sometimes it's easier to avoid everybody and run away and hide. However, in doing so, we are more likely to have to engage with our own company and face our sadness alone. Doing so is painful, but as stated earlier, it is part of our way forward. Follow the path that feels natural for you. For some, it is being surrounded by community and belief in an established religion; for others, a period of introspection may help.

I have added some of my own observations to make the factual references and research seem less dry. But feel free to jump over my personal reflections if you want more factual information. Likewise, you can skip over the factual stuff if you prefer. The four biggest religions are covered first. I hope you enjoy them.

Part 1: Religious Beliefs

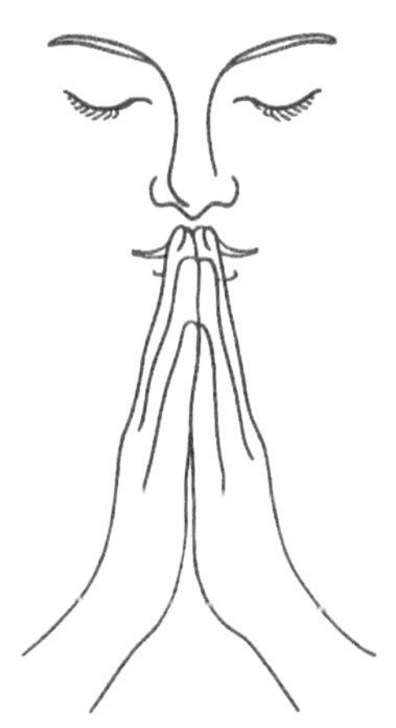

The Major Beliefs

Christianity

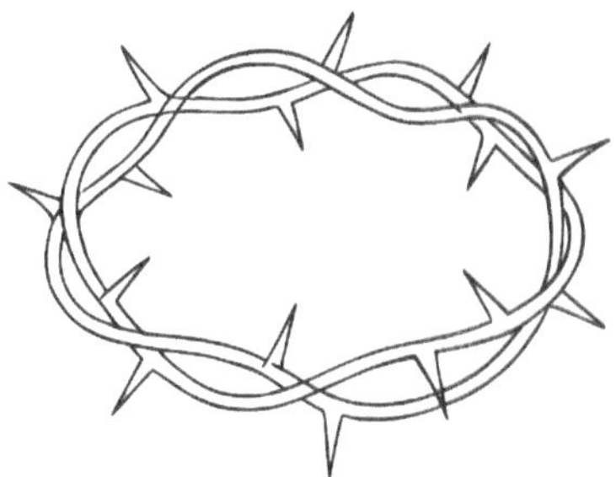

Now is your time of grief, but I will see you again, and you will rejoice, and no one will take away your joy.

(The words of Jesus, according to the Gospel of John (16:22), written around 90-110 AD.)

These words from the Gospel of John seemed to be a fitting way to start my exploration of what Christianity believes happens after you die. Initially, the quote came up in a search because of the word *grief.* Still, it was particularly appealing because it seems to address, in some ways, not only the grief we experience initially but also the eventual feelings of joy that can come later, when we have fond memories and we *see* our lost ones again. Or is this simply a singular reference to a resurrection and not meant to be considered metaphorically? I don't know.

Theologians differ in their interpretations of the quote. Some see this passage as both that Jesus appears to confirm the pain and suffering his disciples will experience after his crucifixion while also reassuring them that this pain is insignificant compared to the immeasurable rewards and lasting joy of faith. By extension—and referencing other passages in the Bible—one could easily assume that this same eternal joy would also extend to life after death and one's subsequent entry to the Kingdom of Heaven.

Unfortunately, due to my healthy level of cynicism, I couldn't help but wonder how the author (or the community) behind the Gospel of John could have accurately represented Jesus' words 60 or more years after they were said. I often can't remember things people say, even after a day—but then again, I acknowledge that if I were present as a disciple and witness to such a meaningful and influential leader, the words wouldn't be as easily forgotten. I do question how accurate they would have been after so long, though.

(To be fair to Christianity, there are very few religious events that were systematically recorded at the time of the particular events in question.)

As it turns out, there aren't as many direct references to our going to heaven as you might expect from a religion that offers such a significant reward, and most of the references I could find use metaphors and figurative speech, which don't clearly state what will happen after death. Of course, it's hard to describe literally that which is so genuinely imaginary and not concrete. Nevertheless, the declaration of what will happen to your soul is explicit enough in several passages, including this one:

Not everyone who says to Me, "Lord, Lord," will enter the kingdom of heaven, but he who does the will of My Father who is in heaven will enter.

(Mathew 7:21)

The verse Matthew 7:21 above comes from the Sermon on the Mount. It suggests that Jesus believed that simply saying the name *Lord* and professing faith through words and deeds isn't enough. One must have genuine faith, not just claim to have it.

A Wonderful Community

As I explain later, there are many positive aspects of Christianity. In my view, the most important of these is the sense of *community and purpose* it provides. In addition, there is no doubt that many churches and their members do wonderful things such as *helping the poor.* And of course, as is the case with all religions, Christianity *offers us hope* of a continuation of some sort after we die.

Notwithstanding the positive aspects of Christianity, it would be remiss of me not to point out that the foundational text of Christianity, the Bible, is contradictory in many ways, particularly about the entry to heaven and what current Christians seem to practice today. If you follow the Bible literally and think you're going to be judged by God, who then decides whether you go to heaven or hell, you must also believe this passage:

It is easier for a camel to go through the eye of a needle than for a rich man to enter the kingdom of God.

(Mark 10:25, Luke 18:25)

These words suggest that even if a rich man has true faith, he's almost certainly going to find it challenging to enter the kingdom of God if he is rich.

* * *

As I do at the beginning of many chapters in this book, I would like to share a little story. (I hope my reason for doing so will become more obvious as you progress through the chapter.)

A Moonies Corporate Pilot

During the early '90s, between airline jobs and a few years I spent working on Wall Street as a trader, I flew part-time as a corporate pilot. One job I picked up was flying Reverend Sun Myung Moon around for a few weeks in his new corporate jet. (The previous pilot had not bowed sufficiently upon Reverend Moon's arrival at the aircraft.)

Reverend Moon was a Korean religious leader who founded a highly successful Christian offshoot, which he named the Unification Church. (His followers are often referred to as Moonies.) He declared himself a self-professed messiah and also established a media empire that included newspapers such as *The Washington Times*. Even though many experts suggest the numbers were much lower, the Unification Church at the time I was flying their leader around was claiming a following of over 3,000,000 devotees.

To raise money *for the church*, members frequently took part in fundraising activities such as selling flowers, candy, or trinkets on street corners or to drivers at traffic lights. Because of my personal experiences working on that particular contract,

I can certainly confirm that some church leaders live a very lavish lifestyle that does not match that of the people raising money for them.

Notwithstanding the Unification Church's desperate need to raise money by selling trinkets on street corners at the time, I was delighted to report that on first meeting Reverend Moon and his wife when they boarded the aircraft (while I bowed), I got a superb look at Mrs Moon's hand. She was wearing the biggest diamond ring I had ever seen in my life! I was also delighted because the Reverend and his associates paid another pilot and me $1,000 a day each to sit in a luxury hotel in Montenegro while they were surf fishing and enjoying a religious retreat. (I will state for the record that I have no knowledge of any misappropriation or misuse of funds by the Unification Church. All of their expenditure may well have been covered from sources other than the church.)

The reason I share this specific little experience with you is to pass on from personal experience how absolutely opulent and excessive the lifestyles of some of these religious leaders actually are!

* * *

Particularly amongst many people who publicly declare themselves to be staunch, upstanding members of the Christian community, there certainly seems to be a fair amount of selectivity in using convenient passages from the Bible and ignoring the ones that are not to their liking. To me, the unspoken message from these mega pastors seems to be that we should definitely believe in the parts about going to heaven but not necessarily the other, often less convenient words of the Bible.

If you believe the extract from Mark 10:25 previously quoted, few of the mega-church pastors would ever make it to heaven!

Billy Graham, who had a reported net worth of $20 million to $25 million when he died, doesn't even make it into the top five in terms of wealth. In fact, Billy Graham did not live a lavish lifestyle and avoided a prosperity gospel, unlike many Christian religious leaders today.

According to public reports and newspaper articles, Billy Graham's meagre wealth is well and truly surpassed by modern pastors like Kenneth Copeland. Copeland's wealth is reported to be somewhere between $300 million and $750 million. His ministry owns multiple jets, a large estate in Texas, and a number of other real estate assets. Kenneth Copeland states that *his wealth does not come from offerings alone*, but it appears clear to me that he is one of many who have found the role of an evangelist financially rewarding. He is also famous for other statements such as *You are not created for poverty*, and he points out that *Abraham was extremely wealthy and had a covenant with God* when justifying his wealth. (Both are verifiable quotes). I do wonder, however, why, if he feels *we are not created for poverty* as he states, he doesn't just share 75% of his wealth with the poorest people in the world who are starving. I am sure he has a well-thought-out response to that question, though.

In his teaching on prosperity and giving, Copeland, like many of his peers, often emphasises that giving generously (such as offerings or tithes) is spiritually rewarding and that God multiplies what is given to Him. It's just a shame that the flow of money doesn't seem to go back in the other direction as quickly. Does God really want a six-month-old child dying on his mother's breast because she can't produce enough milk due to malnutrition? All while a church pastor is flying around in one of his jets? (Or while I am enjoying my boat, for that matter!) I doubt it.

A Warning:

Sadly, these observations also suggest that many people who proclaim themselves as religious leaders take advantage of those who need community and a belief in a higher being. More often than not, these fundraising pastors and church leaders use God—as defined by their particular religion—and the promise of redemption and happiness to feed the human need for community and a sense of belonging—all the while fundraising for their own benefit.

> *It is critical to remember that in our moments of most tremendous pain and grief after loss, we are the most vulnerable. As with many religions, Christianity is not without those who will take advantage of you if you are grieving.*

It is apt that I use the following quote to remind you of that. Harrison's mother and I were taken advantage of in our time of grief, and I write about that experience later in the book. Jesus's words in the Gospel of Matthew specifically relate to this:

Beware of false prophets, who come to you in sheep's clothing but inwardly are ravenous wolves.

~ Matthew 7:15 (ESV)

Having issued my warning about the less scrupulous, I want to state, equally clearly, that there are, obviously, also millions of Christian leaders who are good people with honest and meaningful intentions. Christianity, regardless of the credibility of its roots or the validity of its doctrine, has billions of followers, and its charitable outreach is significant. Christians also enjoy a wonderful sense of community, compassion, and love in their faith and then move on.

Afterlife

Although theologians hold differing beliefs, the stereotypical view among Christians is that the soul and body are two distinct entities. At the moment of death, the soul separates from the body and goes to its eternal reward of heaven or hell. In English Bible translations such as the King James Version, the word *Heaven* appears hundreds of times, while terms associated with hell or *Hades* appear far less frequently. Notably, the word *Afterlife* does not appear at all.

As it turns out, there are apparently 712 references in the Bible to the word *Heaven* (57 to the word *Hell* and 78 to *Hades*) but only 12 references to the more specific word *Afterlife.* Relatively speaking, not many of the references to Heaven actually deal with us *going to Heaven.*[5]

The primary usage of the word Heaven in the various printings of the Bible commonly refers to a somewhat indefinable place above that God created when he created the Earth—an ethereal location containing the stars and from which light, birds, and

5 "Numbers vary depending on the Bible translation."

rain come. Coincidentally, it's also the place from which all the fire and brimstone came when the Lord decided to teach the people of Sodom and Gomorrah a lesson and from where, at Moses's behest, God rained hail, locusts, and fire upon Egypt. It's definitely not a place to be messed with!

In one way or another, every religious myth, including Christianity, speaks of the afterlife and assures us we'll meet the creator and those we love after we die. Wouldn't it be fantastic if, in our grief, we could be assured we'll see those we love again… and that we'll eventually *rejoice* in that pleasure! The temptation to surround oneself with the warm belief that this may be true is especially tempting when you're suffering and grieving from the loss of a loved one.

Once agaïn, is this just an attempt to sell a belief system by offering a reward?

I could have spent a year investigating the various religions and what they say and promise, but if there's no reasonable certainty of the end game, it made no sense to me at first to even go there. Should I do that to determine which religion tells the most convincing story and then grasp onto that? I'm just too analytical, I suppose. Maybe I've spent too many years living and working in the physical world as a pilot who sees how an action results in an often immediate reaction, or maybe it's just a lifetime of experience that taught me to think critically about what goes on around me—to challenge what people say or believe until I have some reasonable certainty that it's true.

I remembered something my father said to me, years before writing this book:

> *Words are just words unless they are true words. Then they start to take on meaning.*
>
> (Donald Dunnett)

So, I started this book looking for facts, proof, and reliability. As this relates to religion, I surmised that if the words around the origins of various religions are not factual representations, and if the words of the people who preach to us are not real, then the beliefs about what happens after you die are not worthwhile either.

However, another part of my brain kept asking whether it's even essential to find proof that there's a heaven above; perhaps the simple, absolute belief that there's a heaven is all that's necessary and all that matters for those left behind?

> *We were with her in her last moments, and although our hearts are broken, we are at the same time comforted by our faith knowing that Anne is now with our heavenly father.*
>
> (A quote from the parents of Anne Pressly, who died in 2008, taken from her obituary)

The parents of a 26-year-old TV personality from Little Rock, Arkansas, wrote the passage above after their daughter was brutally attacked in her home in 2008 and later died in the hospital from her wounds. Anne Pressly wasn't well known outside Arkansas. I could have quoted words from thousands of obituaries worldwide, and most reflect the same sentiment. I used hers because she was a typical example of the terrible injustice that so many families face. These words of consolation about the departed returning to their eternal home are so often used to help families cope with the crushing pain associated with the sudden loss of a loved one.

The same year, my sister, Pamela, died unexpectedly five days after going into the hospital for a hernia operation. At her funeral, the priest from her church said:

We should all receive solace from the fact that she is now with Jesus Christ in Heaven.

His short sermon mentioned *Jesus Christ, our God*, at least 30 times. I was so mad that I wanted to rip the microphone from his hand and yell to the crowd that if there were a merciful God, he never would have let my sister die due to the sloppy work of professionals in a hospital or allowed a girl like Anne Pressly to be murdered, or any young child to die of cancer. But I said nothing—and for good reason.

When I looked at Pam's three children and her husband sitting across from me, I realised they were calmed by the priest's promises that their beloved mother and wife had gone to Heaven and that God was caring for her as she looked down upon us. They *believed*, and their belief gave them the comfort and solace they needed. Who was I to ruin what little comfort they were feeling by broadcasting my disbelief? It seems from Anne Pressly's obituary that her parents found some solace in their faith as well.

Hundreds of thousands of people die each year, and I often wonder how people would cope if they didn't have faith in an extraordinary being or purpose and are therefore able to gain comfort from the fact that their loved ones have gone to a better place. Many would say that this benefit alone should be reason enough to justify a belief in God. I find it hard to disagree with this simple fact. A belief in God or the promise of everlasting life, common to various religions and faiths, has given billions of people the strength to endure troubled times, and faith can be an excellent panacea for those who need it.

Others, however, who aren't believers in Jesus Christ as the son of God, have trouble believing that someone with a long beard is sitting out there somewhere creating virgin births while allowing gross injustice and unnecessary death. They move through their suffering with the support of friends and community, their inner strength, and the belief that there may be something greater than themselves—a force unknown and undefinable, perhaps a collective and global energy. This creative force exists in other dimensions that we can't see or understand. They believe in a power greater than themselves—just not the particular story of Christianity. They may be wrong, of course.

I don't want to criticise a belief in whatever feels best to you. For me, Christianity isn't the best fit. From my point of view, there are just too many contradictions, unrealistic and mythical stories, and misuses of Bible text as a foundation for graft, death, and harm. My doubts surrounding Christianity don't subtract from the fact that I'm becoming increasingly convinced that our souls experience an afterlife. It's just a question of which road to take to understand and believe in that outcome.

Even though Christianity doesn't work for me, it does for over 2 billion other people, so I am open to the possibility that there's a real chance I could be wrong in dismissing it so easily. I probably wouldn't be so dismissive if tens of millions of people had not died in Christian religious wars and literally hundreds of thousands of children hadn't been sexually molested while under the protection of the church[6]. Perhaps by the end of my journey writing this book, my views will have changed. (Refer: *Injustice and Death* in the *Commonality* chapter for further details.)

Proof of God and Christ as His Son

To explore if there's any proof for Christian claims regarding all this rhetoric about Heaven, I referred to a widely watched series of fascinating debates among philosophers, theologians, professors, and authors online that can be found through a simple search. Watching these debates at length gave me the initial sense that the discussion is as simple or complex as you'd like to make it. Whatever direction you lean, you'll find points that ring true from the side of the debate that supports your theory. The discussions can be complex, and often there's no clear conclusion.

Still, through a confessed gross oversimplification of the following points made in a debate between Dr William Craig and Christopher Hitchens, you should start to see a pattern that you find believable or not. You can watch this presentation in full on YouTube or explore further some key points that struck me from each.

The bottom line is that critics of religion such as Christopher Hitchens declare that there's no proof of God's existence or the claims made by Jesus.

---

6 The Associated Press, "About 333,000 Children Were Abused within France's Catholic Church, a Report Finds," NPR, October 5, 2021, https://www.npr.org/2021/10/05/1043302348/france-catholic-church-sexual-abuse-report-children.

William Lane Craig, PhD (Philosophy), D.Theol (Research Professor of Philosophy, Talbot School of Theology) vs. Christopher Hitchens, B.A., Economics, Politics and Philosophy. (Author of *God Is Not Great* and many other nonfiction works before he died in 2011)

Dr Craig's main points supporting the existence of God (as I interpret them):

- There's no reasonable argument that atheism is true. Thus, God is.
- Nobody has ever been able to disprove the existence of God, so it's likely he exists.
- Dr Craig also challenges the modern multiverse theories that are becoming popular, which point to the possibility of an infinite number of universes.7 The multiverse concept appears most notably in cosmology, quantum physics, and philosophy. This theory isn't based on the idea of a divine creator, nor is it discussed in the Bible.
- Several good arguments, according to Dr Craig, show that theism (belief in God) is justified:
    - The Big Bang Theory suggests that the universe arose from nothing, so there must be a creator who made that happen out of nothing. (How else could this improbable miracle of humanity have occurred?)
    - The assumption that the Big Bang and all the improbable conditions that needed to arise to support the eventual development of man were ***fine-tuned with***

---

7 Anthony Aguirre, "Multiverse: Cosmology," in *Encyclopaedia Britannica*, March 27, 2025, https://www.britannica.com/science/multiverse.

a delicacy that defies nature and thus were almost impossible to occur without the existence of a creator's design.

- The moral argument: *If God doesn't exist, then objective moral values wouldn't exist.*
- The resurrection of Christ is factual, and this *divine* miracle supports the presence of God. In Dr Craig's mind, no scientific alternative explanations are plausible or have been proven. Dr Craig—supported by his assertion of the resurrection — primarily relies on the following three tenets that he believes to be true.:

» On the Sunday after Christ's death, his tomb was found empty.

» On separate occasions, according to the Bible, there are groups of people who say they witnessed Jesus after his death. Those sightings were seen by not just his disciples but also by non-believers.

» The fact that his disciples so firmly believed in his resurrection (who, as Jews, wouldn't have been predisposed to such belief) is also proof of the occurrence.

– The direct experience of God; i.e., individuals can personally feel and know God exists without any evidence; this feeling arises from within and needs no explanation or proof. The existence of God is based on individual, internal experiential evidence rather than on various external arguments.

Mr Hitchens' main points, against the existence of God (as I interpret them):

According to Mr Hitchens's argument in this debate, a belief in God is essentially the same as a belief in the supernatural.

The argument in favour of both is the same, with a few crucial distinctions. *Pre-suppositionalists* assume that God has already been proven, and that it's only necessary to better understand God's inner workings. In contrast, *evidentialists* recognise that proof of God would be nice to have at least!

- Mr Hitchens' main points were as follows:
- It's now relatively straightforward and widely accepted by scientists that we (humans) are here through evolution, not through a design process overseen by a divine entity (which was the belief of most Christians before recent times).
- Now that it's becoming difficult to refute the facts of the evolutionary process, Christians are changing gears and saying that evolution itself is a part of the design. To do so, it's necessary to believe that an ultimate creator designed the painful death of species over eons of time, resulting in 99.9% of all species that have appeared on Earth becoming extinct. Humans, too, nearly became extinct 74,000 years ago[8] when the world population was reduced to 30,000-40,000 following a cataclysmic event in Indonesia. It's also necessary to believe that all this suffering and death occurred so that we humans should be on this Earth and have the opportunity to be Christians! In Mr Hitchens' own words…

  It seems strange that Christians should be so self-centred and arrogant that they believe this extraordinary and capricious process of evolution happened just for them.

8 Hitchens incorrectly mistakes this figure as 180,000 in the debate.

- Atheists shouldn't have to prove that there's no God, as Christians seem to expect. The position of atheists, in general, is that there's no plausible or evidentiary explanation for or proof of God, and they doubt his existence. Theists are convinced that there's a God without a doubt—yet they have no actual evidence of this.
- Other theories that don't rely on a creator fully explain all the phenomena of human life and our existence. Believing that by following certain rituals, one can overcome death—or that if there were some divine creator, he'd care about you—represents an outstanding level of hubris.
- The absence of any actual proof of God from followers of the Bible is of primary concern to Hitchens. Yes, the lack of evidence doesn't mean something isn't valid, but if you're talking about something as important as God and Christian teachings—which tell people how to live, sanction the taking of life in God's name, and so on—it seems there should be at least a little proof that God exists.
- Using the life of Mother Teresa as an example, Hitchens suggested that it's disappointing when you realise how simple it is to get a spiritual rumour started amongst an uneducated, superstitious, and frightened population. He was referring specifically to the disputed *miracle* of Monica Besra, whose tumour was reportedly healed by the touch of a medal featuring Mother Teresa's image. According to Hitchens, the Catholic Church required such a miracle to make Mother Teresa a saint; therefore, it was officially recognized, even though the woman's husband claimed that it was actually the medical treatment that caused the recovery.

– According to Christopher Hitchens, after reading countless books and studies on the subject, *there is not a single literate, written-down, properly attested witness of any real sort in the Gospels* that would attest to the resurrection of Christ or the existence of God.

He continued in his well-known cynical tone and with a sly smile…

> *If you assume that all religions are man-made, it explains a lot of their failures.*
>
> ~ Christopher Hitchens

Life of Jesus - Proof

Even though there's no conclusive evidence that Jesus existed beyond the various writings about his life and words, scholars widely accept that there was a historical figure named Jesus. Unfortunately, there's no empirical evidence that he lived or was resurrected and was the son of an omnipotent God. (To be fair, one wouldn't expect to find archaeological evidence because there's no archaeological record of 99.9% of people who lived in those times.) At the risk of being cynical again, it's hard to understand why God wouldn't want to leave some proof of His existence!

According to history.com, which references the work of Bart D. Ehrman (author of *Did Jesus Exist*?):

Documentary evidence [of Jesus being a real person] outside of the New Testament is limited. The most detailed record of the life and death of Jesus comes from the four Gospels and other New Testament writings. *These are all Christian and are obviously and understandably biased in what they report and have to be evaluated critically to establish any historically reliable information*, states Ehrman.

But their central claims about Jesus as a historical figure—a Jew, with followers, executed on orders of the Roman governor of Judea, Pontius Pilate, during the reign of Emperor Tiberius—are borne out by later sources with a completely different set of biases.

Several Jewish and Roman Historians mentioned Jesus. He is also mentioned in the Quran many times. Unfortunately, just because there was a person called Jesus doesn't mean he was the son of God or that God exists.

Many of the standard arguments put forward as proof of God's existence seem to centre around intricate and impressive descriptions that suggest that there could be no other explanation for these types of wonders except for the existence of God as our ultimate creator.

Also referenced by Christopher Hitchens, another typical example often arises when speaking about the intricacies of human evolution or the origin of the Big Bang theory. It is often argued by believers in God that, because we have no logical explanation as to the cause of the Big Bang, we should therefore naturally assume that a greater creator of some sort caused it. How else could this wonderful thing called *evolution* have occurred if not for the existence of a god!

It should go without saying that just because we don't understand something, it doesn't mean a god of some sort created it. Nevertheless, this seems to be a satisfactory sort of twisted reasoning for many who are determined to believe blindly in a religious faith without question.

Another example of this typical argument has to do with the modern version of the Atomic Clock developed in 1967. This clock was built utilising Cesium 133 atoms because they vibrate at a frequency of 9,192,631,770 times per second. This means that, over 30 million years, this clock would have an accuracy within one second! The vibrational frequency of Cesium 133 atoms never changes. They're consistent and dependable. Proponents of an ultimate creator suggest that it couldn't be just *chance* that the vibrational frequency of Cesium 133 remains constant over eons and was discovered by human scientists. They argue that this occurrence represents absolute proof of divine design and of God's existence. Unfortunately, this seemingly persuasive argument falls apart upon closer consideration.

> *The amazing scientific discoveries that occur almost every day only confirm that there's a lot we don't know, not that there is a divine creator. More importantly, they help us realise that we just don't know how much we don't know!*

I believe the following well-known example is the best way to approach this argument for God's existence. Assume you're a native living in an isolated and untouched Amazonian village. You find a wristwatch on the ground. The arms on the watch point to the exact figures every day when the sun goes down and rises, and both arms point to the top of the dial at midday when the sun is overhead. You share this incredible discovery with your tribe, and everyone begins to worship this mysterious object. You all agree that it must have been sent from above and is, therefore, absolute proof that there's a God or creator more significant than you and your tribe. But is that true?

> *The fact that we don't fully understand the complexities of life, the origin and wonders of the universe, the initial creation of energy, the inner workings of a molecule, or even the human brain doesn't in any way prove that there's a creator. It only means we don't know how these things came to be.*

In any case, what I've learned is that proof of God isn't actually needed; belief alone seems to be more than enough for billions of people. Who am I to argue with them because of a simple lack of proof! Perhaps God is the culmination of a powerful collective belief, and that alone may be even more powerful than the story of an individual provider.

(For access to additional key-point discussion and summary notes, refer to the section in the back of the book titled Appendix: Notes by Religion just before the Bibliography.)

Islam

Do not grieve over what has passed unless it makes you work for what is about to come.

Attributed to ~ Ali ibn Abi Talib

Alī ibn Abi Talib (born c. 600, Mecca, Arabia [now in Saudi Arabia], died January 28, 661 CE) was the cousin and son-in-law of the Prophet Muhammad. He became the fourth caliph and the first imam of Shiʿism (according to Shiʿi belief). (Disputes over his right to lead the Muslim community after Muhammad's death led to the major division of Islam into Sunni and Shiʿi branches.[9])

To me, this simple quote, attributed to Ali, the first imam of Shi'ism, is profound. We must grieve to survive and make it through life. It's that or death! And how cruel and selfish it would

9 Seyyed Hossein Nasr and Asma Afsaruddin, "Ali | Biography, History, & Facts," in *Encyclopaedia Britannica*, February 20, 2025, https://www.britannica.com/biography/Ali-Muslim-caliph.

be for us to choose this latter option. However, if we must grieve and choose life, we must use that grief as a source of strength and an incentive to do good in the world, or at least to access more of our potential, or, perhaps, grief can simply make us more loving. However it manifests, hopefully we can use our grief to work toward the next—and often very different—chapter of our lives.

As grievers, we are changed forever, so if we are destined to live a new life, we may as well try to design a better one. For me, the cataclysmic loss of my son in my life caused me to ask…

Why am I here, and why am I alive?

That question spurs a response in many—as it did in me—to move forward and find some sense in our ongoing existence. After I lost Harrison, and after making the decision to try and live, I knew I couldn't just go on wasting life's precious moments. I co-founded a charity that I speak about later in the section called *A Hero's Journey* in the Community chapter. And now, hopefully, writing this book will help me, and others, find a path forward.

Are you going to use your grief to create change in yourself and the world around you? If that's what you decide to do, it may help you find a way through the darkness of loss, as it has me. (Keep in mind that you don't have to form a charity to change the world around you. We all know that just chatting with a lonely older person, or a smile, is enough to help others, and possibly yourself.)

The quote from Ali ibn Abi Talib is simple but pretty powerful, I think.

* * *

The Islamic religion began on the Arabian Peninsula in the early 7th century CE (Common Era—same as AD but more secular), where the prophet Muhammad lived and taught. According to Islamic belief, Allah (God) spoke to Muhammad through the archangel Gabriel and gave him teachings that later became the Quran, the holy book of Islam.

There's a second collection of texts that's also important to the Islamic religion called the Hadith, which chronicles Muhammad's words and actions and explains more about Islam's spiritual, political, and social goals. Muhammad is traditionally said to have been born in circa 570 CE in Mecca and to have died in 632 in Medina, spending his entire life in the Arabian Peninsula (Primarily Mecca and Medina).

Five pillars represent the most important aspects of the Islamic faith:

- Shahada, which means *faith*, is the statement that there's no god but Allah, and Muhammad is His Prophet.
- The second important necessity for Muslims is that they pray five times daily at specific times in front of the Kaaba in Mecca or wherever they are at the appropriate time of day. This prayer is referred to as Salah.
- The third pillar is called Zakat (or almsgiving), which is the obligation to give a portion of one's wealth to people in need.
- Another must is the tradition of Sawm (fasting) during the holy month of Ramadan, in which followers of Islam fast from dawn to dusk.

– The final requirement for Muslims is, if possible, that every Muslim must go on a pilgrimage to Mecca at least once in their life. This journey is called the Hajj.

I will never forget flying for one well-known airline in the early '90s. The majority of pilots were Muslim, and it was fascinating to see the faces of tourists when the Captain of the plane would, on occasion, come out of the cockpit prior to a flight, lay a mat on the floor of the galley and start praying to Allah. (Unfortunately, departures would sometimes occur around the time Muslims are called to prayer.)

The tradition of fasting during Ramadan also led to some interesting times. Once, a Captain I was flying with, having not eaten for hours, was absolutely confused about the direction of the runway we were about to enter. The result of some of low blood sugar or fatigue I expect. It took a lot of convincing before he acknowledged we were actually heading toward the wrong runway.

Also very important to note is that, in Islamic thought, there are two aspects of life: the spiritual and the physical. Allah rules both. Islam (as in Judaism) isn't just a faith; it's a way of life that offers guidance on social justice, economics, politics, and personal growth.

There are two main sects within Islam: Sunni, which has the majority of followers, and the smaller Shia sect, which represents 10-15% of all Muslims worldwide. Sunni Muslims believe that Muhammad's legitimate successors were the first four caliphs. Shia Muslims, on the other hand, believe that Muhammad's cousin and son-in-law, Ali, was the rightful successor. This division, which occurred in the mid-seventh century after the death of Muhammad, has led to different interpretations of the

Prophet's words. As a result, religious practices and personal behaviour differ among Sunnis and Shias. However, the basic values that all Muslims share are the same.

Extremism: Muslims in America and around the world have incorrectly been labelled by people unfamiliar with the teachings of Islam as dangerous extremists, and all Muslims have been discriminated against because of the actions of small extremist factions. The vast majority of Muslims are peaceful and loving followers of a faith that has countless references prescribing inclusion, kindness, peace, and doing good in the world. I did not know this, but according to the Online Etymology Dictionary[10]:

> *The literal translation of the Arabic word Islam is "submission" [to the will of God] and is related in origin to the word Salaam, which means "peace."*

> Also noteworthy is that Islam is one of the few major religions whose name is not related to a person or ethnic group but to the central idea of the religion.[11]
> ~ [The Heart of Islam: Enduring Values for Humanity, Seyyed Hossein Nasr, 2002]

Many religions in the world have extremist factions that take extracts from the fundamental teachings of their faith and twist them as justification for perpetrating horrific acts of violence upon those who reject or are seen to be enemies of that religion.

---

10 Douglas Harper, "Islam (n.)," in *Online Etymology Dictionary* (Online Etymology Dictionary, 2025), https://www.etymonline.com/word/Islam.

11 Seyyed Hossein Nasr, *The Heart of Islam: Enduring Values for Humanity* (San Francisco, California: HarperSanFrancisco, 2002), https://archive.org/details/heartofislamendu0000nasr.

Islam is no exception. However, according to the Pew Research Centre,[12] in 2017, the American public's general perception of American Muslims' support of Islamic extremists was twice that of actual Muslim support of Islamic extremists. As it turns out…14% of the U.S. general public thought that targeting and killing civilians can be justified in order to further a political, social, or religious cause. The number was actually lower for Muslims (12%).

> *Interestingly, twenty-one percent of Republican-leaning participants thought that targeting and killing civilians can be justified in order to further a political, social or religious cause could be justified! This is almost twice that of the general Muslim population in the USA. (The number of Democrats was 10%.)*

Unfortunately, there is probably still a great deal of mistrust and misconception about the dangers inherent in the American Muslim community. Political leadership that creates fear and hatred of the Muslim community does not help this incorrect perception.

For me, and, I assume, for many others, our primary distrust of Muslims was fostered by the attack on the World Trade Centre in New York City on September 11, 2001, where I'd worked until three years prior to the attack. I was still living not far away, and

---

12 Pew Research Center, "American Muslims' Views on Terrorism and Concerns About Extremism" (Washington, D.C.: Pew Research Center, July 26, 2017), https://www.pewresearch.org/religion/2017/07/26/terrorism-and-concerns-about-extremism/.

I watched smoke streaming from the rubble of the Twin Towers for over a week and grieved for the friends who perished on 9/11.

At the time, it was hard for many Americans and me not to draw the conclusion that Muslims are our enemies. But the fact is, they're not. Certainly no more so than any other religious group in the U.S.

If extremists in all religions believed the following quote, the world would certainly be a much better place:

> *The ink of the scholar is more sacred than the blood of the martyr.*
>
> ~ Attributed to the Prophet Muhammad
> (in later hadith tradition)

For more in-depth reading on Islam, I recommend John Esposito's book, *What Everyone Needs to Know About Islam*, which was the source of some of the information above.

Afterlife

The idea of life after death is central to Islamic belief. Muslims believe in a Day of Judgment when everyone will be judged for how they lived their life and either be relegated to eternal Heaven (Jannah) or eternal hellfire (Jahannam) based on their thoughts and actions. The Quran describes Jannah and Jahannam in great detail, and the place where one ends up will be determined by the weight of their good and bad deeds during their lifetime.

Muslims also believe in the existence of a soul separate from the body. This is mentioned several times in the Quran. Even though there are slightly different translations of the specific reference in the 39th chapter of the Quran, Surah Az-Zumar, 39:42[13], on Quran.com, describes how Allah deals with the soul and what happens after death.

It is Allah Who calls back the souls of people upon their death as well as the souls' of the living during their sleep. Then He keeps those for whom He has ordained death, and releases the others until 'their' appointed time. Surely in this are signs for people who reflect.

This isn't surprising to me, of course. As stated previously, I believe that if organised religions didn't offer some path after death and a heaven or some vision of an afterlife, I doubt they'd have many followers! That assumption doesn't preclude the possibility that their claims and promises could be valid, of course.

Proof

The fact that the Islamic religion emerged at such a later date than that of Christianity and certainly much later than the East Asian religions, in my mind, suggests that there should be more verifiable proof available to the casual inquirer such as myself. Although I don't see myself becoming a Muslim, I was interested in how credible the belief is and what proof was available.

Unfortunately, even though Muhammad was born approximately 570 years after Christ, no written records were generated during his lifetime. The Quran was compiled and standardised

---

13 Quran.com Team. "Quran Surah Az-Zumar [39:42] — Juz 24 / Hizb 47." Quran.com, 2025. https://quran.com/39/42?translations=18,19,20,21,22,84,95,85,101.

within a few decades after Muhammad's death from writings created by his companions, but it provides few specific references to the name *Muhammad*; there are, however, many indirect references using descriptions such as the Prophet or Messenger.

Many references to the Prophet Muhammad are also found in writings that occur outside the Quran. One such example is *Sirat Muhammad Rasul Allah* (Life of Muhammad, the Messenger of God) by al-Malik ibn Hasham,[14] which was compiled 120-200 years after his death

As is the case with Jesus, there are enough credible references from multiple sources and stories written after the fact to assume that Muhammad was a historical figure.

Clearly, both Jesus and Muhammad were considered to be wise men, but were they really able to communicate with God?

The only evidence for Jesus's or Muhammad's conversations with God comes from religious texts written by their followers, not from independent historical documentation. These long-standing religions are based on books and records created long after the events described. The stories welcome people into the fold through their grandeur and complexity, and by providing a shining light into the afterlife for followers of the faith, but regrettably they are just stories, not necessarily factual events.

---

14 William Montgomery Watt and Nicolai Sinai, "Sīrat Muhammad Rasūl Allāh," in *Encyclopaedia Britannica* (Chicago: Encyclopaedia Britannica, Inc., February 25, 2025), https://www.britannica.com/topic/Sirat-Muhammad-rasul-Allah.

Having said that, it does seem (according to Britannica) that carbon dating indicates that a number of early Quranic manuscripts were created around 650 CE, not long after the death of the Prophet Muhammad in 632 CE. To me, that time-line suggests that the Quran would contain a more accurate representation of what Muhammad said and did than those from other religions written centuries after the activities of the person described. Whether God delivered the words spoken by Muhammad through the archangel Gabriel is a matter of debate.

It's not lost on me that there never seemed to be any witnesses when these divine pronouncements were handed down.

In the chapter on Commonality, I take a closer look at this question and why these interactions with God are very rarely witnessed in the religions I examined. As in Christianity, Islam offers no proof regarding what will happen to you after you die, but the basic tenets of the Islamic religion, like Christianity, promote following a positive life full of good deeds and offer an eternal reward for doing so.

Even if Muhammad's interaction with the archangel Gabriel was totally made up, clearly, there is nothing wrong with following a life of good intentions… if that is the path you actually choose, or have chosen, to follow.

(For access to additional key-point discussion and summary notes, refer to the section in the back of the book titled Appendix: Notes by Religion just before the Bibliography.)

The Hindu Faith

For most of us in the Western world, our fleeting interactions with Hindus are occasional at best. We may see a woman or a man with a red dot on their forehead and assume them to be Hindu, but in most cases, we feel removed from the influences of the Hindu religion. For many in the West, this faith has a much greater impact on our daily lives than we think.

As I repeatedly emphasise throughout this book, for me, writing *Dance with Angels* was intended to be a personal journey of discovery and a way to find a belief structure that resonated with me. It was not designed to be a comprehensive overview of religions and beliefs, just a simple journey by a lost father in pain. It has, however, over time, morphed into a way to form my own belief structure for support and recovery rather than to wholeheartedly adopt someone else's. As a result, when examining religions in general, the first things I considered were whether they intersect with my life or represent concepts I can believe in. Each reader's level of resonance will obviously be different.

The most apparent way that Hinduism intersects with my current life was not at first realised until I started researching for this chapter. We don't consider this in our daily lives, but the practice of yoga and meditation is integral to Hinduism, aiding spiritual growth and self-realisation. The contortions we follow, silently straining our bodies to the whispers of enlightened yoga instructors on mats that cost hundreds of dollars, were first described in one of the Hindus' sacred texts, the Rigveda, which dates back over 3,000 years. The Yoga Sutras of Patanjali, considered the foundational texts of classic yoga philosophy, were reportedly composed by an ancient Indian sage (rishi) and serve as a key to the philosophy and practice of yoga. You will find yoga and meditation being practised in just about every town you choose to live in America, so the Hindu religion is, in fact, already a large part of the daily lives of many.

My first anecdotal exposure to Hinduism in a minor form has been through participation in Bhakti yoga classes that are somewhat aligned in a non-confrontational way with the Hari Krishna movement. The Society of Krishna Consciousness is an offshoot of Hinduism that originated from the popular (devotional) Hindu Bhakti yoga tradition in India and was introduced to the USA in 1965. The beautiful chanting and hymn-like mantras at the beginning and end of the first Bhakti class I attended brought tears to my eyes. There is something incredibly cathartic about being in a room of people all singing with a loving heart! It's easy to see why many religions incorporate singing or group-like verbal participation, as the heart warms deeply when surrounded by a group of people all singing, saying, or doing the same thing.

Is it the feeling of community, the experience of brotherhood… or just the incredible sense of being, the escape from the loneliness of singularity that draws people to classes like these? It certainly worked for me; it feels good, and thus, people want to return again and again to recreate the wonderful feeling of belonging and community. For me, the feeling was just as powerful as that of sitting in a temple chanting or in a church singing. It is just a wonderful feeling.

Hinduism is considered the oldest of the world's major living religions and deserves much more of my time and exploration, so I went searching for facts.

Facts

I have taken a few trips to Paris over the years, both before and after my son's death. However, around seven years after I started writing this book, I ended up there again to try to finish a few missing chapters of this book. It seemed like a strange place to work on a chapter about Hinduism (India would have been better!), but what a magnificent place to clear the mind, sit in beautiful parks, and try to regain faith in the world, disregard its struggles, be alone and research an ancient religion!

(If you want to replace some of your sorrow with beauty and clarity in your life and can scrape together the money and an excuse, consider renting an apartment in Paris for a few weeks or a month. Even if you are not a writer, I suggest you read a beautiful little book called *A Writer's Paris* by[15] Eric Maisel. Stay away from the tourist attractions and crowds and wander

15 Eric Maisel, *A Writer's Paris: A Guided Journey for the Creative Soul* (Cincinnati: Writer's Digest Books, 2005).

its streets to admire its architecture and history. Sit in its parks and cafes and watch life go by.)

> *When we lose somebody dear to us, we need to learn to live without them. When the time feels right, give yourself a well-deserved break, avoid the stress and grief, and replace them with calm, beauty, and inspiration. It doesn't have to be in Paris, of course; anywhere beautiful and removed will do.*

Yes, Paris is a strange place to be working on a chapter about Hinduism, but one day, I found myself sitting on a bench in a quiet but outstanding little neighbourhood park called the *Square Louvois*, looking up at a majestic fountain. It was a different visit from the one I had years before with my wife and two children in tow. Although I loved the rushed visits to explore the sights with my family, years later, I found myself alone in this beautiful place, taking breaks to admire the 300-year-old fountain and the 700-year-old buildings that surround it. Now, in semi-retirement and after the loss of my son, I was admiring Paris and life from a totally different perspective.

When admiring the 700-year-old architecture of Paris, or even considering the Roman history that preceded it, which dates back 2,000 years, it is easy to be humbled when discussing Hinduism, the world's oldest continuously practiced religious tradition. Archaeological evidence suggests that the practice of Hindu worship dates back over 4,500 years ago, encompassing a rich tapestry of traditions and philosophies with over one billion followers, making it the third-largest religion globally, after Christianity and Islam. If I am in awe of the history of Paris, what level of respect is deserved by a religion that is twice as old as the Roman Empire!

The majority of the world's Hindus live in India, accounting for approximately 90% of the global Hindu population. Fortunately, one of the oldest Hindu temples in America is in San Francisco. In addition to my online research and writing chapters of this book while travelling, upon my return to San Francisco, I was able to gain a more personal glimpse into the world of the anglicised Hindu by simply travelling 10 minutes from my floating home (and then spending another 30 minutes looking for parking in San Francisco).

Hindus believe in a supreme God/creator called *Brahma (a deity and creator)*. But in the Vedanta literature I was given when I visited San Francisco, it states… *the Supreme Reality, Brahman, cannot be described; the most one can say is that it is Sat-Chit-Ananda—Absolute Existence, Consciousness, and Bliss.* It is easy to be confused as I initially was. The significance is in the difference between:

Brahma *~ Is the creator god in Hindu cosmology, who Hindus believe is the deity responsible for bringing the universe into existence.*

Brahman *~ A type of formless reality that is the essence of all beings, and like an infinite, eternal spirit. (A form of universal consciousness, not a deity).*

Hindus believe that the absolute *Brahman* becomes manifest in a number of forms, known by various names and represented by several gods and deities. Thus, Hindu practice is often described as being *henotheistic*, meaning individuals may worship one deity as primary while acknowledging the existence of others.

This results in different Hindu traditions practicing different deities as supreme – Vishnu for Vaishnavas, Shiva for Shaivas, Devi for Shaktas – while still acknowledging the validity of other forms of the divine.

Hinduism is also a religion deeply rooted in ritual, and a social characteristic associated with the religion is the *caste* system, which classifies individuals into four main groups of varying levels of *purity* and social standing, with the Brahmin group (priests and teachers) considered the purest. The lowest castes are Shudra and Dalits (comprising manual labourers), often referred to as Untouchables. An aversion to this elitist hierarchy is one of the reasons that many Hindus turned to Buddhism.

I believe that we are all created equal and shouldn't be discriminated against due to the conditions of our birth. The caste system has historically been an integral part of Hindu philosophy, which is not particularly attractive to me. However, I am glad to point out that many modern Hindus and Hindu organisations actively oppose caste discrimination. Also, notable is that the Indian constitution outlawed caste discrimination in 1950. That is reassuring to hear, because there are certainly aspects of Hinduism that resonate with me. Mahatma Gandhi's philosophies of nonviolence, austerity, and passive resistance come to mind first. As I've said in other sections of this book, I now hold a revised disdain for those who covet wealth after the dramatic realization of how empty that pursuit is when faced with the stark reality of losing something more important, like a loved one.

As I worked on this book, I started to gravitate more to the possibility that a process of rebirth of our soul or essence is an outcome I'd like to believe in. The process of rebirth, the effects of karma, and how we live our lives within that process are core aspects of Hinduism that resonate with me in this way. The rebirth of a soul that carries one's karma is also more appealing to me than the Buddhist concept that we do not have a rebirth of the soul after death but rather a continuation of one's karma.

Also appealing to me is the Hindu view that not all answers can necessarily be found through a pluralistic, dogmatic interpretation of one's religious beliefs and scriptures. This perspective is expressed beautifully in the Hindu words of prayer:

May good thoughts come to us from all sides.

Although the caste system puts me off, it is refreshing that Hinduism maintains that truth must be sought from multiple sources, not simply proclaimed through just one belief. Since I haven't come across a single religion or philosophy that offers irrefutable answers, I've lost respect for any belief system that isn't open to other possibilities and realities—another check mark in the Hindu column, and indeed a philosophy I would include if I were to create my own religion. The altar in the Vedanta temple in San Francisco has representations of Jesus, Buddha, and the Hindu mystic Sri Ramakrishna, signifying respect for all three as great teachers.

Within Hinduism, there are six primary philosophical systems: Samkhya, Yoga, Nyaya, Vaisheshika, Mimamsa, and Vedanta. The Vedanta Society of Northern California has a Hindu temple in San Francisco that holds educational classes. I recommend a visit for anyone living in the Bay Area, even if you have no intention of becoming a Hindu. It's always worth experiencing and being open to others' faith, in my mind. Since you are reading this book, I assume you agree. Although the classes are not in the same building, the Vedanta Society owns the first Hindu temple in the western United States, which was built in 1905.

Their website states: *Vedanta teaches that the essence of all beings and all things is Spirit, infinite, eternal, unchanging, and indivisible.* It emphasises that a person's true nature is this divine Spirit, identical with the inmost being and reality of the universe, and that the goal is to actualise this truth in one's life.

Hinduism is a far more interesting religion than I first thought, and I haven't done it justice by oversimplifying its intricate concepts and history. You can find just about everything you need for a full and more comprehensive, well-rounded viewpoint at Britannica.com.[16]

Some significant terms are worth mentioning here, though:

Atman – *self* or *soul*. One of the most fundamental concepts of Hinduism, the universal self, refers to the eternal core of the personality that, after death, either transmigrates to a new life or attains release (moksha) from the bonds of existence. This is, of course, very similar to Buddhist beliefs due to its origins, but as I point out in the chapter on commonality, the cycle of rebirth of a soul or the *eternal core* of one's personality is a common thread among many belief systems. (Some sceptics even suggest that even if you don't believe in religions or the existence of a god at all, the concept of an *eternal core* being recycled through various lives is possible if you believe in simulation theory. If so, you could assume that the basis of each human's code is recycled

---

16 Arthur Llewellyn Basham and Brian K. Smith, "Hinduism | Origin, History, Beliefs, Gods, & Facts," in *Encyclopaedia Britannica* (Chicago: Encyclopaedia Britannica, Inc., April 3, 2025), https://www.britannica.com/topic/Hinduism.

or reused over and over again during different simulations. But more about that later in the book.)

The most holy of books in the Hindu faith is the Rigveda, which translates to *The Knowledge of Verses* in English, is the oldest of the four sacred books of Hinduism. Other important texts include the Mahabharata and Ramayana epics, the Bhagavad Gita, and the Puranas. The *Rigveda* was created around 1500 BCE (before the common era) and consists of a collection of 1,028 poems (10,600 + versus) that were preserved orally before they were written down about 300 BCE.[17] This ancient collection of poems and hymns is called the *Four Vedas*.[18] Unfortunately, the Rigveda was passed down verbally for many centuries before being written down, and was composed in an ancient language called Vedic Sanskrit, which gradually evolved into classical Sanskrit. I suspect that the numerous oral and manual translations and transcriptions of these poems and texts would have changed them substantially over that period.

If you have ever played a game where you're told a particular phrase and have to whisper that phrase to the person next to you, and they, in turn, whisper the information to the person next to them, and so on, you will understand that I am correct to be a little bit sceptical about the accuracy of the specific wording of the texts. By the time the phrase makes its way around a circle to the last player, it's completely changed. It's hard to imagine

---

17 Encyclopaedia Britannica Editors, "Rigveda | Definition & Facts," in *Encyclopedia Britannica* (Chicago: Encyclopaedia Britannica, Inc., 2025), https://www.britannica.com/topic/Rigveda.

18 Wendy Doniger, "Veda | Definition, Scriptures, Books, & Facts," in *Encyclopaedia Britannica* (Chicago: Encyclopaedia Britannica, Inc., March 13, 2025), https://www.britannica.com/topic/Veda.

how many stories and hymns would change over 1,200 years; without doubt, they'd be embellished and altered. Nevertheless, these texts are revered by and serve as guidance to over one billion people worldwide. The belief in the importance of these texts by so many, in itself, makes them a potent force, regardless of some changes that may have occurred.

Other essential and often-used terms, not only employed by enlightened Western yoga instructors but also followers of Buddhism, include dharma and karma, which originated in Hinduism. I use them several times in this book, so I had to grasp the difference. I thought I had a pretty good understanding of karma, but people have occasionally told me that I am living my *dharma*, so I thought it was essential to understand them and the often-missed nuances between them.

Karma is a word that most people have heard used as if it were a cosmic scoreboard, as when people say, *Do good, and good will come back to you; do bad, and you will get that back in return*. That's true, but it's important to note that karmic consequences—not only the large ones but the quiet ones—are what Hindus and Buddhists believe in. Every word, thought, and deed plants a seed, shaping this life and, for believers, the hereafter. Everything you do creates your own karma.

Dharma gets less attention. Dharma is about your calling in the current life; in my mind, it relates to your correct role, or what you are meant to be doing, your purpose. Hindus associate dharma with their familial duties, stage of life, and social status—students learn, kings protect, and so on. To Hindus, dharma is what creates balance in the universe.

In Buddhism, Dharma has a slightly different meaning. It's the Buddha's message about why we suffer and how to end it, not your societal role. Whatever your background, following the Dharma in Buddhism involves living with knowledge, compassion, and mindfulness.

In simple terms, in Hinduism, karma is the rule of cause and effect, or how the things you do have effects that go out into the world and then come back to you. Dharma is the way to go; it directs you on what to do so that your deeds are in line with the universal order of life. What happens because of your actions and thoughts is one. The other is your correct purpose.

Afterlife

Both Buddhists and Hindus believe in reincarnation, but they understand it differently. Hindus believe that the soul is reborn progressively through good actions, over and over again, until it eventually reaches liberation, called moksha.[19]

As I mention in the next chapter of this book, Buddhists also believe in cycles of rebirth, and they call the goal of liberation nirvana. (However, most Buddhists don't believe in a *soul*, as most people would define it. Instead, most Buddhists think of this cycle as a collection of mental karmic imprints that are reborn into the next life rather than a soul.) In Hindu mythology, however, there is a soul and a colourful god of the dead called Yama[20] who is in charge of the dead's resting place. (Buddhists

---

19 Patrick Olivelle, "Moksha | Salvation, Dharma & Karma," in *Encyclopaedia Britannica* (Chicago: Encyclopaedia Britannica, Inc., 2025), https://www.britannica.com/topic/moksha-Indian-religion.

20 Matt Stefon, "Yama | Ruler of Dead, Judge of Souls & Lord of Dharma," in *Encyclopaedia Britannica* (Chicago: Encyclopaedia Britannica, Inc., 2025), https://www.britannica.com/topic/Yama-Hindu-god.

also recognise Yama, but to a lesser degree.) Yama is said to be the one you will face as he weighs the good and evil deeds of your life and determines retribution. You will recognise him because of his majestic appearance, wearing red or green garments, and having red eyes. If that doesn't do it, just look for the god-like character riding a buffalo, carrying a noose and a mace, and accompanied by his two, four-eyed dogs. He certainly sounds like a pretty terrifying character!

In Part 3 of this book, you'll find numerous references to a publication called *Journey of Souls,* in which a similar process of rebirth and evolution is described in multiple case studies of people under deep hypnosis. (Some Jews and followers of the Kabbalah (from Jewish mysticism) also believe in reincarnation (called *Gilguil*) in which souls experience multiple lifetimes to achieve spiritual perfection.) It is fascinating to me that many belief systems suggest a progressive series of incarnations through which we hopefully grow and eventually draw closer to the divine source of all creation and power. I love that storyline. If we're essentially spirits, it makes sense that the spirit would go through periods of growth and rebirth rather than be discarded or disappear.

It's essential to note that for Hindus to fully embrace the enticing belief in reincarnation (the cycle of samsara) and the potential for rebirth after death, as well as the cycle of life, it is crucial to understand and follow the key concepts of karma and dharma as a path to the ultimate goal of moksha. I am not sure if I could have an unswerving belief in moksha, but a belief in a life that promotes good karma and in following one's dharma certainly resonates with me.

Proof

Is there proof to support the statements and beliefs described in the foundational poems of Hinduism that have been passed down for over a thousand years and translated through numerous languages? There is plenty of evidence dating back thousands of years regarding the existence and substantial influence of the Hindu religion; still, there is no actual proof that the assertions of the religion are anything more than myth. I don't want to be harsh in sounding this way. Hindus aren't alone in this. Empirical evidence supporting any of the claims by proponents and believers in the major faiths remains scarce.

However, if *proof* to you means evidence that this ancient faith has real roots in history, not just in stories or myths. Then, yes, Hinduism, without a doubt, has left a trail that we can still see today and has influenced us in many ways.

The earliest indications of Hinduism date back to the Indus Valley Civilisation, more than 4,000 years ago. Archaeologists have uncovered artifacts, seals, and sculptures from that time, among which is a small carving known as the Pashupati Seal.

It shows a figure sitting cross-legged, surrounded by animals, that bears a striking resemblance to Shiva, one of Hinduism's most powerful gods. These discoveries suggest that the seeds of Hindu worship were already present long before the religion entirely took shape.

Then came the Vedic period, when the great hymns of the Rigveda were composed. These are not just old songs—they are some of the world's oldest surviving sacred texts. Passed down orally for centuries before being written, they capture rituals, prayers, and philosophies that still echo in Hindu practice today. To this day, if you hear a priest chanting in Sanskrit, as I mentioned earlier, you may not be listening to the exact words that were spoken when they were created 3,500 years ago, but you will be hearing the exact words that were written down 2,300 years ago—that's still quite impressive.

Later, the grand epics—the Mahabharata and the Ramayana — added layers of story and meaning. They are not just literature but cultural touchstones that shaped the moral and spiritual imagination of India. Some places described in these epics have even been linked to archaeological sites. Although disputed, some archaeological evidence suggests that the ancient city of Dwarka, long believed to be the legendary home of Krishna, has been located off the coast of Gujarat. What was once thought of only as mythology, may now be showing up as stone foundations and ruins beneath the sea.

So, while Hinduism doesn't hand us proof in the sense of a single relic, it does offer many archaeological remains, some enduring texts, and old established traditions. These are threads that connect modern-day rituals to ancient civilisations, showing that Hinduism is not just a faith of stories. It is a faith with history carved into the earth and etched into human memory. We even practise some of those rituals in the West.

(For access to additional key-point discussion and summary notes, refer to the section in the back of the book titled Appendix: Notes by Religion just before the Bibliography.)

Buddhism

I thought I was losing him, but he is everywhere.[21]

~ Quote from The Five Invitations – Frank Ostaseski

A journey to explore spirituality and investigate a more internal path can't just be carried out in libraries and on the internet. Part of my journey to hopefully find some answers and improve my chances of recovering from my grief would clearly need to be experiential…at least anecdotally. Of course, Buddhism, being among the world's five largest religions, had to be included in my search for meaning!

The Sanskrit root of the word Buddha—budh or budd — *means to awaken*, or to know. Others define it as *divine intellect*. In Buddhist texts, Buddha is applied as the title for Siddhārtha

---

21 Frank Ostaseski, *The Five Invitations: Discovering What Death Can Teach Us about Living Fully*, Deckle Edge (Hardcover) (New York: Flatiron Books, 2017).

Gautama — *the Awakened One*. The words Bodhi (enlightenment) and Bodhisattva (being striving toward awakening) are all derived from the same root word -budh- as well.

* * *

Around the time I was starting to think about the context for writing a journal or book, one of my neighbours in my little floating-home community just north of San Francisco went into her 16-year-old son's bedroom to wake him up for school and found him dead. There had been no foul play or distress in his life. He'd died suddenly in his sleep and without warning because of a heart issue!

> *Why is it that when the axe of tragedy is swung without warning, it seems so blunt and often more traumatic than a death we see coming?*

One would assume it's because we have time to process the approaching event psychologically over time and get somewhat used to it. In any case, according to the *American Journal of Psychiatry* and other expert references, sudden unexpected loss is often much more traumatic than an expected death, as in the case of a long illness, and has much greater potential to cause deeper psychiatric upsets.[22]

---

22 Katherine M. Keyes et al., "The Burden of Loss: Unexpected Death of a Loved One and Psychiatric Disorders across the Life Course in a National Study," *The American Journal of Psychiatry* 171, no. 8 (August 1, 2014): 864–71, https://doi.org/10.1176/appi.ajp.2014.13081132.

Clearly, any loss of life is tragic, and just because the person you lost knew about it ahead of time doesn't mean you miss them any less. The sense of loss is just as great, and, for many, the subsequent grief can last just as long if not longer. But, as mentioned later in this book, when the loss is sudden and unexpected, it's like being thrown into an icy-cold, raging river rather than immersing oneself in that cold, dark water slowly. That analogy is one I heard at a workshop I attended, run by David Kessler, author of a number of great books on grief, at least one of which you will find in my curated list on LighthouseLaneBooks.com.

> *My big question is, how long do we have to spend in that freezing water until we're eventually able to drag ourselves to shore?*

I still shudder at the thought of what a terrible, devastating experience it would be to find your only child dead and what that would do to the mother. Perhaps my own experience has made me more acutely aware of the pain of sudden loss; I wouldn't wish it on anybody. I wanted to let my neighbour know that I felt her pain in the hope of possibly easing some of it.

By the time I actually connected with Elana (the mother of Ez, the boy who'd died), six months or so had passed since she'd gone into his bedroom and found him lifeless. As it turned out, when we finally did meet and started to spend time together, she seemed to be dealing with her very tragic loss in a way that I didn't expect. Although Jewish, Elana was also a serious follower of Buddhism and, because of that belief, was convinced that her son had not disappeared but that his spirit had transitioned to another plane. This more supportive way in which she was dealing with her loss made me excited about exploring Buddhism as part of my journey. It was also a reaffirmation for me of the book's premise—that having a belief structure often helps one recover from grief more quickly and with less pain.

I also instinctively wanted to find out more about Buddhism because it isn't founded on a belief in an ultimate creator, which was my initial assumption about all religions when I started writing this book. Generally speaking, Buddhists don't believe that the world was created and is ruled by a god (although there are supernatural figures who get involved). Instead, adherents follow the teachings of the Buddha along with some basic tenets about the nature of reality. The primary belief is that human life is a cycle of suffering and rebirth, but that if one achieves enlightenment (nirvana), one can escape this cycle forever.

Many followers of Buddhism don't consider it a religion at all. To them, it's a philosophical approach to life, a way of living and understanding. Due to input from several people, I had to acquiesce and eventually change the name of this section of the book from The Major Religions to The Major Beliefs so I could be sure to include Buddhism appropriately.

Religion (according to Webster's dictionary): *An institution to express a belief in a divine power.* Or ... *a strong belief in a supernatural power or powers that control human destiny.*

Indeed, Buddhism doesn't fall into the category of being a religion if you listen to Mr Webster. It was, instead, created around the teachings and philosophies of a living, charismatic figure whose insights and perspectives appealed to many people. Siddhārtha Gautama, who became known as the Buddha, isn't revered as a deity but as a wise man. Actually, various traditions believe that he wasn't the first buddha nor will he be the last. All

Buddhist traditions agree that he attained, through meditation and reflection, the ultimate state in Buddhism, nirvana—the end of the cycle of death and rebirth.

***Faith dispels doubt and hesitation. It liberates you from suffering and delivers you to the city of peace and happiness.*[23]**

~ Tenzin Gyatso, His Holiness, the 14th Dalai Lama

The Story of Buddha

The story of the origin of the Buddha is an intriguing tale of kings, golden chariots, and royalty living lives of radiance and beauty that, interestingly, resulted in a worldwide following and philosophy that denounces ***attachment*** to those very same mantles of wealth.

As legend has it, a little over 2,500 years ago, a young prince was born in northern India; his name was Siddhārtha Gautama. The city in which he was born was shining with the splendour of gems, where darkness, like poverty, could find no place.[24] *It was a wonderful, radiant place where sunbeams fell on golden palaces set high in the sky.*

---

23 Dalai Lama, *The Dalai Lama's Little Book of Buddhism* (Newburyport, MA: Red Wheel Weiser, 2015),

24 Aśvaghosa, *Buddhacarita, or, Acts of the Buddha: Complete Sanskrit Text with English Translation*, New enl. ed. 1984, repr (Delhi: Motilal Banarsidass, 2004), https://archive.org/details/buddhacaritaorac0000asva.

The young prince eventually left the overwhelming opulence of the city in which he was born and went outside its walls, only to be faced with the ravages of poverty, old age, death, and sickness of which he was previously unaware. He was appalled by the injustice of the disparity between his life and that of those outside, returned his worldly possessions to his parents' palace, and embarked on a journey of internal discovery, enlightenment, and teaching.

The Metropolitan Museum of Art website[25] describes the story of Buddha succinctly on their website. In summary, the website recounts that after leaving his privileged life, Siddhārtha Gautama spent years pursuing extreme asceticism in an effort to overcome physical desire. Near death from fasting, he eventually accepted food and realised that self-denial alone could not lead to enlightenment. He then meditated beneath what later became known as the bodhi tree, where he attained awakening and became the Buddha.

Afterwards, he remained in meditation before beginning to teach others, encouraging a path he called the Middle Way—one that avoids punishing oneself by going without but also eliminates the opposite of that: excess. His teachings, which began around the fifth century BCE, emphasised balance, awareness, and moderation as the route to liberation.

On learning about the concept of the Middle Way and its importance in the Buddhist faith, I was reminded once again of Viktor Frankl's iconic work, ***Man's Search for Meaning***, which I have mentioned previously in this book. I'm not too concerned

---

25 Kathryn Selig Brown, "Life of the Buddha," Museum educational resource / Art history essay, Timeline of Art History, October 1, 2003, https://www.metmuseum.org/toah/hd/buda/hd_buda.htm.

about avoiding self-denial (never been a problem for me!), but avoiding the extremes of physical and psychological desire are dark recesses that I (or my inner child, perhaps?) have at times embraced with passion. As Frankl references in *Man's Search for Meaning*, that sort of behaviour often reveals a desire to fill what he calls man's existential void. We often try to fill that void with an unfruitful attachment and need for more power, sex, or wealth.

* * *

Another core idea in Buddhist thought resonated strongly with me—the parallel between the cycles of rebirth described in Buddhism that occur before reaching nirvana and the stories described in *Journey of Souls* by Michael Newton about what happens to our soul after death is striking.

In my view, there are also some loose similarities between this type of ongoing journey and that suggested in the *Egyptian Book of the Dead.* What we call the *Egyptian Book of the Dead* is actually a term of modern origin used to describe a series of ancient Egyptian rituals, spells, and writing developed from multiple sources, such as inscriptions on papyrus scrolls, figurines, mummy wrappings, and other sources. These are all designed to help the deceased find their way on the journey through the afterlife and be reunited with the sun god, which the Egyptians called Re, and the god of the nether world, called Osiris. These stories, too, are a part of a continual cycle of renewal and rebirth.

The journey described in Buddhism and that in the ancient Egyptian texts isn't the same by any means. Nevertheless, in his *Journey of Souls*, Newton describes the spiritual growth that occurs in these multiple cycles of rebirth. In his case studies,

Newton states that the souls that have achieved certain levels of continued growth each time they're on earth eventually change in status and get closer and closer to *The Source* of all beings and ultimately are freed from the cycle of rebirth.

Among Buddhist writings, the collection of texts known as the *Bardo Thödol* (often referred to as *The Tibetan Book of the Dead*) most piqued my interest. This work arises from *Vajrayāna* (Tantric) Buddhism, which developed in Central Asia and later flourished in Tibet. Vajrayāna teachings describe bardos—transitional states of consciousness that occur during life, death, and rebirth. In Tibetan tradition, the period between death and rebirth is often described as lasting up to 49 days, during which consciousness passes through several bardos.

The first of the bardo is at the actual moment of death. The soul of the recently dead thinks about its past life and comes to terms with the fact that it has died. Things that look like ghosts appear in the second bardo. If the mind isn't able to discern that these ghosts aren't real, it gets confused and, based on its karma, may be drawn into a rebirth that stops it from becoming free of the cycle of death and rebirth. The birth of the soul in a new body is the third bardo.

A central tenet of all schools of Buddhism is that attachment to and craving for worldly things spurs suffering and unease (dukkha). This suffering influences actions whose accumulated effects, or Karma, bind individuals to the process of death and rebirth (samsara). Those who have attained enlightenment (bodhi) are thereby released from this process, attaining liberation (moksha). Those who remain unenlightened are drawn by Karma, whether good or bad, into a new life in one of six modes of existence: as a sufferer in hell (enduring horrible torture), as a wandering ghost (driven by insatiable craving), as an animal (ruled by instinct), as a demigod (lustful for power), as a human being (balanced in instinct and reason), or as a god (deluded by their long lives into believing they are immortal).[26]

~ Encyclopedia Britannica 2025

Buddhism is complex and, at the same time, simple; at its essence is what's known as The Four Noble Truths,[27] which the Buddha taught in his first sermon. According to Britannica, all four Noble Truths relate to suffering in one way or another:

The First Noble Truth identifies the existence of suffering.

The Second Noble Truth seeks to find the cause of suffering.

The Third Noble Truth states that an end of suffering is possible.

---

26 Matt Stefon, "Bardo Thödol," in *Encyclopaedia Britannica* (Chicago: Encyclopaedia Britannica, Inc., 2025), https://www.britannica.com/topic/Bardo-Thodol.

27 Donald S. Lopez, "Four Noble Truths," in *Encyclopaedia Britannica* (Chicago: Encyclopaedia Britannica, Inc., February 24, 2025), https://www.britannica.com/topic/Four-Noble-Truths.

The Fourth and final Nobel Truth states that the path (Pali: magga; Sanskrit: marga) to the cessation of suffering is achieved through understanding and embracing the following eight elements:

The eight elements of the path:

1. **Correct view**: *an accurate understanding of the true nature of reality, specifically the Four Noble Truths.*
2. **Correct intention**: *avoiding thoughts of attachment, hatred, and harmful intent.*
3. **Correct speech**: *refraining from verbal misdeeds such as lying, divisive speech, harsh speech, and senseless speech.*
4. **Correct action**: *refraining from physical misdeeds such as killing, stealing, and sexual misconduct.*
5. **Correct livelihood**: *avoiding trades that directly or indirectly harm others, such as selling slaves, weapons, animals for slaughter, intoxicants, or poisons.*
6. **Correct effort**: *abandoning negative states of mind that have already arisen, preventing negative states that have yet to arise, and sustaining positive states that have already arisen.*
7. **Correct mindfulness**: *awareness of body, feelings, thoughts, and phenomena (the constituents of the existing world).*
8. **Correct concentration** *and single-mindedness; meditative awareness.*

The two main branches of Buddhism, Mahayana and Theravada, combined have an estimated 360-500 million followers worldwide.

> *One critical insight I learned from my exploration of Buddhism is the concept that life is all about balance and is expected to contain both pain and pleasure. To experience one entirely, you must also experience and embrace the other.*

A simplistic example of this would be to imagine a person living on a meagre diet of potatoes and rice for years but who is suddenly offered a fantastic meal and has a greater appreciation of it. Or the reverse—a spoiled young adult has had abundance all their lives and suddenly finds themselves living through a worldwide financial depression, loses everything, and then starts to appreciate more fully all the things they've lost. One could also immediately refer to Buddha's personal journey when he first left his opulent palace and was faced with poverty for the first time in his life, but for Siddhārtha Gautama, his sudden and dramatic change of environment didn't create an appreciation for his past wealth—quite the opposite. He developed an awareness of compassion for those around him and a desire to forgo his wealth.

I'm not saying that a person needs to undergo trauma to understand this philosophy correctly, but there's no doubt that the loss of my son has given me an even greater reason to cherish the wonderful memories I have of him. Thinking about the hugs, holding his little hand on a walk, and the excitement of playing make-believe used to immediately bring a flood of tears to my eyes. After a while, the tears were fewer, and the warm feeling from that memory grew because his loss has given me a greater appreciation of what I had, and the memories and songs I still have.

I first encountered the concept of how loss can often create greater appreciation while reading Joe Biden 's book, *Promise Me, Dad*[28]. Joe Biden has faced much grief, first losing his wife and daughter in a car accident and then one of his two sons, Beau, later in life. In his role as Vice President, Joe was often the person who'd speak to the Gold Star parents of the US soldiers killed. One great memory from reading that book is this line where he talked to all these parents. I paraphrase…

> ***It's impossible to believe now, but I promise you that someday, when you have a memory of your child, your first reaction will be to smile, not cry.***
>
> ~ Former President Joe Biden – Promise Me, Dad

When I read Biden's book not long after my son's death, I couldn't believe that his promise would ever happen to me, but, around three years later, I found that more often I started to smile than tear up when I was reminded of my son (although sometimes I still do both simultaneously). From my experience, to speed up the transition from tears to a smile that Biden described, it's essential to realise that…

> *We are actually better off not spending our time trying to avoid the anguish and grief of loss, but instead, recognising and acknowledging it.*

If you face your grief, it will become less overwhelming and potent. For me, sometimes grief is like a shroud—a heavy, cold,

28 Joe Biden, *Promise Me, Dad: A Year of Hope, Hardship, and Purpose* (New York: Flatiron Books, 2017).

grey fog of pain that envelopes me. I don't think that shroud will ever disappear entirely. I can still see it lurking in the distance. Sometimes, I realise I'm once again under its influence and have to live with that. But the periods of being in a foggy, confusing world of pain, sadness, and grief are now fewer each day. Joe Biden's words are slowly coming true.

The Buddhist belief that life is a journey of suffering and pleasure was foreign to me until my early 50's. Beforehand, I had a truly remarkable and *blessed* life full of joy, adventure, and passion. I sailed boats around the Caribbean, divided the sky for years as a professional pilot, dated beautiful women, climbed mountains, and chased wild horses through the tall, golden grass of the Australian Outback while mustering cattle from the air. I had eventually found a wife and had two tremendous children, whom I loved dearly. That all changed when I suddenly received an unexpected call while on holiday with my family on the French Riviera. My sister had died of septicaemia! I hadn't even known she was sick.

Before that call, I'd never been to a funeral, lost a friend to cancer or alcoholism, or had to face the realisation that perhaps I wasn't destined for the greatness that I'd always expected and anticipated. Nor had I yet to deal with aging, being alone and unhappy, or, more impactful than all these, feeling the depth of suffering one endures when one loses a child.

My sister's unexpected death was followed by the loss of my Uncle Peter, who looked after me when I was young. After that was my father's death, the loss of my wife through divorce, and the passing of my loving dog. And then came the most impactful experience of my life—the loss of my son. The suffering part of life had certainly arrived!

When considering the concept of balance in one's life, I had to ask myself if what I had experienced was payback for all those years of wonderment or if it was just the normal ebb and flow of pain and pleasure, as taught by the Buddha. Suffering was predominant for me on this journey now, so I wanted to find out more about it. I desperately wanted to know how Buddhists viewed it. Perhaps these monks I'd often seen, clad all in orange, could tell me how to free myself of that suffering by understanding it correctly!

Phillip Moffitt

He doesn't walk around wearing orange robes, but Phillip Moffitt is one of the better-known Buddhist teachers in California. Phillip left his world as a successful publisher and CEO of *Esquire* magazine in his forties to become a Buddhist meditation teacher. He has published several books and has helped people integrate Buddhist principles into their everyday lives to create a more authentic and enjoyable journey.

As it happened, when I was working on the chapter on Buddhism for this book, I was invited to attend a full-day seminar called The Art and Practice of Forgiveness, which was offered online by the long-established meditation centre in northern California called Spirit Rock. Phillip Moffitt was the teacher.

I sat with a friend as we listened to Moffitt discuss Buddhist views on forgiveness and its importance in the healing and grieving process. There were periods of thoughtful, guided meditation in the seminar, and during one of these, much of the anxiety, guilt, sadness, and tension I'd been feeling disappeared. This sense of release lasted for the rest of the day. I felt like the younger Warwick—full of potential, happiness, and warmth. I so wanted to be able to make that last! Unfortunately for me, I realised I didn't have the time for daily meditations with Phillip Moffitt. Or did I? Perhaps a life with more understanding of the Buddhist way and a mindful, more present existence was possible!

This is the definition of forgiveness provided by Phillip Moffitt in his presentation, The Art and Practice of Forgiveness:[29]"

> ***Forgiveness is a voluntary, intentional letting loose of emotional and mental thoughts of anger, revenge, hatred, and resentment toward someone or some group of people that have harmed you, or someone that you care about.***

I certainly had and still have some of those thoughts of anger and revenge, and it would be wonderful to let them go. I wondered if perhaps doing so is one of the ways out of the darkness that surrounds us all during the times after a loss.

What is the connection between forgiveness and grief according to the Buddhist religion? Why should we forgive, and who should we forgive? How will this help release the suffering and grief of those who've lost a loved one and are having trouble moving on? That seminar by Moffitt, along with a talk by another well-known and highly regarded Buddhist psychologist, Dr Jack Kornfield, gave me some answers—or at least interpretations

---

29 Phillip Moffitt, "The Art and Practice of Forgiveness (PM3D21)" (Meditation retreat, Spirit Rock Retreat Program, Spirit Rock Meditation Center, November 21, 2021), https://spirit-rock.secure.retreat.guru/program/the-art-and-practice-of-forgiveness-pm3d21/.

that were relevant to those of us who've experienced great loss and particularly to me.

The following are my takeaways and interpretations from my experience with Buddhist thought:

Forgiveness isn't the same as in the Christian religion, in which we're effectively asked to turn the other cheek. In Buddhism, you can still hold people accountable for their wrongdoing, and forgiveness is about letting go of the attachment to the anger that arises from our experience of it. That anger, if held, is doing more damage to us than to those who wronged us. It makes *us* suffer, not the person who did wrong.

> ***When someone betrays you, you can hate them, or at some point, you can just say... It's not worth it. It's not worth it to live day after day with hatred.***[30]
>
> ~ Dr Jack Kornfield

Often, you're the one you need to forgive, not others. Be kind to yourself. I've carried a lot of guilt for not protecting my son from the people who killed him and for not being there to save him or being able to stop them from taking advantage of him. Do you have regrets that make you feel guilty and blame yourself? If so, the key to releasing those feelings is to forgive yourself.

You must be able to let go of anger to move on and feel joy again. Forgiveness is part of the necessary process of moving through—not bypassing—the suffering of grief.

---

30 Jack Kornfield, "The Ancient Heart of Forgiveness," *Greater Good Science Center*, August 23, 2011, https://greatergood.berkeley.edu/article/item/the_ancient_heart_of_forgiveness.

According to Buddhist teachings, the consciousness of our loved ones passes into another plane and will eventually be reborn according to one's Karma. *Your loved one isn't lost. They're just no longer with us in the same form.* The suffering you experience and, in particular, the attachment to that suffering, is what creates the anger and grief. In Buddhist thought, attachment is regarded as the primary cause of all suffering.

Desire and suffering go hand in hand.

I do know that the overwhelming *desire* to have my son around—to watch him sing, laugh, and grow—was and is the source of much of my suffering. But can one learn to detach from that desire and move forward? Keep in mind the distinction between eliminating the attachment to the desire and the desire itself. One can still have the desire to hold their loved one's hands again or see their smile, hear their laughter, and so on, but it is the need and attachment to that desire that causes a lot of our pain.

If you're reading this book, you're mindful enough to at least care about your mental well-being. In all likelihood, you've lost somebody dear to you and are suffering in some way from their loss. Or you may be embarking on a new journey and want to know how to proceed most effectively.

> *You may very well feel your loss is so acute that nobody could feel the depths of darkness the way you do. I can assure you that anybody who's lost someone dear to them also suffers in their own darkness. You are not alone.*

A simple yet profound insight that resonated with me was my interpretation of an analogy in one of Phillip Moffitt's many books, titled *Dancing with Life.*[31] In this book, Moffitt writes about the Four Noble Truths—the centrepiece of the Buddha's teachings—and how to incorporate the insights they represent in dealing with the suffering in your life. Here's an analogy for how to view pain, grief, suffering, and pleasure that I find helpful to remember:

Life is a dance, and you must dance with it.

For me, the visualisation of dancing in tune with a partner, moving with them and not fighting them, made it easier to understand one of the messages of Moffitt's book—we must move with the ebb and flow of life, the pleasure and pain, in ways that don't define and control us. I longed to free myself from being controlled and defined by the grief I felt at the loss of my son—but could I do it?

Facts

As mentioned earlier, my initial intent was a reference book of sorts that compared the facts and proof from various religions in a more systematic way, but that unintentionally changed as I started to write this chapter. Buddhism and some of the other religions I examined began to merge into a journey of emotion as well as fact.

31 Phillip Moffitt, *Dancing with Life: Buddhist Insights for Finding Meaning and Joy in the Face of Suffering* (Emmaus, Pa.; Godalming: Rodale : Melia [distributor], 2012), http://www.vlebooks.com/vleweb/product/openreader?id=none&isbn=9781605298962.

It is easy to be overwhelmed by the feelings various philosophies and religions evoke. However, I also wanted to maintain some level of detachment and scepticism by stepping away from personal experience and going back to some facts. Combining the two concepts into a memoir is challenging, as I must find a way to transition smoothly between feelings and facts and then back to more personal stories. As a result, I decided to place a lot of facts and research in the back of the book while still trying to keep some of the most relevant concepts that I found necessary in the narrative. I suppose that is the way my mind works—combining emotion and fact to make decisions. I hope short intermissions of fact, such as those interludes in this book, don't subtract deeply from my personal journey.

Origin: Many modern scholars believe that the historical Buddha lived from about 563 to about 483 BCE. Some others think that he lived about 100 years later (from about 448 to 368 BCE). At that time in India, there was much discontent regarding Brahmanic (Hindu high-caste) sacrificial practices and rituals. In northwestern India, several ascetics tried to create a more personal and spiritual religious experience than that found in the Vedas (Hindu sacred scriptures).[32] One of the more charismatic of these ascetic leaders was Siddhārtha Gautama. His following grew, and Buddhism was born.

In the centuries that followed the death of Siddhārtha Gautama around the age of 80, Buddhism diverged into two main groups, the Theravada community and the Mahayana

32 Frank E. Reynolds and Donald S. Lopez, "Buddhism | Definition, Beliefs, Origin, Systems, & Practice," in ***Encyclopaedia Britannica*** (Chicago, IL: Encyclopaedia Britannica, Inc., April 7, 2025), https://www.britannica.com/topic/Buddhism.

community, each of which placed different emphases on the various teachings of Buddha. Even though the Buddha himself didn't leave any written works, hundreds of teachings (called sutras) were attributed to him, which are recognised by the Mahayana. The Sutta Pitaka (Pali: *Basket of Discourse*) and Vinaya Pitaka (Pāli and Sanskrit: *Basket of Discipline*) are collections that comprise Theravada scripture.

Because Buddhism emerged from the same ancient Indian spiritual traditions that gave rise to Hinduism, there are several similarities. Although the Buddha explicitly rejected many Brahmanical beliefs and practices, both religions share concepts such as karma and rebirth; however, their interpretations and paths to liberation (moksha in Hinduism and nirvana in Buddhism) differ. On the other hand, Buddhists, unlike Hindus, don't center their practice around a creator god. Instead, they focus more on individual spiritual practices like meditation.

My own preference is to relate this individualised seeking of enlightenment to an awareness of the *God* that I imagine to be within each of us, rather than a god outside of us. Some would call that philosophy sacrilegious, of course; others will recognise and believe as I do—that we each have an aspect of divinity within us. Many Buddhist texts refer to the *Buddha nature* that all beings possess. But for me, I think—or possibly hope—that the divinity and power within us is something greater than just a Buddha nature. I haven't read any Buddhist references that refer to the power within each of us as divine; perhaps it's just my way of reminding myself of my singularity and how special we *all* are. I believe we all contain some form of power and greatness within ourselves. Personally, I would rather worship at that altar than at one in a church.

Meditation

I think 99 times and find nothing. I stop thinking, swim in silence, and the truth comes to me.

Attributed to — Albert Einstein

I first started a meditation practice in 2012 when the whole world seemed to be coming down around me. My father had died, and my wife announced that she was leaving me; my beautiful dog and only true friend had died when I was at my father's funeral. My uncle, with whom I was close, and my sister had also died in the preceding few years. It all seemed too much, so I started playing guided meditation tapes to escape for periods during my rest periods on the 747 way up in the sky.

One could hardly create a place to escape that was physically farther from my troubles than lying in a darkened bunk room listening to the drone of engines at 38,000 feet above the Earth's surface. But that's where I found my escape from the world and all its tension. Of course, now, I've realised that you don't need to be six miles above the Earth to make meditation work for you. The result is just as good if done sitting in your living room. Little did I know that later, I'd also lose my son and that, for a period of time, it would feel like there was no world at all, and my need to escape the anguish and suffering would be even greater. Meditation provided that escape for me.

In large part because of the numerous benefits that meditation provides when time allows, I strive to establish a daily morning routine. I have my decaf coffee, sit in the sun, catch up on the news, etc. And then, typically still tired from the night before, I use my morning meditation to recharge before launching my workday.

When I first started, I was using a 29-minute meditation that I had previously done during my rest periods on the aeroplane. The recordings I listened to were a combined hypnotherapy/subliminal talk that would allow me to sleep, meditate, and get a mental booster shot of self-esteem, happiness, weight loss, overcoming grief, or whatever topic I thought I needed to address at any given time.

Then, after I retired from my job as a pilot, I would use those same self-help-type meditations to get quick naps in during the day or in the morning. Eventually, though, I realised that to experience true meditation, eliminating daily noise and learning how to be mindful within oneself without guidance offered a more valid form of meditation. Listening to somebody telling you how good you are or trying to help you become motivated by directing you subliminally toward self-improvement helps, but it doesn't connect you deeply within yourself. Yes, there were benefits, and I think that subliminal programming, if repeated enough, can help, but I needed something greater—a paradigm shift to a different place.

After speaking to friends who were into meditation, they suggested a meditation teacher named Jon Kabat-Zinn and his latest book, *Wherever You Go, There You Are.*[33] I have placed some of his books in my bookshop at LighthouseLaneBooks.com.

I have done so because he's spent his life in the realm of mindfulness meditation and is a terrific resource. You can check out his website at jonkabat-zinn.com.One of Jon Kabat-Zinn's more than a dozen books is a co-authored work called *The Mindful Way through Depression*,[34] which has over four stars on Goodreads. I highly recommend this book if you're trying to free yourself of the depression that many of us face after the devastating loss of a loved one. The book's collaborator is Mark Williams, Emeritus Professor of Clinical Psychology at the University of Oxford. Prof. William collaborated with John Teasdale and Zindel Segal in developing mindfulness-based cognitive therapy (MBCT) techniques to overcome chronic unhappiness.

There are thousands of meditation gurus available on YouTube, in bookstores, via apps, at temples, and in just about every yoga studio. You don't have to follow JKZ (Jon Kabat-Zinn). Any good practice, teacher, or methodology should be able to show you how to connect more deeply with the soulful person within.

In the chapter on Spiritualism later in this book, I mention Edgar Cayce, who was a hugely popular spiritualist in the early 1900s. A diagram in one of his books resonated with me while

---

33 Jon Kabat-Zinn, *Wherever You Go, There You Are: Mindfulness Meditation in Everyday Life*, 10th anniversary ed (New York, N.Y.: MJF Books, 2005), https://www.barnesandnoble.com/w/wherever-you-go-there-you-are-jon-kabat-zinn-phd/1102636030.

34 Mark Williams et al., *The Mindful Way through Depression: Freeing Yourself from Chronic Unhappiness* (New York: Guilford Press, 2007).

I was researching for this book. It represents a deeper state of meditation as a buffer and a pathway between our material lives and the spirit realm beyond—what he called *Universal Consciousness*. If you believe in a spirit realm, and you want to be as close as possible to the spirits of those you've lost, I suggest exploring Cayce's premise that entering a deep state of meditation will bring you much closer to them.

Edgar Cayce may be correct. I feel I've only been directly visited by Harrison on one occasion. It was during a period of deep meditation that he came to me, and we sat together on a bench. After we spoke to one another, he eventually got up, walked away, turned, smiled, and waved goodbye. I feel it was the last time I saw him in a real way. Everything since then has been memories that I recall clearly, but sadly, they lack the sense of a real presence.

Afterlife

What Buddhists believe about the hereafter differs among schools and traditions. According to Buddhist teachings, all beings are subject to the cycle of rebirth after death. This cycle, and the world of suffering we all live in, is called samsara,[35] which is originally a Hindu (Sanskrit) term. Hindus, the Ajivika school which coexisted with early Buddhism, and followers of Jainism (one of India's most ancient religions and closely related to Hinduism and Buddhism) all believe in the existence of a soul that goes through a cycle of death and rebirth that keeps it locked in

---

35 Patrick Olivelle, "Karma | Indian Philosophy & Its Impact on Life," in *Encyclopaedia Britannica* (Chicago: Encyclopaedia Britannica, Inc., March 28, 2025), https://www.britannica.com/topic/Karma.

samsara. However, many modern Buddhist teachers emphasise the concept of non-self and the belief that we don't have a *soul* that lives through numerous rebirths. It's more a cumulative effect of an individual's deliberate deeds, or karma, that determines the outcome of this life cycle. Freeing oneself from this endless cycle and achieving enlightenment—sometimes called nirvana or freedom—is the supreme aim of Buddhism.

I initially found it hard to grasp the concept of these Buddhist teachings regarding rebirth, considering most don't acknowledge the existence of a soul! It's natural to ask—if there's no soul and one isn't supposed to believe in the concept of individual ego and self—what lives on after we die and are reborn repeatedly?

I eventually found the answer to my question explained more clearly when exploring the definition of the term skandhas, which is Sanskrit for *aggregates.* Although most Buddhists don't believe in a soul, they do believe in the five elements that comprise the entirety of one's mental and physical being and existence. The term used to describe these five elements is skandhas.[36] A direct quote from Encyclopedia Britannica describing the meaning of the five skandhas and their relationship to what many of us describe as a soul is as follows:

The self (or soul) cannot be identified with any one of the parts, nor is it the total of the parts. They are:

(1) ***matter or body*** *(rūpa), the manifest form of the four elements—earth, air, fire, and water;*

(2) ***sensations or feelings*** *(vedanā);*

---

36 Olivelle, Patrick. "Karma | Indian Philosophy & Its Impact on Life." In *Encyclopaedia Britannica*. Chicago: Encyclopaedia Britannica, Inc., March 28, 2025.

***(3) perceptions of sense objects** (Sanskrit: saṃjñā; Pāli: saññā);*

***(4) mental formations** (saṃskāras/sankhāras); and*

***(5) awareness or consciousness of the other three mental aggregates** (vijñāna/viññāṇa).*

And an awareness that all individuals are subject to constant change, as the elements of consciousness are never the same, and man may be compared to a river, which retains an identity, though the drops of water that make it up are different from one moment to the next.

I do love the analogy that the sum of our parts is like a river that's constantly in flux, made up of thousands of ever-changing components rather than being one unchanging body. It helped me understand that, according to most Buddhist traditions, what passes on after death is also based on a principle of impermanence and an interconnectedness referred to as *dependent origination.*[37] Yes, another impressive term and one that isn't easy to grasp. In my own interpretation, in very simplistic terms, it means that we're each the result of a multitude of influences, and, as a result, we are always changing and have no real permanence. This interpretation makes sense to me, but the topic itself is far more complex.

If you want to delve deeper into this significant subject, a good place to start would be with the reference I've provided for Britannica or simply typing *dependent origination* into a YouTube

---

37 Encyclopaedia Britannica Editors, "Paticca-Samuppada | Buddhist Doctrine of Dependent Origination," in *Encyclopaedia Britannica* (Chicago: Encyclopaedia Britannica, Inc., 2025), https://www.britannica.com/topic/paticca-samuppada.

search. Numerous excellent videos delve into this phrase and its meaning for hours.

According to most Buddhist teachings, yes, we reincarnate, but what's reborn is a stream of consciousness or a continuum of mental energy shaped by past actions or karma—which is different from what many of us think of as a spirit or soul. This stream of consciousness—often referred to as the mindstream—carries the imprints of previous experiences, tendencies, and habits, which in turn influence the circumstances of future lives.

It's also believed that after death, there is a transitional state of consciousness before rebirth that involves three stages. During the intermediate, 49-day state of the three bardos (mentioned earlier),[38] one's karma and actions from the previous life play a significant role in determining one's next rebirth. In the first of the three bardos, the person who has died comes to terms with the fact that they're dead and reflects upon their past.

During the second bardo, the deceased is said to encounter frightening apparitions, which can cause confusion. How the deceased responds to these apparitions affects their future karma and rebirth. The third bardo is the process of rebirth itself.[39]

I wrote earlier in the book, in the Hindu section, about the similarities between Hinduism and Buddhism due to their shared roots. There is also an interesting parallel between the journeys suggested in those religions and the development and reincarnation that Dr Newton lays out in the case studies in his

---

38 Stefon, Matt. "Bardo Thödol." In *Encyclopaedia Britannica*. Chicago: Encyclopaedia Britannica, Inc., 2025. https://www.britannica.com/topic/Bardo-Thodol.

39 Olivelle, "Karma | Indian Philosophy & Its Impact on Life."

book, *Journey of Souls,* which I hadn't previously distinguished. Although it is a transitional state of consciousness discussed in the bardos and not a soul that undertakes this journey, there is still a similar philosophy of progression along a path and some form of reconciliation. (Luckily, the frightening apparitions of the second bardo aren't described in Dr Newton's case studies; I'm not looking forward to that part of the process when I die!)

Proof

Since I was so quick to point out that the first known teachings of the Hindu religion weren't written down until 1,200 years after the reported creation of the poems of the Rigveda, it would be remiss of me not to point out that the first Buddhist scriptures were reportedly not written down until approximately 29-17 BCE, several centuries after Buddha's death. As I mentioned in the earlier section titled Facts, there doesn't seem to be a significant consensus among scholars about when Buddha lived and died. According to Encyclopedia Britannica, estimates differ by as much as 100 years. Stories of the origins of Buddhism are found in ancient biographical texts and poems that vary greatly. In many cases, these were written hundreds of years after Siddhārtha Gautama's birth. Even the years of the Buddha's birth differ.

One of the earliest extended literary biographical descriptions of the Buddha appears to be a Sanskrit poem called the Buddhacharita (The Life of Buddha), originally written at least 600 years after his death. Alas, there is no direct archaeological evidence conclusively tied to the Buddha, or even accurate and verifiable recordings of what he said. The various translations from that text vary dramatically. Once again, we're presented with a mythical story that was transcribed well after the actual occurrence.

So, we're faced with a dilemma: If we feel the proof within us, is that good enough? Sometimes, we know when something feels true. I don't want to be the person who tells you that's wrong, but often our feelings mislead us because, subconsciously, we desperately need something to believe in. Even though the facts—or often, lack of facts—are like a big neon warning sign to somebody outside looking in, we can't see what is logical or likely because our need for faith blinds us. If you need any proof of this phenomenon, look no further than some of the lies told by high-profile politicians running for the highest leadership role in America. There is no shortage of blatant lies being told, but they are totally ignored by the faithful.

I placed Buddhism last on the list of major religions not just because it's the smallest of the five in terms of the number of followers but also because it resonates most convincingly with me and provides me the most consolation. Having said this, none of the beliefs in this book will offer much satisfaction if you don't also believe in spirituality and an afterlife of some sort. Of course, if there's no proof, all we're left with are these attractive myths and stories written a very long time ago… and our gut feelings! It's easy to feel an affinity with these myths, but to me, they're all just different boats taking us to similar destinations. Like the various rides at an amusement park, they give us pleasure, often cost us money, and provide enjoyment while we're on the ride, and then they come abruptly to an end.

Is there more? If the conclusions I reach by the end of this book lead me down a path that focuses more on *my* life now rather than where ***Harrison*** is now, Buddhism will definitely be at the top of the list—particularly if I give up on searching for assurances about where my son's soul has ended up and start to focus on how to live my life while trying to understand grief and impermanence better.

Yes, the stories that form the basis of the Buddhist religion are lacking in verifiable proof, just as Christianity is. But to me, the story of a man who realises the injustice of inequality between those with wealth and those who suffer and then sits under a tree and meditates to understand what he believes to be the nature of life's purpose seems to be far more believable than that of a man being born of a virgin because he is the son of an omnipotent creator. Anything is possible, of course, and if there is an all-powerful creator, I'm sure a virgin birth wouldn't be complicated to figure out.

Nevertheless, I believe that the best solution for me is to combine the best aspects of Christianity and Buddhism, while disregarding the parts that don't resonate well. I guess we all follow a path that feels best in one way or another and often ignore the rest.

(For access to additional key-point discussion and summary notes, refer to the section in the back of the book titled Appendix: Notes by Religion just before the Bibliography.)

The Meaning of Life ... and what makes that life well-lived?

Is the answer to this question of finding one's meaning to continually grow and achieve as much as possible before we die? Or is it as simple as finding peace, satisfaction, serenity, and companionship... In other words, contentment?

In pursuit of the answer, around seven years after the death of my son, I finally thought it possible to distance myself from memories of Harrison's childhood, the place where his ashes are buried, and my daily reminders of him. I moved back to Sydney and into a lovely little loft apartment, which I then spent six months renovating.

During four of those months, I was dating a beautiful, well-educated, Thai woman who had lived in Australia for over 20 years. When we were together, I felt absolute contentment and happiness. I enjoyed the simplicity of life, taking it one day at a time, and appreciating the basic pleasures such as food and sunsets. There were no profound conversations of great meaning or attempts to solve world problems—just a thoughtful appreciation of life on a day-to-day basis.

Having been married to a hyperactive overachiever for 18 years, this new relationship felt like simplicity and bliss encapsulated. No striving for wealth and constantly wanting more but just appreciating life with only one goal—to bring happiness to the people around us and ourselves.

And yes, as one might expect given that introduction, she was a practising Buddhist and had even completed some monastic training to become a lay Buddhist nun (mae chi) in Thailand. She could easily meditate for an hour or more without effort, whereas I struggle to meditate for 10 minutes. She was loving in every way. Joining her in this more appreciative way of being was calming and a lovely experience after years of stress with other partners who seemed perpetually unhappy due to our driven Western lifestyle and upbringing.

This very different, giving, and loving experience stimulated some parts of my brain more than others. I experienced extra doses of dopamine and serotonin from the feeling of love and calming energy! As a result, my actions and state of mind were more driven by the emotions of pleasure rather than by rational and practical thinking.

However, when we were not together, and I was not experiencing her energy, my brain was dominated by my more rational frontal cortex. When I was not overcome with those feelings of love, compassion, and generosity, sadly, I would start to think about the way we were not in sync in certain aspects of our life: How little we had in common or how she had no interest in world affairs, politics, and economics or how our lives had been so different up to that point and whether it was possible for us to succeed as a couple long term.

I am not sure if you, the reader, have experienced these conflicting feelings about life, love, and relationships, but I have, and far too often.

> *Particularly after a loss, we feel a greater sense of emptiness than others do. As a result, when someone comes along who will hold your hand and fill you with love again, it is a wonderful feeling. We need it as part of our recovery.*

I have come to realise that contentment, receiving unconditional love, and expressing love are crucial to the recovery process from grief and cannot be overlooked. However, on a day-to-day basis, it is essential not to be *fully* guided just by the need to be loved by others. It is very tempting to focus on just that. For an ongoing, happier life after loss, I know in my heart that it is, and will be, more rewarding to bring balance to all three: finding contentment, giving love, and receiving love, together.

> *On my deathbed, if I can say, "I loved, I was loved, and I lived a full and rewarding life," then, I believe, I will have fully understood the meaning of life.*

What I do not want as I lie on that deathbed, drawing my last few breaths, is to be wondering, "What would have happened if…?" What would have happened if I had finished my book? What would have happened if I had stayed really healthy and eaten natural foods and done everything I could to stave off dementia? What would have happened if I had settled down with one of the people I loved and found contentment in the relationship instead of avoiding the intimacy?

What I want to be able to say to myself when that final moment comes is, "I tried to explore my potentiality fully, I took risks, and my life was an adventure." And yes, I also want to be able to say that I gave love to those around me, and I took the time to appreciate the taste of a meal someone made for me or to smell the beautiful flowers I see each morning on my walk.

Finding contentment in life is about striking the right balance among the opposing desires of good and bad, drive and passion, grief and joy while being aware of the internal drive for peace and happiness and still pursuing personal growth. With great certainty, I can guarantee you that the meaning of life and the source of joy are not dependent on the continued acquisition of material possessions.

The Smaller Faiths

Although the big four religions all have aspects that I found appealing, I also wanted to research other faiths. Knowing that I'd not found *my tribe* as a Muslim or Hindu, I also pondered the practicality of changing from Christianity to another faith. Is that even likely?

To the point: how many of us who were raised around the influences of Christianity gravitate to Sikhism or become a Mormon or a Jew? Surprisingly, according to a report by the Pew Research Center[40] published in 2017 (collected in 2015):

> *It is fairly common in the USA for adults to leave their childhood religion and switch to another faith (or no faith). For example, many people raised in the U.S. as Christians become unaffiliated in adulthood, and vice versa—many people raised without any religion join a religious group later in their lives. However, in some other countries, changes in religious identity are rare or even illegal.*

Nevertheless, changing one's faith is relatively rare among people worldwide who have had a religious affiliation since childhood. It's far more likely that people who view themselves as atheist or agnostic, as I do, discover what they believe is *their path* later

40 Pew Research Center, "The Changing Global Religious Landscape," Research Report (Washington, D.C.: Pew Research Center, April 5, 2017), https://www.pewresearch.org/religion/2017/04/05/the-changing-global-religious-landscape/.

in life and embrace it. Perhaps it's the desire for community or to fill a void, find answers, ease the pain of loss, or alleviate the uncertainty about what happens after death that leads us to adopt and hold new beliefs. I started this writing journey for all these reasons.

In 2015, which is the year that data was collected for the Pew report mentioned above, 2.3 billion people identified as Christian, and 1.8 billion identified as Muslim. Only about 15 million were Jews. In 2017, Pew predicted that by 2035, the total number of babies born to Muslims would outnumber those born to Christians. As a result, the percentage of Muslims and Christians in the world was predicted to be about the same by 2060, ringing the bell at around 3 billion each. The religiously unaffiliated population worldwide was estimated at 16% at the time, and this was expected to decrease to around 12% by 2060 due to the projected growth of major religions over the next 35 years.

In a study that occurred approximately five years later by Gallup, it became apparent that those projections were not playing out as expected, or certainly not in the USA. According to later Gallup[41] research, the percentage of households moving away from a church affiliation was increasing at an exponential rate. In the year 2000, generally speaking, around 70% of households in the USA belonged to a church. By 2015, that number had dropped to around 55%; by 2021, it was at 47%. Unverified recent studies at the time of this publication suggest a slight resurgence among Millennials, particularly among non-white Millennials.

---

41 Jeffrey M. Jones, "U.S. Church Membership Falls Below Majority for First Time," *Gallup*, March 29, 2021, https://news.gallup.com/poll/341963/church-membership-falls-below-majority-first-time.aspx.

It would not surprise me to see more people seeking spiritual community and meaning in such confusing times.

Thousands of churches have closed over recent years in the United States due to the steep decline in membership. It's occurred to me that I may eventually end up in a church, but if I do, it may be more likely that I've bought one and converted it into a cool house! Notwithstanding my distrust of Christianity, there's unquestionably something calming and lovely about a church. The collective positive energy from the thousands of people who've prayed in a church, the children baptised there, the magnificence of being surrounded by light streaming through stained-glass windows, and the singing and joy in places of worship far exceeds the historical and empirical evidence of external wrongdoing. If my thoughts about Christianity seem to be conflicted and confusing, it's because they are. If I were clear about the faith I want to follow, I wouldn't have written this book. The path we each chose to follow is a collection of learned inputs and impressions. I am still inputting the data, I guess. Nevertheless, I can say with certainty that I'd love to buy one of those churches.

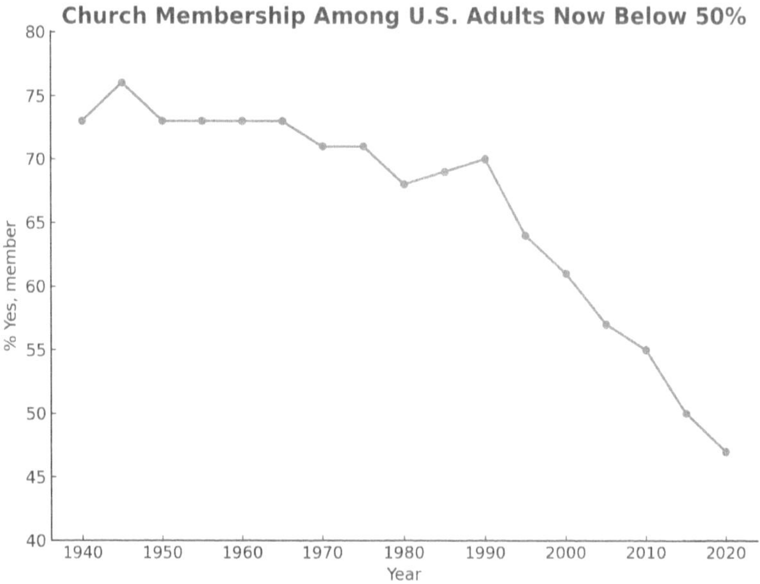

Source: GALLUP, based on annual aggregated data, usually based on two surveys

The bottom line is that nowadays, many more people are leaving the traditional church affiliations they were born into and are therefore open to hearing about alternatives. I'm one of them, and perhaps you are, too. I thought it would behove me to at least take a look and research some of the following minor world religions.

Sikhism

Men in some ceremonial roles or religious leaders in Islam and Hinduism wear headgear, as do some men in desert cultures. However, if you ever see a man with a long beard and a colourful turban, there is a pretty good chance he may be one of the approximately 25 million followers of Sikhism worldwide. Their traditional headgear is very distinctive. It's interesting to note that although they wash and tie their hair daily, observant Sikhs never cut their hair. The turbans they wear not only protect and control their bountiful manes but are also seen as a sign of devotion, dignity, equality, and responsibility before God.

Realistically, becoming an observant Sikh will probably not be in my immediate future; still, their religion promotes equality for all people and encourages a way of life that includes earning an honest living, meditating, sharing with others, and serving the community, which are obviously admirable goals. Goals that I would be happy to try and emulate.

Many of Sikhism's core beliefs are based on spiritual teachings that combine both Hindu and Muslim influences, but they developed a distinct theology and scripture of their own. Founded in the 15th century in the Punjab region of India, like Christianity, it is a monotheistic religion, meaning it emphasises devotion to only one god. Included in the teachings of its founder (an Indian religious leader known as Guru Nanak), the fundamentals of the religion seem to contain a healthy emphasis on equality and social justice, which is certainly a positive factor in my mind. (This emphasis also exists in many of the modern-day teachings of Buddhism, which I have found personally appealing.)

Guru Nanak, the founder, was born in 1469 and died in 1539. The religion was further developed by nine successive gurus starting with Guru Angad, who was chosen by Nanak as his spiritual successor. Fortunately, because Sikhism is relatively recent in origin, there is substantial verifiable evidence of its historical development, texts, and cultural impact. Although the religion itself isn't that old, it is essential to note that Sikhism was heavily influenced by much older religions and ancient texts that are far less verifiable.

Historical Foundations

Guru Nanak's Life and Teachings:

- There's well-documented evidence of Guru Nanak (1469-1539), the founder of Sikhism, as a historical figure. His life and teachings are preserved in the Janamsakhis, which are biographical accounts written by his followers. These texts provide a detailed narrative of his travels, teachings, and interactions with people from diverse religious backgrounds, which established the foundation of Sikhism. Additionally, historical records from Mughal sources mention Guru Nanak and his growing influence in a number of places. (Refer to reference by McLeod, 1968[42]).

Formation of the Khalsa:

- The establishment of what Sikhs call the Khalsa by one of the later gurus, Guru Gobind Singh, in 1699 is a pivotal moment in Sikh history and changed the religion into what it is today. This event is well documented in Sikh historical texts. The formation of the Khalsa formalised Sikh identity and practices and redefined religious authority by emphasising collective identity, equality, and discipline rather than clerical hierarchy. It also introduced a new initiation ceremony and code of conduct, providing the community with a new religious and political vision. Included in this new direction was the introduction of what some called *the five K's* (kesh, kara, kanga, kachera, and kirpan), which are still observed by many Sikhs today (and also the reason that we are often immediately aware that a person is a follower of Sikhism.) These changes were implemented as a way of giving Sikhs a strong, united identity at a time when they were facing real persecution. Each *k* is a physical reminder of what it means to live with courage, discipline, and integrity.

The five k's are as follows:

---

42 William Hewat McLeod, *Gurū Nānak and the Sikh Religion* (Oxford: Clarendon Press, 1968), https://search.worldcat.org/title/1015130383.

Kesh

This simply means uncut hair. Sikhs keep their hair natural as a symbol of accepting themselves the way God made them. It's a quiet statement of surrender to the divine, without needing to *improve* on nature. You'll usually see Sikh men (and many women) wearing a turban to protect and honour their hair, which soon became a symbol of dignity and spiritual pride.

Kanga

To accompany their uncut hair, Sikhs carry a small wooden comb, known as the kanga. This isn't just about grooming; it's a reminder to keep life tidy on the inside too. Order in your hair, order in your thoughts. I like that—spirituality doesn't have to be lofty or mysterious; sometimes it's as practical as brushing your hair and keeping your mind uncluttered.

Kara

The kara is a simple steel bangle worn on the wrist. It's circular, with no beginning and no end, symbolising the eternal nature of God. But there's also a wonderfully down-to-earth purpose: when you look at your hand and see the kara, it makes you think twice about what you're about to do. It's a built-in conscience check: *Are my actions honourable?* If only we all had one of those reminders before sending certain late-night texts we regret later!

Kachera

These are specially designed cotton shorts—modest, practical, and comfortable. They represent self-respect, sexual self-control, and living with dignity. When Guru Gobind Singh introduced them, it was a direct shift away from the idea of holiness being separated from daily life. You were meant to be ready for action, ready to defend the vulnerable if needed—not sitting in robes on a cushion waiting for enlightenment to show up.

Kirpan

The one that catches everyone's attention: the kirpan, a small ceremonial sword. It's not about violence—it's about the responsibility to stand up for truth and protect others. Sikhism takes the idea of compassion seriously, but it also insists that compassion includes courage. You don't just wish people well; you defend them if they're being mistreated. The kirpan is a reminder that spirituality doesn't mean stepping back from the world. It means showing up, bravely.

Collectively, the five k's turn faith into something you wear, carry, see, and feel every day. It's hard not to respect that sort of dedication.

Afterlife

Like Hindus, Sikhs also believe in the existence of a soul and the cycle of birth, death, and reincarnation. For Sikhs, liberation (mukti) from this cycle is achieved through devotion to God, living a truthful life, and rendering selfless service. Therefore, the concept of what happens after death is intricately tied to belief in karma, reincarnation, and one's union with God.

There are three fundamental terms that represent key beliefs in understanding Sikh views on the afterlife.

1. **Reincarnation**:

   Sikhs believe that the soul is eternal and passes through various life forms (reincarnation) based on one's actions (karma) in past lives. The cycle of birth, death, and rebirth continues until the soul is purified and united with God. This belief is rooted in the teachings of the Guru Granth Sahib and emphasises the importance of living a righteous life to achieve liberation (Cole & Sambhi, 1995).[43]

2. **Karma**:

   The law of karma plays a central role in determining the nature of future births. Good deeds and devotion to God lead to a favourable rebirth, while negative actions result in a less favourable one. The ultimate goal is to accumulate good karma and devotion to escape the cycle of reincarnation and merge with God (McLeod, 1989).[44]

3. **Mukti (Liberation)**:

   The ultimate aim for a Sikh is to achieve mukti—liberation from the cycle of birth and death. This is attained through devotion to God, righteous living, and meditation on God's name (Naam Simran). Once liberated, the soul merges with the divine essence, achieving eternal peace and unity with God (Singh, 2006).[45]

---

43 W. Owen Cole and Piara Singh Sambhi, *The Sikhs: Their Religious Beliefs and Practices*, 2nd Revised, The Sussex Library of Religious Beliefs & Practice (Liverpool: Liverpool University Press, 1998),

44 William Hearst McLeod, *The Sikhs: History, Religion, and Society*, Lectures on the History of Religions 14 (New York: Columbia University Press, 1989), https://search.worldcat.org/title/1025956184.

45 Nikky-Guninder Kaur Singh, *The Name of My Beloved: Verses of the Sikh Gurus*, Sacred Literature (New Delhi: Penguin Books, 2003), https://www.goodreads.com/book/show/2708762-the-name-of-my-beloved.

Proof

The beliefs in karma, reincarnation, and liberation are profoundly spiritual and rooted in faith. As is the case in my study of the other religions, I couldn't find any empirical scientific proof of these concepts as they pertain to the afterlife, primarily because they fall outside the scope of scientific investigation, which focuses on the observable and measurable. Reincarnation, for example, is a metaphysical belief and hasn't been proven (or disproven) by scientific methods that I could find. Studies on near-death experiences and consciousness have explored related themes but don't provide concrete evidence for reincarnation or liberation as described in Sikhism (Stevenson, 1974; Greyson, 2000).[46]

* * *

In Sikhism, life after death involves the soul's journey through reincarnation—guided by the principles of karma—until liberation is achieved. These beliefs are central to the Sikh faith and, like those of Hindus and Buddhists, reside within spiritual understanding rather than being supported by empirical proof. The concept of an afterlife in Sikhism, as is the case with all the religions I researched, seems to, once again, be a matter

46 Stevenson, Ian. *Twenty Cases Suggestive of Reincarnation*. 2nd ed. Charlottesville: University Press of Virginia, 1974.; Janice Miner Holden, Bruce Greyson, and Debbie James, eds., *The Handbook of Near-Death Experiences: Thirty Years of Investigation*, 2nd Printing (Santa Barbara, CA: Praeger, 2009), https://search.worldcat.org/title/The-handbook-of-near-death-experiences-:-thirty-years-of-investigation/oclc/876613447.

of personal faith and religious conviction rather than based on any verifiable facts.

(For access to additional key-point discussion and summary notes, refer to the section in the back of the book titled Appendix: Notes by Religion just before the Bibliography.)

Judaism

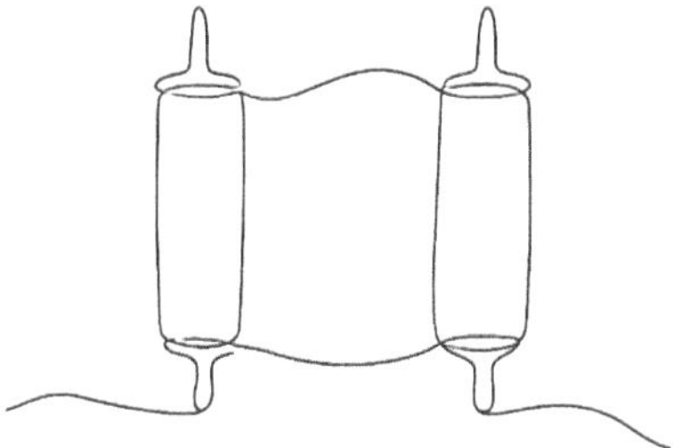

We could all die any day. But before I'll let that happen, I'll dance my life away.

1999 ~ Prince

Prince lost his first child when the boy was just one week old; later, he lost another as a result of a miscarriage. Like so many of us, he wasn't a stranger to grief. He wrote the lyrics above years after his son's death, but they reflect his perspective on the fragility of life and the importance of embracing it while we can—dancing, enjoying, and celebrating all the way up to the last minute. Sadly, Prince died the same year that my son Harrison died, in 2016. Ironically, both of them died of an opioid overdose. In Harrison's case, the drug was prescribed, unnecessarily, by a crooked doctor, nurse, and rehab.

> *Prince and Harrison both danced and entertained others until the very end. We all remember something beautiful about those we've lost. This is what I remember most.*

Before researching this chapter, I never realised a fact that had eluded me during 18 years of marriage to a Jewish woman: Jews have long used dance to express joy to God, and it plays a significant role in their religious observance. The traditional dances of the Ashkenazi and Sephardi are an essential element of important events such as weddings or ritual celebrations. (Come to think of it, there was a heck of a lot of dancing at our wedding!) So, I guess, in a way, Jews dance their lives away more than Christians and Muslims do, at least. I know it is a thin thread between the Prince quote and the Jewish religion, particularly because Prince was not Jewish, but I enjoy the image of Harrison and Prince both on stage, dancing and entertaining. And for some reason, it seems like an appropriate segue to this chapter. I never saw Harrison smile as much as he did when he was dancing and singing on stage!

Because Harrison's mother is Jewish, according to Jewish belief, Harrison was also Jewish. We, as parents, had never pushed him to one religion or the other. Still, coincidentally, in the year or so before his death, he had just started to familiarise himself with the faith and the sense of community it provides. As a tribute to Harrison's heritage, and to the tremendous persecution and struggle that this religious group has endured, I thought it appropriate to look closely at what Jews believe about the afterlife and consider whether I could align myself with Judaism. I think Harrison would have embraced the religion, if for no other reason than simply the sense of community and identity that it offers.

When our twins were born in 1996, we had to address what kind of religious upbringing to provide for them. I was brought up as a Protestant, and neither of us felt strongly about how to raise our children in terms of religion. However, our in-laws were more insistent about picking a religion for our children. Also, more as a tongue-in-cheek gesture, we decided that it would be best not to take any chances regarding the remote possibility that there actually is an omnipotent and all-powerful God who may be insulted by our lack of interest! For us, the obvious choice was to have the children baptised and, for my son, to have a bris (brit milah) performed. (Although the term *bris* sounds very lovely, it is actually a painful circumcision for the poor little boy.) Jacqueline and Harrison also received a ceremonial Jewish naming ceremony on the first Sabbath after their birth. Thus, we covered all the bases (with an intention of some agnostic flavouring when they were old enough to understand!).

When we initially presented this idea to my priest and my wife's rabbi, neither was pleased with our solution, but they nonetheless agreed to it. Our respective in-laws were equally upset, but they didn't find out until both ceremonies had been carried out individually with the respective denominational parents. We were informed by everyone who knew about this that we'd probably created a life of religious confusion and sacrilege for our lovely little children. Fortunately, they were never told of these ceremonies until much later in life. As it turned out, they really didn't care. And neither Gail nor I was struck by a bolt of lightning.

Many of us, including me, gain comfort from the thought that there's more to us than just a body and a mind, yet are uncomfortable enrolling in the dogmatic structures of an existing religion. As do many people, I tend to define God differently with phrases like, ***God is the communal energy that holds us together as humans,*** and ***God is love.*** They are phrases that have been used for centuries to describe something we feel exists but can't define in tangible ways. If I do have to refer to God, definitions such as those seemed more acceptable to me, certainly at the outset of this book at least.

Our son also subscribed to this broader understanding of what God is. However, he also enjoyed the sense of belonging and community that is an essential part of the Jewish faith and identity.

The Story

When Abraham was 99 years old, the LORD appeared to Abraham and said to him,

> *"I am Almighty God; walk before Me and be blameless. And I will make My covenant between Me and you, and will multiply you exceedingly." Then Abraham fell on his face, and God talked with him, saying: "As for me, behold, my covenant is with you, and you shall be a father of many nations."*
>
> Genesis 17:1-8

... And thus starts the journey of the Jewish people, beginning with Abraham.

Over the 3,800 years or so since Abraham supposedly spoke with God, the Jewish people have risen, fallen, struggled, overcome, and been persecuted. Today, the Jewish population numbers approximately 16 million people worldwide—about 2% of the global religious population. Roughly 45% live in the United States and another 40% in Israel. Despite their relatively small numbers, Jewish communities have had a significant impact on global culture, education, business, and public life. In the United States, in particular, their emphasis on learning, civic engagement, and community building combined with financial status has contributed to a significant influence in both economic and political spheres.

Interesting Facts:

It's not just because my son considered himself Jewish that I investigated Judaism more deeply than some of the other minor religions. With less than 20 million followers, Judaism is tiny compared to the Christian and Islamic faiths, both of which have well over 2 billion followers each. Significantly, though only a small religion, the Jewish population has the highest average income among any religious group in the USA,[47] and holds more individual wealth.[48] This pattern of achievement is often attributed to a historical emphasis on education, professional achievement and urban professional life.

Although only representing an insignificant portion of the American population, nearly a quarter of the people on the Forbes list of the 100 wealthiest people in the USA are Jewish. As a result of this combined wealth, those of the Jewish faith have significantly more political influence in the USA and worldwide than their relatively small number would warrant based solely on their followers.

Judaism isn't just simply a religion founded on a belief in the existence of one God. It is also an identity that carries with it a pride in being part of a worldwide community with a rich, long, and intricate history of cultural traditions and historical struggles. In our uncertain world, this provides an inherent sense of belonging to those who call themselves Jews. I think Harrison would have gravitated to his Jewish roots for that reason alone, and I would have been glad for him to do so.

The primary authority for the Jewish religion is the Hebrew Bible, which comprises 24 books (one for each scroll on which they were originally written). These 24 books constitute a

---

47 David Masci, "How Income Varies among U.S. Religious Groups," Pew Research Center, October 11, 2016, https://www.pewresearch.org/fact-tank/2016/10/11/how-income-varies-among-u-s-religious-groups/.

48 Sammy Said, "The 10 Richest Religions in the World," *Church and State* (blog), December 8, 2013, https://churchandstate.org.uk/2016/06/the-10-richest-religions-in-the-world/.

significant portion of the Christian Bible and are often referred to as the Hebrew Scriptures, the Old Testament, or the Tanakh. This collection of texts (except for a few Aramaic portions in the Book of Daniel) was initially written in Hebrew between 1200 and 100 BCE. The Hebrew Bible's present form was most likely finalised around the second century CE and is organised into three main sections:

- **The Torah** *(Teachings)*

  The first five books of the Hebrew Bible (Old Testament), also known as the Law, are commonly called the Torah (or the Pentateuch in Christianity). The Torah in Judaism represents God's revealed instruction or direction for humans, and the writings are attributed to Moses, who was the initial recipient of God's revelation on Mount Sinai. The five books of the Torah are: Genesis, Exodus, Leviticus, Numbers, and Deuteronomy.

- **The Nevi'im** *(Prophets)*

  As the name suggests, this section of the Hebrew Bible contains books, stories, and traditions relating to the significant and minor Hebrew prophets. It includes the books of Joshua, Judges, Samuel, and the Book of Kings (comprising two books that describe the monarchies in Israel and Judah over the progressive years of 930 BCE to the collapse of Judah in 586 BCE). The Nevi'im also includes the books of Isaiah, Jeremiah, Ezekiel, and The Book of Twelve, which includes stories of 12 of the lesser prophets.

- **The Ketuvim** *(Writings)*

  The last section of the Hebrew Bible is devoted to sacred poetry and songs, theology, and drama. It comprises Psalms,

Job, Song of Songs, Ruth, Lamentations, Ecclesiastes, Ester, Daniel, Ezra-Nehemiah, and Chronicles.

Afterlife

Jewish beliefs about the afterlife vary. Some Jews believe in a World to Come (Olam Ha-Ba) and the resurrection of the dead (Techiyat HaMetim), while others feel it is more relevant to focus on the legacy that individuals leave in this world and not what happens afterwards. The primary scriptural references of these discussions are the Hebrew Bible in books like Daniel (12:2), Isaiah (26:19), and later rabbinical writings.

Even though beliefs about what happens after death vary among different branches of Judaism, there are some common themes. What follows are definitions of terms and philosophies that may help provide a general overview.

The Jewish texts that reference these beliefs include the Torah, the Talmud, and Kabbalistic writings. Obviously, it's important to remember that there can be variations in beliefs and interpretations within the Jewish community, and not all Jews hold the same views about the afterlife. For example, even though my ex-wife is Jewish, I'd be surprised if she knows what Olam Ha-Ba is, and I'm sure there are millions of Jews like her.

As stated previously, it's been my personal experience that, for many, a powerful sense of community and identity is what primarily appeals to the many Jewish people I have known, not an in-depth knowledge of the Talmud! I certainly acknowledge that my narrow experiences may not represent the majority, and may be ill-informed.

* * *

The following terms and beliefs are essential as a starting point if one wants to understand Judaism's view of the afterlife.

1. **Olam Ha-Ba** (The World to Come): Judaism believes in an afterlife known as Olam Ha-Ba, which is translated as The World to Come. This concept is often associated with a state of spiritual existence after death. The specifics of Olam Ha-Ba can vary, but it's generally seen as a reward for a righteous life.
2. **Resurrection of the Dead:** Traditional Jewish belief includes the idea of a resurrection of the dead when the Messiah comes. This concept is particularly emphasised in Orthodox Judaism, which holds that the righteous will be resurrected to enjoy eternal life.
3. **Gan Eden** (Paradise) and **Gehenna** (Purgatory): Jewish tradition includes the idea of Gan Eden, which is often equated with paradise or a heavenly garden. This is where the souls of the righteous may find rest and reward. Conversely, Gehenna is sometimes seen as a place of purgatory or punishment for the wicked.
4. **Reincarnation** (Gilgul): While not a universally accepted belief, some Jewish mystics and Kabbalists believe in reincarnation—*gilgul* in Hebrew. According to this belief, the soul may undergo multiple lifetimes until it achieves spiritual perfection.
5. **The Importance of Mitzvot** (Commandments): Regardless of their specific beliefs about the afterlife, many Jews emphasise the importance of living a righteous life and fulfilling mitzvot (commandments) to prepare for whatever comes after death.

It's important to note that several differing belief structures exist within the Jewish religion. One belief is that the soul goes to either paradise or purgatory, and another belief is that the soul experiences a series of ongoing reincarnations. The most traditional belief is that the dead who were righteous during their lives will be resurrected to enjoy eternal life when the Messiah comes.

At this stage in my journey, I've become comfortable with the idea that we have a soul that lives on in some way rather than life ending with the death of the physical body. I'm also starting to accept the possibility of a series of reincarnations and periods of soul journey during the afterlife before being reborn, rather than waiting for a messiah to trigger that (it could be a long wait!). Because of this, I decided to look more closely at the mystical aspect of Judaism, called the Kabbalah. The tenets of this tradition are similar in some ways to Hindu and Buddhist beliefs and the experiences of Dr Newton, mentioned in Spiritualism in Part 3, which were aligned with the concept of rebirth and growth.

During my exploration of Kabbalah, I was acutely aware that I was leaning toward a sort of self-proclaimed confirmation bias in seeking out proof and viewpoints that seemed more closely aligned with my newly formed beliefs—or, more accurately, beliefs I'm trying to create in myself. Nevertheless, the path was too intriguing to disregard, so I gladly embarked on research to find out more about this mysterious and mystical part of Jewish history and folklore—Kabbalah.

Kabbalah

(also known as Kabbala or Cabala)

I'd never heard of Kabbalah until Harrison's mother became interested in it about five years after our son's death. For her, the beliefs expounded in Kabbalah were helpful, so I wanted to research it.

My go-to source when looking for an accurate definition and explanation of a subject is Encyclopedia Britannica.[49] In Britannica, Kabbalah is described as a form of esoteric Jewish mysticism that appeared in the 12th century—more than 1,000 years after the current version of the Hebrew Bible was written! As one may expect, it's indeed esoteric and mystical! (Let's not forget that many Christian beliefs are as well.)

I think it's important to consider how recently the main text of Kabbalah was written and put that into perspective. It was during the 12th century that the Second Crusade was launched. The Knights Templar were organised to protect Christian pilgrims in Jerusalem. Genghis Khan was born in that century, and there was a 50-year drought in the American Southwest. In short, this was a long time after the birth of Christ and the writing of the original Hebrew texts. Why did Kabbalah emerge so late in the timeline of Jewish history?

---

49 Encyclopædia Britannica Editors, "Kabbala | Definition, Beliefs, & Facts," in *Encyclopædia Britannica* (Chicago: Encyclopædia Britannica, Inc., March 25, 2025), https://www.britannica.com/topic/Kabbala.

The first significant text of Kabbalah, the Sefer HaBahir[50] (Book of Brightness), is essentially a symbolic commentary on the Old Testament. The Jewish Virtual Library[51] notes that this isn't the work of a single author but rather a collection of 140 passages comprising an anthology of contributions written and edited by many Jewish esotericist.

Although the Sefer HaBahir was created in the late 12th and early 13th centuries, it includes references to and interpretations of symbology that date back to the early Jewish tradition around the first century AD. As a result, there's the incorrect assumption that Kabbalah is much older than it really is. To be fair, however, the Kabbalistic tradition does have links to earlier forms of a Jewish-related mysticism called Merkabah, which became prevalent in Palestine in the first century. The Sefer Yetzirah[52] (Hebrew for Book of Creation) is the oldest known Hebrew text and focuses on white magic and cosmology. It appeared sometime between the 3rd and 6th centuries.

Notwithstanding the late arrival of the prominent Kabbalistic texts, as with most religions, this belief system depends on how convinced one is by wondrous stories of golden chariots and other romantic, exciting, mystical, and often fanciful adventures. But

---

50 Encyclopædia Britannica Editors, "Sefer Ha-Bahir | Kabbalah, Mysticism, Wisdom," in *Encyclopædia Britannica* (Chicago: Encyclopædia Britannica, Inc., 2025), https://www.britannica.com/topic/Sefer-ha-bahir.

51 Encyclopaedia Judaica Editors, "Sefer Ha-Bahir," in *Encyclopaedia Judaica* (Detroit: The Gale Group, 2008), https://www.jewishvirtuallibrary.org/sefer-ha-bahir.

52 Encyclopædia Britannica Editors, "Sefer Yetzira | Mystical, Kabbalistic, Jewish," in Encyclopædia Britannica (Chicago: Encyclopædia Britannica, Inc., 2025), https://www.britannica.com/topic/Sefer-Yetzira.

no religion would have many followers if the stories about its history and what happens after you die were boring, would it?

After Britannica, I looked at other articles and websites to better understand this mystical tradition. The websites promoting Kabbalah have varying descriptions of what Kabbalah is. Ironically, my ex-wife had been trying to steer me toward Kabbalah for several years to help me recover from the loss of our son. I never got around to it at the time, but having done so, now while researching for this book, I think it certainly offers some solace and is worth incorporating into one's life in part at least.

From my cursory and only skin-deep research into the concepts of Kabbalah, I am left with the impression that it's a belief structure that seems to view growth as an ongoing process, emphasising awareness over perfection and engagement with life rather than escape from it. It also seems to offer a non-dogmatic framework for understanding consciousness and responsibility, teaching that meaning is created through small, intentional acts that help restore balance within ourselves and the world—all very positive concepts to include in any belief structure if you wanted to build your own.

I have actually conceptualised my next book, which includes only the good from various religions. I am going to circle back and take a closer look at Kabbalah if it becomes a reality.

As is the case with Christianity, there is sufficient evidence of Judaism's early origins, as documented in texts and historical references, to confirm that it has been practised and respected for a long time. But, once again, as is also the case with Christianity, even though there are historical references that confirm the origins of these texts, there's no proof within those texts of what happens after we die. To me, what's most believable and relevant isn't proving that the text of the Hebrew Bible is factual. Instead, the tremendous value of this religion is the sense of belonging, identity, and community that provides members of the Jewish faith with a shawl of comfort and meaning to wrap around their shoulders.

What Can We Actually Prove About Judaism?

When I first began exploring the world's religions, I was searching for answers about what happens when we die and evaluating the historical foundations of each belief.

> *What is becoming glaringly apparent to me now is that none of the religions I have looked at so far deal in proof to any significant degree. What they do offer is tradition, community, faith, and hope.*

That said, Judaism does have some verifiable records, at least. For those curious about how historically grounded it is, there's quite a bit to go on—at least when it comes to proving that Jewish people and beliefs have been around for a very long time. And that matters. Maybe not in the *Where do we go after we die?* Sense but more so in the relevance and truthfulness of what people cling to before death when they start to ask that question.

Here are some facts that stood out to me when looking for factual proof:

Some of the earliest references to the people of Israel outside the Bible come from a stone inscription known as the Merneptah Stele, dated to around 1200 BCE. It suggests that a group called

Israel was in existence at that time—not conclusive proof, but something. There is also the Tel Dan Stele—an inscription that actually mentions the *House of David*. Sceptics treated the stories of King David like myths until this find. It turns out that he likely wasn't a myth at all. Another story that refers to the Babylonian Exile—in which Jerusalem's elite were taken captive after the conquest—has been confirmed by Babylonian records.

The Dead Sea Scrolls, unearthed in the mid-20th century, were another really significant find. They comprise ancient Jewish writings, some predating the birth of Christ, that include pieces of the Hebrew Bible and a host of other documents. Whatever you believe about the supernatural claims inside the Hebrew Bible (the Tanakh), it seems that (like the New Testament for Christians) the text is tied to real places and people. Some of those details have been verified by sources like the Siloam Inscription, another archaeological find that links biblical stories to real-world geography. We do not, however, have proof of the truthfulness of the stories, only that they can be connected in many cases to real places and people.

Continuity of Jewish law, or Halakha: This has been studied and practised for over 1,500 years. Such cultural continuity is rare. The Talmud, the heartbeat of rabbinic Judaism, continues to shape how observant Jews live, eat, argue, and celebrate today. The Western Wall in Jerusalem, the ancient synagogues of Galilee, and other holy sites are all physical echoes of that past. You can walk through the remnants of these places and know that for thousands of years, people have gathered there, asking the same big questions we ask now.

Still, none of this confirms what happens after we die. For me, the most meaningful strength I can observe in Judaism isn't in confirming whether Abraham heard voices or whether the Red Sea really parted. It's in the sense of identity, of belonging, of having a spiritual home. There's something deeply moving about the idea of a faith tradition that has endured exile, persecution, and reinvention yet still holds a people together.

Judaism did not provide me with any conclusive proof about what happens after we die, but like most religions, it clearly holds a lot of other meaningful benefits for those who embrace it.

(For access to additional keypoint discussion and summary notes, refer to the section in the back of the book titled Appendix: Notes by Religion just before the Bibliography.)

Mormonism

Although Mormons represent only a small fraction of the Christian population in the USA and only 1.6% of the total US population, I wanted to research this group to gain an understanding of their beliefs, as they're close to home in several ways. Apart from Utah's proximity to California, a few years before Harrison's death, he attended a small boarding school near Salt Lake City, home of the Church of Jesus Christ of Latter-day Saints, more commonly known as the LDS or Mormon Church. Also, I have wondered about some quirky traditions like *Temple garments*—religious underwear, which sounds pretty interesting.

I have also always admired the healthy lifestyle of Mormons, which makes them seem so radiant. Apparently, not drinking and smoking really does have its benefits! If you doubt that, go to the Salt Lake City area and look at all the sparkling eyes, clear skin, and bright smiles. Additionally, I thought it was appropriate to do more than see the hit musical, *The Book of Mormon,* to gain a deeper understanding of Mormons and their beliefs.

Notwithstanding the positive aspects of the Mormon religion, the fact that gambling, drinking and swearing are frowned upon didn't make it likely that becoming a Mormon would be at the top of my list. (I couldn't help wondering if by donating my 10% tithing [donation] every month, they would allow some daily swearing and a couple of beers? I suspect not.)

The Church of Jesus Christ of Latter-day Saints, currently based in Salt Lake City, Utah, was initially established in Fayette, New York, on April 6, 1830[53] by a self-proclaimed prophet named Joseph Smith. Smith was born in 1805. According to Encyclopedia Britannica, his parents were farmers who disagreed with others in the Christian faith on several religious issues. One would assume that his parents' conflicting views had a significant impact on Joseph as a young man.

At the age of 14, while struggling with his parents' beliefs and praying for guidance on which Christian church to follow, Smith said he was visited by both Jesus and God, who told him that none of the Christian-denominated churches were correct. Four years later, in 1823, he reported having another similar experience. During prayer, he claimed that an angel called Moroni appeared in his bedroom. According to Smith, Moroni informed him of a collection of golden plates that held a historical record of the ancient people of America. Smith then apparently found the plates hidden inside a stone box buried near his father's farm.

Four years after that, during another of his revelations, the angel permitted him to take the plates and guided him to

---

53 Richard Lyman Bushman, "Joseph Smith | Biography & Facts," in *Encyclopædia Britannica* (Chicago: Encyclopædia Britannica, Inc., March 27, 2025), https://www.britannica.com/biography/Joseph-Smith-American-religious-leader-1805-1844.

translate the characters that were carved on them using special stones known as ***interpreters***. Smith maintained that he didn't write the book but rather translated it with divine guidance. He finished the work in under 90 days and published it in March 1830 as a 588-page volume titled *Book of Mormon*.

Again, my scepticism abounds, and I can't help but wonder how many plates there must have been to produce a 590 page book! Of course, that's no less realistic than two of every animal on Earth making their way onto Noah's Ark. Despite the highly unrealistic nature of claims like this, I do really try to remain open to the possibility that not all knowledge is within my grasp. When discussing omnipotent beings and unworldly influences, it is not entirely fair to judge these claims solely on the basis of the laws of physics and reality that we currently understand. After all, what don't I know? Obviously, I do not know the answer to that question! Nevertheless, even when trying to be open-minded, I still can't buy into the story of Joseph Smith, Moroni, and the golden plates.

In fairness, I must point out that there were reportedly eleven witnesses who saw these plates—all but two happened to be Joseph's family members. The two who were not family, were clerical and business associates. Sadly, Joseph Smith eventually returned them to Moroni. They were never truly verified by independent sources.

According to the family members who claimed to have seen the plates, they were thin metal sheets that appeared golden and were bound together like the pages of a book. It may only be a coincidence that Joseph and his father were treasure hunters who'd previously searched the hill on which the book of golden plates was said to have been found. It was also unfortunate that the Smith family, who were very poor, had to wait several years before Moroni would let Joseph retrieve the plates and allow people to see them. Even a greater shame is that Moroni took them back so that they couldn't be closely examined by anyone else. The legitimacy of the plates doesn't ring true to me, but as I have stated above, the belief in itself becomes the truth for many and can be just as potent a nectar to a faithful believer.

Once again, it seems—as is the case with most religions—followers are faced with the choice of accepting these stories in blind faith or questioning them based on a lack of actual proof. Even though stories such as these are not ones I chose to believe, I do recognise, as I have come to acknowledge for all religions, that the belief itself can provide comfort and be a form of truth in itself.

Sadly, in 1844, Joseph Smith and his brother, Hyrum, were killed by a mob in Carthage, Illinois. Following Smith's passing, Brigham Young took charge and guided the majority of Mormons to Utah, where the Church of Jesus Christ of Latter-day Saints has continued to thrive. The Mormon Church is reportedly has well over $100 billion in assets. Many websites list this organisation as the second-wealthiest church in the world! As a member of the church, one is morally obligated and expected to donate 10%[54] of all earnings and gains to the LDS Church's resources and further its work.

---

54 Church of Jesus Christ of Latter-day Saints. "Section 119, The Law of Tithing." *Doctrine and Covenants Student Manual*, July 8, 1838. Https://www.churchofjesuschrist.org/study/manual/doctrine-and-covenants-student-manual/section-119-the-law-of-tithing?lang=eng#title.

> *According to a whistleblower report filed with the IRS late in 2019 and described in a Newsweek.com*[55] *article, one subsidiary investment arm of the LDS Church, Ensign Peak Advisors (EPA), amassed more than $100 billion over the previous 22 years from tithings and donations. The whistleblower document alleges that EPA used $0 of that amount for religious, educational, or charitable purposes. The church has disputed these claims.*

Following the 2019 whistleblower report, a wave of legal actions culminated in a large class action suit in 2024. However, throughout 2025, federal courts consistently dismissed these claims, citing either the statute of limitations or the *Church Autonomy Doctrine*. As of early 2026, the only remaining hope for these plaintiffs lies in a pending petition to the U.S. Supreme Court to redefine how religious organisations can be held liable for secular fraud.

If you read the section earlier in this book titled *It Doesn't Really Matter, Tim!* And my notations about Viktor Frankl and the meaning of life, you'll recall my unshakable belief that the accumulation of more and more wealth and a continual Gollum-like mania to hold on to that wealth is abhorrent to me. That insight was gained through the loss of my son and the subsequent realisation that there are so many more important things in this world than the continued stockpiling of assets to

---

55 Asher Stockler, "Mormon Church Stockpiled $100 Billion Intended for Charities and Misled LDS Members, Whistleblower Says," *Newsweek*, December 17, 2019, https://www.newsweek.com/mormon-church-stockpiled-100-billion-intended-charities-misled-lds-members-whistleblower-says-1477809.

try to attain personal *freedom* and satisfaction. This is one reason I admire people like Melinda Gates, who donates billions of dollars every year to improve the world. My admiration for people like Mrs. Gates is balanced by my disdain for churches that take money from hardworking people, only to hoard and worship it rather than put it to use helping others.

For this reason alone, becoming a member of the Church of Jesus Christ of Latter-day Saints has no appeal to me. I'll have to figure out a way to live a healthy lifestyle without them. If, on the other hand, you, the reader, feel that you want to know a bit more about LDS, here's more information with references that you can pursue on their website.[56] The religion, like so many others, has a lot of great aspects to it.

One of the things I love about the Mormon religion is that it follows a dietary code known as *the Word of Wisdom*. This code restricts the consumption of alcohol, tobacco, and caffeinated beverages, including coffee and tea. In more recent times, the restrictions have been expanded to include recreational drugs such as marijuana. The Word of Wisdom also lists healthy foods that should be eaten and suggests nutritious diets that include grains and minimal meat consumption. Even though the religion itself doesn't seem valid enough for me to believe in, its dietary code is one positive part of the religion that I could embrace and endorse.

Nevertheless, it would be remiss of me not to point out that, as is the case in most religions, there are inconsistencies and a level of hypocrisy in the Word of Wisdom as well. One example:

---

56 Church of Jesus Christ of Latter-day Saints. "Facts About Mormonism." *Church of Jesus Christ of Latter-day Saints FAQ*, 2025. https://faq.churchofjesuschrist.org/facts-about-mormonism.

Founder Joseph Smith is reported to have owned a hotel that had a bar offering alcoholic beverages. The expansive investment portfolios of the church are also said to include investments in tobacco companies and stocks in companies such as those manufacturing caffeinated drinks, including Coca-Cola. Coca-Cola isn't explicitly mentioned in the Word of Wisdom; it only notes hot, caffeinated beverages such as coffee and tea, but the idea is clear. Religious edicts are often followed... until profit and convenience get in the way. Realistically, I suppose it's unfair to criticise the LDS Church for profiting from those who choose not to follow its guidelines.

All sarcasm aside, the Word of Wisdom provides a healthy approach to living, and I wish I had the strength to follow its recommendations. I'd probably have much more energy and be a healthier person if I did. The membership of the LDS Church continues to grow each year in the USA and worldwide.[57] Its followers in the USA primarily live in Salt Lake City, and worldwide membership exceeds 17 million people.

Belief in the Afterlife

Mormons believe in a plan of salvation that centres around the existence, for each of us, of a pre-mortal soul. Based on LDS scriptures, all humans are God's children and live with Him before being born. They come to Earth to gain a body to become more like Him. After we complete our mortal life, we go to an afterlife that involves resurrection and judgment. Accordingly,

57 History.com Editors. "Mormons." History, April 15, 2025.

those who obey His gospel will receive the gift of eternal life with God.[58]

If one leads a life of obeying the gospel, there's the promise that they will *receive the gift of eternal life with God.* It appears to me that the new souls who are *God's children before being born* are not old souls who've cycled through numerous lives here on Earth to reach the ultimate nirvana of some sort, as is the case with some other religions.

A quote from the LSD website[59] states: *Members of the Church believe that through the Atonement of Jesus Christ, after physical death, each person's body and spirit will reunite and no longer be subject to disease or death. Latter-day Saints also believe that after the Resurrection, mankind can be exalted to the highest level of salvation. He that overcometh shall inherit all things, and I will be his God, and he shall be my son.*

(Revelation 21:7).

At the risk of offending all the Mormons and Scientologists out there, the stories that Joseph Smith created are, in my mind, are about as plausible as the teachings of L. Ron Hubbard, the founder of Scientology. Sadly, I consider it more likely that both men were charlatans and storytellers who were just really great salesmen. That is not to say that the benefits of belief and fellowship from the community are any less valid than other

58 Church of Jesus Christ of Latter-day Saints. "Atonement of Jesus Christ." Gospel Topics, April 6, 2021. https://www.churchofjesuschrist.org/study/manual/gospel-topics/atonement-of-jesus-christ?lang=eng.

59 Church of Jesus Christ of Latter-day Saints. "Facts About Mormonism." Church of Jesus Christ of Latter-day Saints FAQ, 2025. https://faq.churchofjesuschrist.org/facts-about-mormonism.

religions out there. They all seem to be based on shaky foundational ground from a historical perspective.

My research on Mormonism made me eager to finish the section on simulation theory that appears later in this book. If you want to seriously consider believing stories like those of Joseph Smith and Ron Hubbard, isn't it just as possible that we aren't actual souls within human bodies but rather pieces of highly advanced code generated and recycled through earthly physical bodies? Of course, if you're a good enough storyteller, there will always be people willing to believe any story! It seems we all need something to believe in, myself included.

Proof

The Church of Jesus Christ of Latter-day Saints was recently founded and is relatively young. Therefore, there is a reasonable amount of evidence proving the life of Joseph Smith and the Book of Mormon that he wrote. Still, the contents of the Book of Mormon and Joseph Smith himself warrant closer examination to be sure.

- When Joseph Smith was still a teenager, he reported seeing or having an interaction with Jesus and God, and then later Moroni, who he said was an angel. As is the case with most interactions with God or God's representatives, there is no proof of this. He is not alone, of course; none of the religious leaders or prophets whom I can think of has a verifiable witnessed account of such visits. Moses and the Prophet Muhammad come immediately to mind.
- There is such a thing as the Book of Mormon, and it is confirmed that Joseph Smith authored it. However, there is no

physical evidence whatsoever of the golden plates from which he claimed it was translated, other than statements from family members and close associates.

- The Book of Mormon describes some advanced civilisations in the Americas, called the Nephites and Lamanites, who were descendants of a prophet called Lehi and his family who left Jerusalem around 600 BC and travelled to the Americas. There is absolutely no archaeological evidence to support the existence of these civilisations.
- There is evidence that he lived, and contemporaneous accounts do provide detailed information about Joseph Smith. Unfortunately, those records do not significantly enhance his credibility. It is a fact that he was tried in 1826 for something called *glass-looking*, which was a practice of claiming to find buried treasure using a seer stone, a device he later claimed to have used to help him translate the Book of Mormon. There is no proof that seer stones actually work. In other words, he tended to tell tall stories. (There are further references in the back of the book under the section titled *Appendix: Notes by Religion*. A study by Richard Bushman called *Rough Stone Rolling* explores Smith's claims regarding faith and challenges the historical evidence provided.)
- In earlier versions of the Book of Mormon, Joseph Smith claimed that Native Americans were descended from Israelites. DNA evidence proved that fact to be incorrect. Native American populations primarily share ancestry with East Asian groups, not Middle Eastern populations.
- The 1981 introduction to the Book of Mormon stated:

...after thousands of years, all were destroyed except the Lamanites, and they are the principal ancestors of the American Indians.

In a later edition (2006) of the Book of Mormon, that language was revised to say the Lamanites are ***among the ancestors*** of the American Indians rather than the principal ancestors.

Conclusion Regarding Proof

In my mind, the foundational stories of the Mormon Church lack a lot of credibility. That shouldn't minimise the fact that there are clearly many people who believe in the faith, that it's beneficial for them, and the religion offers a lot of positive aspects. However, these truths are worth knowing if you are considering becoming a Mormon. Unfortunately, there's no factual evidence that would make a belief in Mormonism a credible option for me. It may be a great option for others due to its healthy lifestyle, sense of support, community, and positivity.

(For access to additional key-point discussion and summary notes, refer to the section in the back of the book titled Appendix: Notes by Religion just before the Bibliography.)

Seventh-day Adventist Church

For the living know that they will die, but the dead know nothing; they have no more reward, and even their name is forgotten.

~ Ecclesiastes 9:5

The above statement of belief isn't specific to Seventh-day Adventists alone. Ecclesiastes 9:5 is part of the Old Testament and is included in the Hebrew Bible in the section known as the Ketuvim (Writings). However, it holds great significance for Seventh-day Adventists because it is often used to support their belief that death is a state of ***unconscious sleep*** until the resurrection.

Origins of the Seventh-day Adventist Church

The Seventh-day Adventist (SDA) Church started in the middle of the 1800s as part of what was initially called the Millerite movement, a religious awakening led by an Adventist[60] Baptist preacher, William Miller.[61] Miller initially predicted that the Second Coming of Christ would happen in 1843 and then later refined that to March 1844. Unfortunately for Miller, it didn't happen on either occasion. Nevertheless, he'd been preaching and prophesying about the Second Coming since 1831 (I don't know what donations he was accepting as part of that process?)

Over the nearly 13 years that he was predicting the imminent second coming, Miller had gathered between 50,000 and 100,000 followers. Of course, in 1844, he lost credibility when his predictions didn't come true. Eventually, he acknowledged his error in setting specific dates, though he continued to believe in Christ's imminent return until his death in 1849.

One of Miller's followers, Samuel Snow, decided to pick up the gauntlet after Miller's departure. Snow had previously predicted October 22, 1844 as date for the Second Coming. Regrettably, that date also came and went with no appearance of Chris. And was later referred to as the *Great Disappointment*. In my view, Samual Snow was short-sighted in picking a date so close to the one chosen by Miller!

As expected, when Jesus didn't arrive on the revised date, many followers lost faith and left the movement. However, a dedicated group of Millerites continued to study the Bible and

---

60 Melton, J. Gordon, and James Hutchinson Smylie. "Adventist | Meaning, History, & Beliefs." In *Encyclopædia Britannica*. Chicago: Encyclopædia Britannica, Inc., February 21, 2025. https://www.britannica.com/topic/Adventism.

61 Encyclopaedia Britannica Editors, "William Miller | Millerite, Adventist, Preacher," in *Encyclopædia Britannica* (Chicago: Encyclopædia Britannica, Inc., 2025), https://www.britannica.com/biography/William-Miller.

eventually established what would later become the Seventh-day Adventist Church. The Church states that it has more than 100,000 congregations worldwide and more than 23 million members—I find this remarkable, considering it was founded on a failed prediction. Once again, this just proves to me how community and belief take precedence over facts and reasoning.

If you believe in Jesus Christ as the Son of God and in His first resurrection, then it would be entirely believable to assume He may return. I get that. What I find more interesting is that the initial followers of William Miller believed he had some way of knowing in which month it would occur!

The foundations of the modern version of the Seventh Day Adventist Church were put in place when, just a few months after the Great Disappointment of October 1844, Ellen G. White,[62] one of the Millerites who refused to give up the faith, experienced the first of nearly 2,000 visions that she claimed were bestowed upon her by God. Her self-declared (and unverified) visions led to the emergence of the new movement. White remained a key figure during the church's formative years until her death in 1915, and her numerous writings greatly inspired and influenced SDA beliefs and practices (Knight, 2000; Douglass, 1998).[63]

---

62 Encyclopaedia Britannica Editors, "Ellen Gould Harmon White | American Religious Leader & Prophetess," in *Encyclopædia Britannica* (Chicago: Encyclopædia Britannica, Inc., 2025), https://www.britannica.com/biography/Ellen-Gould-Harmon-White.

63 George R. Knight, A Brief History of Seventh-Day Adventists, illustrated ed. (Hagerstown, MD: Review and Herald Publishing, 2000), https://adventistbookcenter.com/books/a-brief-history-of-seventh-day-adventists.html; Herbert E. Douglass, *Messenger of the Lord: The Prophetic Ministry of Ellen G. White* (Nampa, ID: Pacific Press Publishing Association, 1998),

Officially founded in Battle Creek, Michigan, in 1863, the SDA's main goals were to prepare members for Christ's imminent return and to encourage healthy living and behaviour consistent with Biblical teachings. Unlike William Miller and Samuel Snow, Ellen White was bright enough not to assign a specific date for Christ's return. As a result, the Seventh-day Adventist Church is still going strong today. Although the SDA Church has a significant number of followers, it remains a small fraction of global faith populations, capturing less than 0.3% of the world's people. Its growth is meaningful, especially in the Global South, but it also faces the twin pressures of retention and engagement.

As with many religions, the continued success of the Seventh Day Adventist Church has more to do with its positive doctrine, sense of community, and people's need to believe in something greater than themselves than its credibility regarding its origins. Notwithstanding my apparent scepticism and sarcasm regarding those origins, on a more serious note, the SDA Church does have several positive belief structures and teachings, specifically regarding its philosophies around healthy living. Ellen White's views on health—particularly her opposition to the consumption of tea, coffee, meat, and drugs—are positive. Her recommendations were eventually officially incorporated into Seventh-day Adventist practice and remain in effect today. Adventists believe that a healthy lifestyle—which is defined as a vegetarian diet, abstaining from tobacco and alcohol, and incorporating regular exercise—aligns with God's will for His people (Fraser, 2003).[64]

---

64 Gary E. Fraser, ***Diet, Life Expectancy, and Chronic Disease: Studies of Seventh-Day Adventists and Other Vegetarians***, 1st ed. (New York: Oxford University Press, 2003), https://global.oup.com/academic/product/diet-life-expectancy-and-chronic-disease-9780195113242?cc=pk&lang=en&.

In addition to her numerous writings and teachings, in 1866, White established an institute in Battle Creek, which was later known as the Battle Creek Sanitarium. This establishment was renowned for its contributions to the field of diet and healthcare, becoming a model for many other institutions nationwide. Many early Adventists were also participants in the abolitionist movement and very active in the movement to end slavery in America. In addition, Seventh-day Adventists were participants in the *temperance movement*, an effort to discourage people from using alcohol and to practice moderation in general regarding eating and drinking—all positive developments.

A couple of additional interesting facts about the SDA church when compared to other Christians:

- Seventh-day Adventists believe that Saturday is the Sabbath. This aligns with their understanding of the Fourth Commandment (Exodus 20:8-11) and differs from most other Christian groups, who regard Sunday as the Sabbath (Douglass, 1998).[65]
- Another one of the Church's unique beliefs, described in the Sanctuary Doctrine, is that Jesus played a major role in making things right with God, and this is seen as one of several actions that will lead to Christ's return (Knight, 2000).[66]

---

65 Douglass, *Messenger of the Lord.*

66 Knight, *A Brief History of Seventh-Day Adventists.*

What Happens After Death

The Seventh-day Adventist Church has a doctrine called the *State of the Dead*, often referred to as *soul sleep*. They believe that we don't automatically possess immortal souls. Instead, immortality is given only to the righteous by God. According to their teachings, until the Second Coming of Christ, after we die, we're asleep, peacefully unaware. Not drifting in heaven or suffering elsewhere—just… paused. If we have lived a righteous life, we are then granted an immortal soul when Christ returns again.

As the quote at the start of this chapter (Ecclesiastes 9:5) suggests, for Adventists, death is more like a deep sleep, with the individual completely unconscious and awakening at the resurrection of the dead (Ellen White, 1911).[67]

In the SDA faith, there are two resurrections of the dead yet to happen. At Christ's Second Coming, *the resurrected righteous and the living righteous will be glorified and caught up to meet the Lord.*[68] (*John 5:28-29; Revelation 20:6*) The subsequent resurrection of the dead occurs after Christ's thousand-year reign. At this second future event, the wicked will be brought back to life for a final judgment and then destroyed forever.

Members of the SDA Church see the second death as a merciful end rather than endless torment, which aligns with their

---

67 Ellen Gould White, *The Great Controversy*, vol. 5, Conflict of the Ages (Mountain View, CA: Pacific Press Publishing Association, 1911), https://text.egwwritings.org/book/b132.

68 Seventh-day Adventist Sabbath School Net. "Death and Resurrection - Seventh-Day Adventist Fundamental Belief 26." *Sabath School Net* (blog), June 2, 2011. https://ssnet.org/about-us/fundamental-beliefs-seventh-day-adventists/death-and-resurrection/.

view of a fair and loving God. They also believe that the world will end at the final judgment, where people's eternal destinies are determined. The good will live on in a new Earth, while the wicked will be destroyed, which Adventists see as the end of sin.

Proof

The SDA Church's beliefs about the afterlife are primarily based on its unique interpretation of the Bible, which, in my mind, is problematic to start with. Yes, scientific evidence supports the benefits of healthy lifestyle choices; however, SDA beliefs about the afterlife—such as soul sleep and eventual resurrection—can't be proven by science. They're based only on faith.

Health and Lifestyle Evidence

An investigation by researchers at Loma Linda University (an SDA institution) into Adventist health has found that Adventists tend to live longer and have fewer chronic diseases than non-Adventists. Many people think these results are because Adventists advocate eating only plants, staying away from harmful substances such as alcohol and tobacco, and engaging in daily physical activity (Fraser, 2003).[69] Loma Linda, California, where many Adventists live, has been designated a *blue zone*, which means that people there live longer than average.

69 Fraser, *Diet, Life Expectancy, and Chronic Disease.*

Taoism

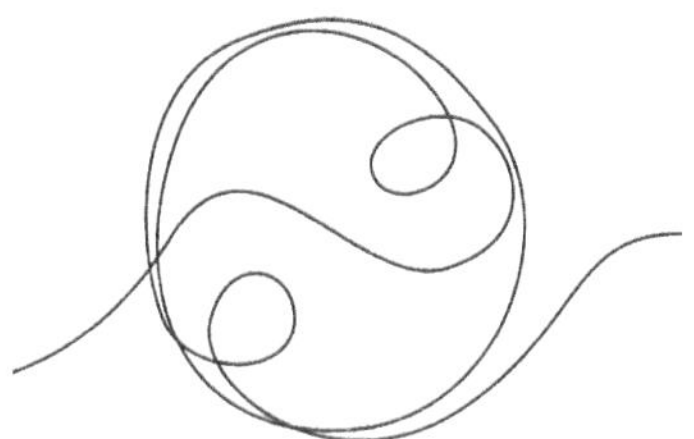

Regard your neighbour's gain as your own gain and your neighbour's loss as your own loss.[70]

(T'ai Shang Kan Ying P'ien (sacred Taoist text attributed to Lao-Tzu)[71]

Taoism[72] (sometimes spelled Daoism) is an ancient Chinese philosophical tradition and spiritual practice that has profoundly influenced Chinese culture for over 2,000 years. Essentially,

70 P'ien, T'ai Shang Kan Ying. "Your Neighbor's Gain." Luminary Quotes, 2017. https://luminaryquotes.com/quote/your-neighbors-gain/.

71 S. Whitfield, "Review of T'ai-Shang Kan-Ying P'ien: Lao-Tzu's Treatise on the Response of the Tao," *Journal of the Royal Asiatic Society* 6, no. 1 (1996): 139, https://doi.org/10.1017/S1356186300015194.

72 Anna K. Seidel and Roger T. Ames, "Taoism | Definition, Origin, Philosophy, Beliefs, & Facts," in *Encyclopaedia Britannica* (Chicago: Encyclopaedia Britannica, Inc., April 15, 2025), https://www.britannica.com/topic/Taoism.

Taoists try to focus on living in harmony with what they call the *Tao* (or Dao).[73] Living in pursuit of Taoist ideals means following what's often referred to as *The Path* or *The Way.*

Some describe the Tao as the universe's natural order, a force that flows through all things and guides the balance of life. Taoism advocates living in a state of harmony with the universe and its energy, which means living a life of passivity, calmness, and non-action—*Wu*Wu *Wei*.[74]

Unfortunately, the lack of a clear definition of what the Tao is and the grandiose description of its *undefined, all-encompassing* nature initially reminded me of The Great and Powerful Wizard of Oz. I know that comparison is irreverent and unfair, particularly given other religions' equally unverifiable insistence that there's a God up in heaven who's the ultimate creator! Nevertheless, that's the association that first came up for me.

At the innocent age of 12, I must have been indelibly impacted by the revelation that the source of the booming voice of the Great Oz was just an old man behind a curtain. Perhaps it was this dramatic revelation during my childhood that unfairly shaped my healthy scepticism regarding religions, deities, creators, and ultimate hidden forces?

When I set aside my reflective scepticism to consider Taoist philosophy, it quickly became apparent that there are clear parallels to some of the conclusions and beliefs that were already

---

73 Matt Stefon, "Dao | Chinese Philosophy & Religion," in *Encyclopaedia Britannica* (Chicago: Encyclopaedia Britannica, Inc., February 18, 2025), https://www.britannica.com/topic/dao.

74 Matt Stefon, "Wuwei | Daoism, Non-Action & Spontaneity," in Encyclopaedia Britannica (Chicago: *Encyclopaedia Britannica*, Inc., 2025), https://www.britannica.com/topic/wuwei-Chinese-philosophy.

forming on my journey of discovery. There were too many beliefs among Taoists that align with my growing worldview not to take a closer look. After all, I also believe that:

- We're surrounded and infused by energy and a life force we don't fully understand.
- Our world is better enjoyed when we're in harmony with it.
- After Harrison's death, I realised that material wealth and greed (beyond our basic needs) are meaningless.
- The world would be a better place if we were more sensitive to each other's pain.
- There's a communal energy that surrounds and guides us if we let it.

All these beliefs align with the primary Taoist philosophy. Where would we be if, over the ages, all the Christians, Muslims, and Jews of the world had communally embraced and lived a life of tolerance that was more in keeping with the precepts of wu wei? Clearly, the world would be a much better place.

While exploring definitions of the meaning of Tao, I kept encountering impressive words like ***metaphysical***, which Webster's dictionary defines as something ***highly abstract and overly theoretical*** or as ***being without material form or substance.*** Then there's ***enigmatic***, which means ***not clear or easily understandable.*** The broad concepts of the Tao are so ***amorphous (without shape)*** that I find it ironic that Tao has come to be described using ***prosaic (dull or unimaginative)*** terms such as The Path and The Way. However, it seems to work because The Way is described in broad yet simple terms that are appealing and make sense. In other words, Taoism is attractive because a term like The Path can mean many things to different people, and it signifies a personal philosophy or direction that isn't easily defined in words. As a result, followers or interested individuals have more freedom to create their own understanding of what The Way truly means. Therefore, simple terms like this offer greater appeal to a wider audience.

The paragraph below about the Tao is from National Geographic's wonderful educational materials for middle-school students (National Geographic Society, 2024)[75]. This simplistic definition offered a helpful level of clarity for me personally:

The Tao (or Dao) is hard to define but is sometimes understood as the way of the universe. *Taoism teaches that all living creatures ought to live in a state of harmony with the universe and the energy found in it. Ch'I, or qi, is the energy present in and guiding everything in the universe.* The Tao Te Ching *and other Taoist books provide guidelines for behaviour and spiritual ways to live in harmony with this energy... One of the main ideas of Taoism is the belief in balancing the forces of yin and yang. These ideas represent matching pairs—light and dark, hot and cold, action and inaction—which work together toward a universal whole. Yin and yang show that* ***everything in the universe is connected and that nothing makes sense by itself.***

What follows is a note I had sent to my lovely daughter years after my divorce from her mother. Perhaps I should have just sent the quote from Lao-Tzu instead (at the front of this chapter). It is what I was trying to say in the following very clumsy letter.

75 The Wise Apple, "Taoism," National Geographic Education, July 23, 2024, https://education.nationalgeographic.org/resource/taoism/.

Jacqueline, I'm so glad you've turned out to be such a wonderful woman who's aware of other people's feelings. It's so important to put yourself in someone else's shoes and allow yourself to feel what they are going through; you seem to be able to do that, which is truly a gift.

As I delve further into the book I'm writing, I come closer to the conclusion that we're all here to grow spiritually each time our soul experiences the cycle of life. That's the most important thing. Personal internal growth, kindness, and awareness of the world around us are paramount.

I hope my lovely daughter continues to acknowledge her more spiritual side and not just follow a path driven by the pursuit of wealth and power as so many others do. Hopefully, she remembers the quote from Lao-Tzu and decides to follow some Taoist principles as well. Her Dad plans to.

Taoist Beliefs About the Afterlife

Taoist ideas about the afterlife centre around the individual being in sync with the Tao, the impersonal and eternal force that holds everything together (Robinet, 1997).[76] In contrast to many faiths that have clear ideas about heaven and hell, Taoism

76 Isabelle Robinet, *Taoism: Growth of a Religion*, trans. Phyllis Brooks, First English edition (Stanford, California: Stanford University Press, 1997).

suggests that people return to the Tao after death, merging with the universal energy and achieving a form of spiritual continuity (Kohn, 1991).[77] In this view, death is a process of returning to the timeless energy and order of the universe.

If the Taoist belief in a universal energetic connection between the body and the soul is true, this would explain why I feel at one with my son when I swim in the ocean. I feel unexplainably closer to him when immersed in water, particularly when all my senses are focused on that singular experience. Whether I'm swimming in the cold, often grey waters directly off the dock of my beautiful little floating home in Sausalito or in the clear, warmer waves off Manly Beach in Sydney, Australia, I feel closer to him and surrounded by his energy. I had inexplicably felt that overwhelming feeling long before researching this book.

One interesting concept in Taoism is the discussion of *Shen*, or spirit, and the idea that an individual's spirit can become an ancestor spirit after death if they've lived in harmony with the Tao and had a positive impact on the living (Girardot, 1983).[78] If someone has upset the balance or gone against Taoist ideals, their spirit might not leave them peacefully. Instead, it might become a wandering or angry spirit. This isn't a universal Taoist

---

77 Livia Kohn, *Early Chinese Mysticism: Philosophy and Soteriology in the Taoist Tradition*, 1st ed. (Princeton, New Jersey: Princeton University Press, 1991).

78 N. J. Girardot, *Myth and Meaning in Early Taoism: The Theme of Chaos (Hun-Tun)* (Berkeley: University of California Press, 1988).

doctrine believed by all; it's similar to Chinese folk traditions (DeWoskin, 1983).[79]

Meditation, controlling your breath, and certain types of exercise are all believed to help increase an individual's *qi* or *life energy*. It's suggested that fully enhancing qi allows Taoists to go beyond death and live longer through *immortality practices* that focus on health and harmony. Most of us have heard about studies showing that spiritual practices are good for our health and may help us live longer and with less stress. Unfortunately, there are no studies that have shown that these practices can stop you from dying or ensure a life after death.

I found no evidence that a spirit can merge with universal forces or become an ancestor spirit, of course. Once again, the lack of empirical evidence of an afterlife in this religion, as in others, means the current scientific consensus doesn't support Taoist beliefs about the afterlife. Still, there's no doubt that Taoist practices and meditation can improve mental and physical health (Wong, 2011).[80]

Notwithstanding the lack of scientific proof, I don't need a test or study to prove what I feel when I'm in the surf or surrounded by redwood trees or the smell of a pine forest. That's my *empirical* study. And it tells me that there's definitely something to the ancient traditions and beliefs of the Tao.

---

79 Kenneth J. DeWoskin, *Doctors, Diviners, and Magicians of Ancient China: Biographies of Fang-Shih*, Illustrated, Columbia Asian Studies Series: Translations from the Oriental Classics (New York: Columbia University Press, 1983), https://archive.org/details/isbn_023105596x.

80 Eva Wong, *The Shambhala Guide to Taoism*, Shambhala Guides (Boston: Shambhala Publications, Inc., 2011)

Proof

I had hoped that, after examining all the references to ancient texts of Taoist philosophies and belief systems, I might find some solid, undeniable proof that the soul lives on. But, once again, what I found was something more nuanced… and maybe, in a quiet way, more honest.

This section on Taoism is the last of the religions I specifically examine in this book. In the next chapter, I examine the commonalities among the religions. There are a striking number of them! It is fitting to have Taoism as the last individual religion because it focuses on a theme that is significant and prevalent across most religions.

> *When you line up all the central spiritual teachings, it's striking how often they point to the same themes—oneness, energy, balance, compassion, and the mysterious sense that there's something beyond the physical shell we call a body.*

Taoists talk about merging with the Tao. Hindus speak of the atman returning to Brahman. Christians place their hope in heaven. In Jewish tradition, the soul is seen as returning to its divine source, while Islam teaches that life is a journey of surrender toward unity with God. The one cohesive thread amongst them all is that there is something more… *beyond.*

The hard truth is this: no religion or philosophy I examined provided empirical, testable proof of what happens after we die. Not even the sincerely held testimonies of those who've had near-death experiences could entirely do that. Still, I came away with something else—a deep respect for the consistency across cultures and centuries. These ancient systems—whether they originated from the Ganges, Jerusalem, or China—are sincere attempts to grapple with the same questions I've been facing since the day I lost my son. They provide answers, but not really in any verifiable way.

So, no, I didn't find definitive proof. But I did find a mosaic of wisdom that continues to point beyond the material world. And while it may not be measurable by a lab instrument, there's something powerfully human in that shared reaching. I suppose that, too, is a kind of evidence—just not the kind that fits neatly in a spreadsheet like I initially hoped.

(For access to additional key-point discussion and summary notes about proof and Taoism, refer to the section in the back of the book titled Appendix: Notes by Religion just before the Bibliography.)

* * *

Upon examining the religions individually, it would be logical and natural to find one that sounds like the right place to be. I hope some of the readers who have made it this far have done so. However, personally, I was left with a humbling sense of uncertainty about life after death and without a belief structure that I found totally fulfilling. I didn't feel my journey was over yet. Fortunately, I found additional resonance when examining the commonalities among religions in the next section, then moving into the book's science and more spiritual beliefs, which follow in Part 3. If you haven't zeroed in on what resonates with you yet, hopefuly you will join soon as well.

Commonality

For many people, there's no better place than your church where you can go when the shit hits the fan... without turning to drugs. You feel prayer around you and are embraced by people who provide care and support.

(A quote from an anonymous Christian friend, when I asked her why she attends church so faithfully every week.)

The all-embracing, powerful sense of community and support people feel from being part of a congregation is a strong magnetic force of appeal for many. It's **one of the strongest similarities many religions share** and the singular, most powerful reason for so many faithful followers of these different faiths (and often of populist political figures as well). Questioning the fundamental stories and legends of the belief and its practicality is swept aside by this profoundly powerful sense of belonging.

* * *

A little personal story about resistance, avoiding grief, and community:

It wasn't my custom, but one night, around seven years after losing Harrison, I found myself, uncharacteristically, sitting and listening to a beautiful cello performance by an artist at a local restaurant in Sausalito called Osteria Devino. I was holding a glass of lovely GSM (a blend of grenache, syrah, and other grapes). The lights were dim, my eyes were closed, and the melodies of Bach and Beethoven soothed my mind, washing away all conscious thought about daily problems, losing my son, or any of the myriad of thoughts that are constantly bouncing around and filling a space in our minds that is better spent dedicated to greater things. It was as though I was temporarily transported to a romantic European city. Then, in this space created by an unintended meditative state, I suddenly remember a quote from a book called *The War of Art* that I had been reading the day before:

> ***Resistance grows greater the closer you are to the finish line.***[81]
>
> Steven Pressfield

I was then suddenly reminded of my father, who had passed away just a few years before Harrison. Dad, a journalist, had always wanted to write a book and had spent years working on a compelling historical novel that followed the journey of a

81 Steven Pressfield, *The War of Art: Winning the Inner Creative Battle* (London: Orion, 2003), https://www.goodreads.com/book/show/24856285.

Chinese family of immigrants who came to Australia and ultimately worked in the gold fields of Victoria during the Australian Gold Rush of 1851. He eventually discarded the manuscript after years of hard work. Sadly, I was never able to find it. During the editorial and revision process, he had convinced himself that a publisher would never accept his book. "It is too full of holes and inconsistencies," he once grumbled. (I had actually read an early draft and thought it was pretty good.)

If he were anything like his son, I assume his resistance was primarily due to avoidance or profound fear of the pain that failure and rejection would cause. Indeed, the closer I get to the end of my book, the more I struggle with procrastination and self-doubt. That struggle relates primarily to the avoidance of potential pain. A subconscious desire to avoid pain of any type is normal. A desire to avoid the pain associated with grieving is no exception.

In the same week that my father died at the age of 92, I had to euthanise my dog, a Rhodesian Ridgeback named Rip—my best and only companion at that time. This was during the period when my wife was in the process of leaving me. I also lost my dream of living in Australia because of the divorce, and thus, a potential separation from my children if I stayed, which I wouldn't accept.

All in the space of a few weeks, I had lost my father, my wife, my dog, and, effectively, my children and my ability to live in Australia. My son was sent away to a far-off boarding school because I was on the road 17 days a month flying, and his mother was running a business and felt that he deserved better attention and help than she could provide. (Like many very talented and creative people, Harrison was on the autistic spectrum, and we had finally found a great school where he could get fantastic support and an environment full of creative opportunity and experiential learning. Nevertheless, I missed him greatly.) All I wanted to do was run away!

I also wanted to reclaim some of my father's legacy by resurrecting his book. Sadly, there wasn't even a draft in all his papers. His personal disappointment had created a sense of failure that was so great that he had to get rid of all *the evidence.* In throwing away the manuscript and the evidence, he was able to move forward and forget. I suspect the feeling is similar to my desire, at times, to run away from the grief of losing my son, and sometimes other troubles. I partially blame myself for my son's loss, and it's easier, sometimes, to want his memory to be so hidden that it doesn't cause so much pain.

My father's resistance to completing his novel became so great toward the end that it ultimately overcame him. As I get closer to the end of this book, I see the same thing happening to me. I procrastinate. Whenever possible, I will do anything but sit down and write. In my case, it's not just the fear of rejection or zero book sales. For me, I think it is also about avoiding the pain associated with journaling about my grief and loss on a daily basis.

As I have discovered on this journey, which many know, one of the stepping stones to recovery and overcoming grief is actually facing it.

Even though, when writing this, I was experiencing tremendous resistance and wanted to run away, I also wanted to find rest for my soul and understand what happened to my boy! Isn't it better to move through whatever's left of life with a lessening of pain and grief by facing it, not avoiding it? (Since you're reading this book, I assume you're familiar with that pain as well.) Considering a possible outcome in which I do not reach my goal to find some peace and permanent escape from grief scares me as well.

In the case of my father, he was not particularly religious; he had very few friends other than my mother and a limited sense of commonality with a larger group of people, spiritual or otherwise. If he had, I believe that with additional support, he might not have wasted all those years of hard work and discarded his manuscript. He lacked a community and support. He struggled with his fears alone. And that is the crux of this story. We don't have to.

> *There is enough good and commonality among all these religions and beliefs to fill your pockets and get lots of support. To me, the commonalities among religions are fascinating. We are all closer than we think.*

I shared the above story about my father and difficult time in my life not in an attempt to gain sympathy but to demonstrate a particular point about running away from pain. I fully realise that millions of people face much greater hardship than I. We all struggle with loss in different ways. To some, the feeling of loss of an unborn child is far greater than that of a 20-year-old boy. To others, a divorce and loneliness may feel greater than losing a child. In fact, many people report grieving the loss of a beloved pet even more deeply than a spouse—especially when that pet was their closest companion. (Actually, not a surprising fact).

Fortunately, regardless of the dubious origins and credibility of most religions, the commonalities among them offer hope for us—not as a refuge to escape but rather as a support while we battle through and face our challenges. They offer inspiration to keep going (on a project or in life) and can also help us recover from grief and overcome sadness and self-doubt. I don't want this manuscript to suffer the same fate as my father's. Nor did I want my life to be an escape path from pain, so finding common ground amongst all these beliefs was important to me before I launched into Part 2 of the book and examined other beliefs that are not religious in nature.

Commonality and Community

What follows is a brief yet profoundly impactful excerpt from one of the most beautiful and inspiring books I have ever read. *Tuesdays with Morrie*, written by Mitch Albom,[82] has sold millions of copies and has been translated into more than 45 different languages. It remains one of the top-selling memoirs of all time. In the book, Mitch beautifully documents his weekly visits with his old college professor and mentor, Morrie Schwartz, who has been diagnosed with a terminal illness, yet manages to spend the last months of his life eloquently passing on some of life's greatest lessons to others rather than focus on himself. (You can purchase *Tuesdays with Morrie* at LighthouseLaneBooks.com)

---

82 Mitch Albom, *Tuesdays with Morrie*, 1st ed. (Sydney: Hachette Australia, 1998), https://www.amazon.com.au/Tuesdays-Morrie-Mitch-Albom/dp/0733609554.

(The following passage is written from the perspective of Mitch Albom, the author and interviewer, and his old mentor, Morrie, as the interviewee.)

> *I heard a nice little story the other day, Morrie says.* He closes his eyes for a moment, and I wait.
>
> *Okay. The story is about a little wave, bobbing along in the ocean, having a grand old time. He's enjoying the wind and the fresh air—until he notices the other waves in front of him, crashing against the shore.*
>
> *"My God, this is terrible," the wave says. "Look what's going to happen to me!"*
>
> *Then along came another wave. It sees the first wave, looking grim, and it says to him, "Why do you look so sad?"*
>
> *The first wave says, "You don't understand! We're all going to crash! All of us waves are going to be nothing! Isn't it terrible?"*
>
> *The second wave says, "No, you don't understand. You're not a wave. You're part of the ocean."*
>
> A smile. Morrie closes his eyes again.
>
> *Part of the ocean,* he says. *Part of the ocean.*
>
> I watch him breathe in and out, in and out.

Tuesdays with Morri ~ by Mitch Albom

Common Gods, Texts and Prophets

Praying with Muslims

On a recent trip to Turkey, I finally found the courage to join a group of men filing into a mosque in Istanbul for their late afternoon prayers. (The particular sunset prayer I attended is called Maghrib and is one of five compulsory daily prayers.) In the past, on hundreds of trips to the Middle East as a commercial pilot, I had always wondered what it felt like to be a Muslim and respond to the enchanting and melodic *adhan*, the call to prayer recited by the *muezzin* (servant of the mosque chosen for his good character and voice). For me, there has always been something a bit magical about the sunset call to prayer. As the day comes to a close, when a cooling calm replaces the often overwhelming heat as the sun slips below the horizon and the dust-filled sky turns a lovely orange-pink, the call to prayer permeates the air, projected from the beautiful minarets of mosques. I am embarrassed to say that, over countless years of listening to the call to prayer, I had not once set foot in a mosque.

Finally, after the death of my son, and on one of my last trips as a 747 Captain, when in Dubai, I found the nerve to participate as if I were one of the faithful and answer the call. Of course, all the men around me knew I was a Westerner and probably not a Muslim, and it was far too apparent that I had no concept of the prayers they were reciting. Given my noticeable presence and the ignorance of a typical non-Muslim, I was expecting at any time that somebody would point toward me and start yelling *infidel* in Arabic. To minimise the chance of public exposure and a forced exit, I did my best to be respectful, carefully following every movement—kneeling when required, bowing from my waist, and touching my head to the ground. Fortunately, no public humiliation occurred, and I was kindly allowed to join the rows of faithful followers and give my adoration and respect to Allah, *the one true God.* I did so assuming that if I were a practising Christian, I would still be okay because I was worshipping the same God. Muslims just refer to Him by a different name.

Christianity, Judaism, and Islam do have a large number of significant intersections and beliefs. It was a surprise to me that, as stated above, they all share the same God! Given that fact, it strikes me as a massive shame that religions that all share the same God would be at war with one another and have remained in a state of continued hatred for so many centuries. In my mind, even if the God they all worship is authentic, it suggests to me that He is not kind, and certainly not logical. Logic would suggest that it is not wise to have your believers and followers kill each other. I am sure that some theologian will have an explanation for this or why those who kill *in God's name* do so, believing wholeheartedly they are on a righteous path. To me, the whole concept of all this hatred and killing in God's name totally undermines any credibility in the idea of God at all.

At the time of this edit, the Jewish state of Israel is exacting revenge and devastation in Gaza in retaliation for a terrible attack by Hamas on a peaceful music festival in Israel. According to the Gaza Health Ministry, over 45,000 people have been killed in the retaliatory response. The war in the Middle East burns like a never-ending fire that cannot be extinguished. The desecration, inhumanity, and anger among different followers of the same God continues!

In search of a religion or belief structure that I can grab onto to help me recover from grief, I find it increasingly difficult to embrace any religion that has been the cause of so much death and inhumanity to man! The question remains, though, whether it is religion that is the cause or bad people who use religion as an excuse.

* * *

The following are some of the *significant similarities* among these three religions and their texts, which could help unite the groups if they put aside animosity and embrace community instead.

Christians, Muslims, and Jews

Similarities

- The Hebrew Bible widely interprets human life and the universe as creations of only one supreme God. This interpretation of an almighty deity and ultimate creator is the foundation for Judaism, Christianity, and Islam. The teachings of *all three view Abraham as a patriarch*. Therefore, they are classified as Abrahamic religions. They all derive from Abraham, and thus, as stated above, *they worship the same God.*
- The numerous parallels continue when you consider that many of the same individuals are mentioned in each religion's sacred books. Jesus, for example, is named frequently in the Quran and is regarded by Muslims as one of the prophets. Christians view Jesus as the Son of God, not a prophet. Interestingly, Judaism does not recognise Jesus or Muhammad

as prophets but does recognise them as significant figures of their times. Although the interpretation and significance of each figure differ in most cases, ***Jesus, Abraham, Moses, David, Solomon, Elijah, and Jonah*** are also recognised in all three religions.

- *All three religions share Jerusalem* as a significant religious site.
- *Jews and Christians both believe in Moses and the revelations he received on Mt. Sinai.* Christians call the Hebrew Bible the Old Testament. The Jewish Torah comprises the first five books of the Old Testament. Christians call these books the Pentateuch or Law.

Buddhism and Hinduism also share many similarities, primarily because Buddhism emerged from the ranks of disgruntled Hindus. When it comes to beliefs in what happens after death, there are significant parallels and some notable differences between the two. While *both Hinduism and Buddhism share important foundational beliefs in reincarnation and karma*, their approaches to the self, the nature of liberation, and the mechanisms of rebirth diverge somewhat.

1. <u>Cycle of Reincarnation</u> (Samsara)

   Both Buddhism and Hinduism believe in the cycle of birth, death, and rebirth known as samsara. In Hinduism, the soul (atman) is eternal and transmigrates from one body to another based on karma (Bhagavad Gita, Chapter 2, Verses 22-23). In Buddhism, there is no eternal soul but rather a continuity of consciousness that passes from one rebirth to the next, and this is influenced by one's karma (Harvey, 1990).[83]

2. Karma

   Both religions hold that actions (karma) in one's life determine the conditions of future rebirths. Good deeds lead to favourable rebirths, while evil deeds result in unfavourable ones (Brihadaranyaka Upanishad, Chapter 4, Section 4; Harvey, 1990).[84]

3. Liberation — Moksha/Nirvana. (Buddhists typically use the term nirvana for this liberation.)

The ultimate goal in both religions is liberation from the cycle of samsara. In Hinduism, this liberation is called moksha, the realisation of the self's unity with Brahman (the supreme reality) (Brihadaranyaka Upanishad, Chapter 4, Section 4).[85] In Buddhism, this liberation is called nirvana, the cessation of suffering and the end of the cycle of rebirth (Harvey, 1990).[86]

---

83 Harvey, Peter. *An Introduction to Buddhism: Teachings, History and Practices.* 1st ed. Introduction to Religion. Cambridge, UK: Cambridge University Press, 1990.

84 Krishnananda, Swami. "Chapter IV, Section 4 - Fourth Brahmana: The Soul of the Unrealised After Death." In *The Brihadaranyaka Upanishad.* Rishikesh, India: The Divine Life Society, 1983.

85 Krishnananda, Swami. "Chapter IV, Section 4 - Fourth Brahmana: The Soul of the Unrealised After Death." In *The Brihadaranyaka Upanishad.* Rishikesh, India: The Divine Life Society, 1983.

86 Harvey, Peter. *An Introduction to Buddhism: Teachings, History and Practices.* 1st ed. Introduction to Religion. Cambridge, UK: Cambridge University Press, 1990. https://www.goodreads.com/book/show/418423.An_Introduction_to_Buddhism.

Differences

4. Concept of Self (Atman vs. Anatta):

   A significant difference between Hinduism and Buddhism lies in the concept of self. Hinduism proposes an eternal soul (atman) that persists through rebirth and ultimately merges with Brahman (Bhagavad Gita, Chapter 2, Verses 22-23).[87] Conversely, Buddhism teaches the doctrine of anatta (non-self), which asserts that there is no permanent, unchanging self. Instead, what continues from rebirth to rebirth is a stream of consciousness without a fixed entity (Harvey, 1990).[88]

5. Nature of Liberation (Moksha vs. Nirvana):

   While both religions seek liberation, their interpretations differ. In Hinduism, moksha is the soul's union with Brahman, ending the cycle of rebirth. In contrast, Buddhist nirvana is the extinguishing of desire and suffering, leading to the cessation of rebirth. Nirvana is achieved through understanding the Four Noble Truths and following the Eightfold Path (Harvey, 1990).[89]

---

87 Mukundananda, "Bhagavad Gita."

88 Harvey, Peter. *An Introduction to Buddhism: Teachings, History and Practices.* 1st ed. Introduction to Religion. Cambridge, UK: Cambridge University Press, 1990.

89 Harvey, Peter. *An Introduction to Buddhism: Teachings, History and Practices.* 1st ed. Introduction to Religion. Cambridge, UK: Cambridge University Press, 1990.

6. Rebirth Mechanism:

   In Hinduism, the soul (atman) undergoes rebirth based on its accumulated karma (Brihadaranyaka Upanishad, Chapter 4, Section 4).[90] In Buddhism, rebirth is driven by the law of dependent origination (paticca-samuppada), which explains how ignorance and desire lead to the continuity of the cycle of birth and death without involving a permanent self.

7. Ritual Practices:

   Hinduism incorporates elaborate rituals and ceremonies—such as the shraddha rites described in the Garuda Purana—to aid the deceased's journey and ensure a favourable rebirth (Garuda Purana, Preta Khanda).[91] Buddhism emphasises individual practice and meditation to achieve enlightenment with less focus on rituals for the dead.

Common Beliefs About Life After Death

It is interesting to research the commonalities among the main religions for the living. However, when I originally started this book, its primary purpose was to gain an overall understanding of how these religions intersect when it comes to life after death. Someone could spend a lifetime analysing the differences and parallels among the world's religions. After spending only a few hundred hours doing it, it very quickly became apparent that, for most people, it all comes down to what you want to believe,

90 Krishnananda, "Chapter IV, Section 4 - *Fourth Brahmana: The Soul of the Unrealised After Death.*"

91 Kausiki Books, *Garuda Purana: Pretha Khanda: English Translation Only without Slokas.*

not whether any of it is verifiable or makes sense. Although many will disagree, there is virtually no verifiable proof available regarding the origin stories of the larger religions, other than the existence of some key characters.

The singular commonality is that they all have a foundation based on exceptionally convenient and singular, unverified interactions with angels and gods. Given the lack of foundational facts, it seemed even more important to see if there was at least some commonality among all these different faiths about what happens after you die.

The following are those beliefs:

Judaism, Christianity, and Islam: A belief in an *afterlife and judgment*

Core Belief: The soul persists after death and faces judgment based on earthly actions.

- *Judaism:*

  Some sects believe in the resurrection of the dead and divine judgment.

  The righteous enjoy Olam Ha-Ba (World to Come), while the wicked face Gehenna (a realm of purification or punishment).

- *Christianity:*

  Belief in Heaven for the righteous and hell for sinners, with some sects including purgatory (e.g., Catholicism).

  Most mainline Protestant and Roman Catholic churches believe that final judgment occurs at the Second Coming of Christ.

- *Islam:*

  After death, souls await the Day of Judgment.

The righteous are rewarded with eternal paradise (Jannah), while the wicked are punished in hell (Jahannam).

Hinduism, Buddhism, Jainism, Sikhism: A belief in *reincarnation and karma*

Core Belief**:** Life is a cycle of birth, death, and rebirth (samsara) governed by karma.

– *Hinduism:*

  The soul (atman) reincarnates until it achieves moksha (liberation) by uniting with the divine.

– *Buddhism:*

  The cycle of rebirth (samsara) is driven by craving and attachment.

  Liberation (nirvana) ends this cycle and leads to peace.

– *Jainism:*

  Souls accumulate karma and reincarnate until they achieve moksha by overcoming passions and ignorance.

– Sikhism:

  Belief in reincarnation, but liberation (mukti) is achieved through devotion to God and ethical living.

Hinduism, Buddhism, and Jainism: A belief in *spiritual liberation*

Core Belief: The ultimate goal is to escape the cycle of birth and death.

– *Hinduism:* Moksha represents unity with Brahman (the ultimate reality).

– *Buddhism:* Nirvana is freedom from suffering and desire.

- Jainism: Liberation is the soul's release into a state of pure bliss and knowledge.

Indigenous and East Asian Religions: A belief in *ancestral connection and spirit worlds*

Core Beliefs: The dead maintain a presence in the living world or in a spirit realm.

- *Shinto (Japan):*

  Ancestors become kami (spirits) and are revered.

- *African Traditional Religions:*

  The dead join the ancestral realm and influence the living.

- *Native American Religions:*

  Souls journey to a spirit world or continue interacting with the natural world as souls or spirits.

Bahá'í Faith and Mystical Sects of Other Religions: *belief in a non-physical afterlife* (distinct from the concept of Heaven or Hell)

Core Belief: The afterlife is a state of spiritual existence.

- *Bahá'í Faith:* Heaven and hell are metaphors for nearness or distance from God.

All the religions I researched believe in some sort of reunion with the divine, eternal peace, or liberation from suffering.

Conveniently Adaptable

Although our children were brought up to be aware of several religions, my wife and I believed decisions about which faith to follow, if any, should be theirs to decide. When my son reached his later teenage years, he started formulating his thoughts on the matter, which I loved and respected tremendously. Harrison believed in the existence of *God* but hadn't exactly figured out how to define what or who God is. He didn't necessarily think of God as a deity or the ultimate creator of the universe. He was comfortable with a general definition of God being ***whatever each person needs him to be.***

Dogmatic religious followers might disagree with that view. Still, I've noticed that many *part-time* followers of religion I've known tend to shape and adapt their beliefs to support them in ways that work best for them. I assume we all know people who identify as Christians but modify their moral code to fit their needs when it's convenient. This occurs in every religion, and for many, I think it's a blessing that people can adjust their understanding of their faith to help them when it's most needed.

Even though few fundamental followers of Christianity will admit it, their hard-and-fast rules have changed. One hundred years ago, Christians firmly believed that God created the Earth and all its animals, including humans. With the eventual advent of and indisputable proof regarding evolution, most Christians changed their view on all this and now say, "God created the mechanism that allowed us to evolve into humans."

It is natural to formulate a philosophy that supports your beliefs or actions. Unfortunately, on this planet, we find far too many people who can justify almost any action or belief. These actions are frequently negative, and, more often than not, they are enthusiastically justified in the name of religion, even though they frequently contradict the tenets of that very same religion.

Reward

The one big thread that connects all religious beliefs is that you are rewarded in some way for following that specific belief structure.

- If you are a good person and a follower, good things will happen to you after you die.
- If you are a terrible person and a non-believer, terrible things will happen to you after you die.

After all, who would follow a religion or belief structure if your reward for being faithful is some damnation rather than eternal happiness, another chance at life through reincarnation, the offer of paradise, or a life of serenity under the wing of the great creator himself? At the very least, shouldn't we receive some reward for all these years living on Earth and being a dutiful servant?

For some, their belief offers them hope of relief from their hard days before death or a life of poverty, pain, and suffering. For others who are more fortunate here in the land of the living, we hope for more of the same after death or possibly a recanting and forgiving of our worldly sins.

Community, Song, Music, and Chanting

As I mentioned earlier in this chapter, one of my most pleasant memories while spending countless days alone in the Middle

East as the Captain of a 747 was the sense of calm and majesty I felt watching the sunset over a skyline of mosques and minarets as the recording of the adhan (Muslim call to prayer)[92] wafted through the air. As if on some magic carpet, the words in Arabic somehow inspired a sense of awe and majesty—even to a nonbeliever who did not know what the words meant. The haunting tone hung in the air, intertwined with the orange sunset filled with dust and smoke. Those daily calls to prayer will always remain in my mind and heart. In some way, they made all those years away from my family and children *almost* worthwhile. Not only does the adhan call people to worship and announce the greatness of Allah and Muhammad as His Prophet, but it also reminds people that they are part of a communal sense of being and the commitment that comes with it. Everybody is connected through the powerful chanting of the adhan.

In my research, I did not find one religion or group of followers that do not engage in some form of communal singing, chanting, or musical-related activity. Not many events bring as much warmth or feel as good as standing in a place of worship and singing shoulder to shoulder or hand in hand. When we sing as a group, life feels wonderful, troubles fade away, our emotions are lifted high, and oxytocin (often called the *bonding hormone*) is released by our body. This enhances feelings of trust, and we feel joyous and warm inside because of a surge of dopamine, the *feel-good* hormone.

Buddhist monks chant and pray together, Muslims kneel and pray in unison, Christians sing hymns together in church,

---

92 Encyclopaedia Britannica Editors, "Adhan | Words, Call to Prayer, & History," in *Encyclopaedia Britannica* (Chicago: Encyclopaedia Britannica, Inc., March 6, 2025), https://www.britannica.com/topic/adhan.

Catholics have a traditional chant-like communal prayer, African American churches join in gospel music, and Jews chant verses of the Torah. Hindus engage in devotional songs and mantras, Buddhists chant the sutras, and Taoists chant religious texts. The list goes on.

During these times—when we feel the warmth of singing together or just experience a sense of community—it can seem like the *grace of God* is enveloping everyone. This inspires a sense of direct evidence of the particular God they worship.

There are many benefits of this sense of community, but the most obvious one is the almost immediate sense of belonging when we are drawn into a group practising their religion. There is the beautiful feeling of being part of a supportive community, and all religions offer this sense of belonging. Even in belief systems in which participants practice extended periods of silence and solitude, they are doing so as part of a spiritual community. In such an environment, we don't ever feel alone when things get tough through loss, struggles, or mental anguish because there are loved ones and friends to listen, support, and comfort us.

Even though religious groups are a great place to find the sense of community and support we need after loss, there are other options. About six months after Harrison died, not having yet decided on a belief system that resonated with me, I went to a weekend retreat to help me deal with the grief. Until that point—and, to a lesser degree, today—I believed nobody could be living through what I was experiencing at the time. However, the simple act of sitting in a room with 20 other people—all of whom had suffered a tragic loss and were also trying to find a way through the pain—was eye-opening for me. They told tales of losing two children at once, a father and a brother who passed in the same week, the death of twin sisters, and the loss of whole families. My heart bled for the people around me, and I started to understand that my pain and suffering were no worse than anybody else's.

Yes, it may feel like your heart has been ripped out, but:

It has helped me to try and remember that I am not alone in my grief.

A Moral Code

Treating others as you would treat yourself is also a common thread among all religions. If I were to create the perfect religion, vital teachings such as the following on the philosophy of respecting and loving your neighbour would definitely be included:

From the Bible:

"Love thy neighbour as thyself."

From the *Tao Te Ching*:

"Regard your neighbour's gain as your gain, and your neighbour's loss as your loss."

From Islam:

"None of you [truly] believes until he wishes for his brother what he wishes for himself."

From the *Talmud*:

"What is hateful to you, do not to your fellow man."

If we all followed these edicts daily, we would definitely live in a wonderful world!

Lack of Original Source Text

As previously mentioned, because of my pragmatic nature, before I could believe religion's teachings about what happens after you die, I needed first to decide if each religion was credible. Unfortunately, evidence for the fundamental stories that underpin Christianity, Buddhism, Islam, Hinduism, and Judaism are primarily subjective and based more on romantic stories rather than solid proof. The claims at the core of most religions cannot, in most cases, be substantiated.

I have done my best to look for and point out areas where I have established objective proof of claims made. Still, unfortunately, the subjective far outweighs the objective when it comes to religion.

It is only fair to add that my scepticism about most organised religions is, of course, subjective as well! If I don't have verifiable proof that stories like the virgin birth or the resurrection are bogus and didn't occur, who am I to say they shouldn't be believed? Here are some facts. You decide.

No Verifiable Source Text

It is intriguing, if not compelling, that none of the religions I have covered can produce a reasonable source text from the period in which the religion or belief system was actually established. The New Testament of the Bible, for example (regarded by many to be the word of God), is actually a collection of individual accounts written between 35 and 80 years after the death of Jesus, not accounts written, witnessed, or confirmed by multiple sources at the time of the events described.

The various books of the Bible—the Gospels composed by Matthew, Luke, Mark, and John—were written by Christ's disciples well after his death and then hand-copied by scribes or translated into different languages from the original Greek writings. Each, without doubt, would have resulted in errors each time they were copied or transcribed. The Gospels of Matthew (one of the 12 apostles) and Luke are said to have been written after the Gospel of Mark. They are similar in structure and tell the same story as that in Mark's Gospel. In fact, Matthew incorporates about 90% of Mark's content, and Luke incorporates about 50% of Mark's content.. That would make sense if the events were real and coming from independent sources, all written around the same time, but the wording, sequence of events, and specific details in Matthew and Luke are strikingly similar to those in Mark, suggesting direct borrowing. (The Gospel of Mark was written around 35-40 years after the death of Christ, the Gospel of Mathew approximately 40-55 years, and Luke approximately 50-60 years after the death of Christ.)

Many believe there were original writings and representations of Christ's words recorded in Aramaic (the language Jesus spoke) referenced in the Gospels of Mark and Luke. If that were true, they would have had to be translated into Greek and, in all likelihood, would have been, in that process, rephrased to fit the writer's situation and understanding of what Jesus had meant. Many question the accuracy of these original Aramaic texts and their translations, or whether they even existed at all. If texts from the Bible were written in Aramaic or any other language while Jesus was alive, alas, there is no record of them.

(If you're keen to explore the possible Aramaic origins of the Gospel of John, you can find an article on this topic along with useful academic papers at jstor.org, a reputable digital library.)

One could spend a lifetime (as many theologians do) trying to understand and elaborate on the meaning and origins of the Bible's different parts and arguing over how accurate they are. One German theologian, Gunther Schwarz, devoted a significant portion of his life to studying biblical passages and exploring the languages spoken during Jesus's time—namely, Hebrew and Aramaic. He retranslated the Greek Bible back into Aramaic in an attempt to clarify any confusing passages. His goal was to create a version that made sense in Jesus's original language. When comparing sources such as the Gospels in Greek and other Aramaic references in the New Testament, Schwarz also turned to a Syriac version of the Bible used by churches in the Syriac tradition, the Peshitta,93 which dates to the 2nd-5th centuries CE. The Syriac Peshitta of the New Testament was translated directly from early Greek manuscripts but somewhat later than the Old Testament Peshitta translations, which were

93 Encyclopaedia Britannica Editors, "Peshitta | Definition, History, & Facts," in ***Encyclopaedia Britannica*** (Chicago: Encyclopaedia Britannica, Inc., 2025), https://www.britannica.com/topic/Peshitta.

written in Aramaic. Unfortunately, his conclusions have not been overwhelmingly accepted.

Notwithstanding the translation issues, it is also worth recognising that the first Bible wasn't printed until 1454 – 1455. Before that, all texts were copied by hand, with the inevitable accompanying mistakes, abbreviations, or changes.

Because there is so much disagreement and insufficient evidence, it seems surprising to me that people feel they can confirm that Christianity is based on events that occurred with any certainty. In short, from what I found, it sems there are no significant original biblical texts surviving from the time of Jesus, and there is too much conjecture about the original source texts to convince me to put the Bible firmly in the confirmed pile.

The Old Testament

Although 2 billion people worldwide call themselves Christians, do they all believe the Old Testament is accurate? I assume not, or perhaps many simply don't think much about it. If they did, and acknowledged that the New Testament is surrounded by conjecture and lacks confirmed validity, it goes without saying that it would be reasonable to consider many of the stories in the Old Testament as being purely mythical.

I mean no disrespect to those who believe in what is, without doubt, a holy book, but let's start with the simple question of who wrote the Old Testament. That, in itself, raises conflicting theories. For over 1,000 years, most people believed in the ***single author*** theory,[94] which holds that Moses was the author

94 Sarah Pruitt, "*Who Wrote the Bible?,*" HISTORY, July 17, 2020, https://www.history.com/news/who-wrote-the-bible.

of the first five books of the Bible: Genesis, Exodus, Leviticus, Numbers, and Deuteronomy. These comprise the Torah (Hebrew for *instruction*) and Pentateuch (Greek for *five scrolls*). However, today, it is more widely believed that it was written by several authors and prophets and eventually compiled sometime in the sixth to fifth century BCE (before the common era). The complete Hebrew Bible took shape over several centuries. Its canon not being finalised until approximately the 2nd century CE..

A credible place to start if you want to explore this topic further is a book called *Who Wrote the Bible?* By Richard Friedman.[95]

So, once again, unfortunately, there is no verifiable original source text to support the stories in the Old Testament. Even if there were proof of actual texts, would you believe that Abraham lived to the age of 175, that the world was created in six days, or that millions of species of animals were placed on Noah's Ark and thus saved from a global flood? I don't think I can.

But, once again, I find myself acknowledging that, regardless of source proof, there is definitely proof of community, a sense of well-being, and charitable giving and support that make most religions valuable in their own right. As many would say:

> *If there are all these good things going on, who cares if there is proof of the origin stories?*

That is a very valid question.

Regarding Proof: Ask Yourself the Following Questions:

---

95 Richard Elliott Friedman, *Who Wrote the Bible?*, Illustrated, Reprint, Revised (New York: HarperCollins, 1997),

Suppose you were a native living in the Amazon jungle today who has had no exposure to a person or civilisation outside your village. What would you think when you look up into the sky and see a silver object with a long white tail moving across it? Is this a divine being—a god—moving across the sky? You would likely assume that this vision proves the existence of a heavenly god, would you not? Likewise, many religious followers would have you believe that the fact that we are currently surrounded by things we do not understand is proof of a creator.

I would argue that the wonder we feel, no matter how great, is not in a singular way evidence that a specific deity like creator exists. We all like to think that we are part of something greater, but does that force have to be a god-like creator? For many people, this is the case, so they understandably draw on the unexplained to justify their beliefs. No matter how good that feels, it just isn't a valid form of proof. The feeling itself is very valid, but unfortunately, that doesn't confirm existence. Having pointed out that the singular feeling within us is not enough, it would be unfair not to consider our beliefs as being valid when one considers that they are often the sum of many parts—perhaps more like a trail of evidence rather than one singular event.

A trail of evidence, not a single smoking gun

When we seek proof of any religion, what we usually find is not a smoking gun, but a trail of evidence—historical hints, cultural continuity, and physical remains. Hinduism's trail stretches back to the Indus Valley seals, the ancient hymns of the Rigveda, and the temples and epics that have carried its voice for thousands of years. However, Hinduism isn't unique in this regard.

Other great traditions also leave behind their own kinds of proof. Take Buddhism, for example. The life of Siddhārtha Gautama, the Buddha, is traced through real places in northern India and Nepal. Archaeologists have uncovered pillars and inscriptions from Emperor Ashoka in the third century BCE that reference the Buddha's teachings and the monasteries he built. These are hard, tangible reminders that Buddhism spread quickly and left physical markers on the landscape.

Looking at Christianity again, I realise I've been somewhat critical, but its foundation rests on the life of Jesus, and while scholars still debate many details, there are references to him in Roman and Jewish historical sources—Josephus, Tacitus, and others. The geography of the Gospels also matches real towns and landscapes in first-century Palestine. Pilgrims today can still walk the same paths from Bethlehem to Jerusalem that the early followers would have known.

Hinduism's evidence, though older and more diffuse, is no less powerful. Instead of a single founder, it offers a continuity of sacred texts, rituals, and archaeological remains stretching back thousands of years. Unlike Buddhism and Christianity, which are tied to historical individuals, Hinduism is tied to civilisations themselves. Its proof is less about one life and more about an entire river of tradition, flowing unbroken from ancient times to now.

What this shows us is that every faith leaves its mark differently. The less sceptical part of me is forced to acknowledge that *proof* is not as simple as finding a piece of validated paper. Sometimes the proof is in the clear ways each religion has changed and influenced our lives. I started looking for simple proof but have been forced by the writing of this book to give the history much more respect in weighing the validity of these various religions. Nevertheless:

There is no actual proof of God—only belief in such.

Hope

Grieving the death of someone we love is like being thrown into a raging river of powerful and conflicting emotions. It pulls us down, down beneath the surface of our lives and into dark waters where we cannot breathe. Frantically, we try to escape the whirlpool of this inner journey. Surrendering, we feel ourselves carried forward by gentle currents to a new destination. Emerging from the water, we step ashore with refreshed eyes, and we enter the world in a new way.

~ Extracted from Frank Ostaseski's Q&A posted on 1440 Multiversity.[96]

For many, a way out of that river of grief that Frank Ostaseski[97] describes so eloquently is the lifeline of community and the most singularly powerful thing all religions and belief structures offer—hope.

---

96 Frank Ostaseski, *"Facing Death with Courage"* (Radical Compassion and Courage, 1440 Multiversity, Scotts Valley, CA, October 7, 2018), https://www.1440.org/blog/dont-wait-talking-about-radical-compassion-and-courage-with-frank-ostaseski.

97 Frank Ostaseski, *"Frank Ostaseski Home Page,"* Frank Ostaseski, January 25, 2025, https://frankostaseski.com/.

Ostaseski is a Buddhist teacher and a pioneer in hospice care in America. He reportedly has helped countless individuals and families through the end-of-life process and the grief that surrounds losing a loved one. I found his visualisation of the raging river of grief so poignant that I referred to it earlier in this book. The more sudden the news, the more turbulent, dark, and cold that water feels. As is the case for many, hope is what keeps me on the shore and out of that raging river that I found myself fighting after the sudden loss of my son.

Even the most atheistic or irreligious often rely on hope to overcome grief. If one believes that death is the end of life, and there's no one godlike creator, there should be recognition and hope that, at the very least, the energy of the person we have lost is returned to the Earth in one form or another. For those who believe in some form of religion or a belief system such as Buddhism, there's also the hope of heaven or a continuation of the soul in one journey or another.

Hope is the cornerstone of survival for people around the world—hope for a better life here on Earth, hope that we will win the lottery, live happily, or have good health. For many, the lifeline of hope that carries us through the day and provides a way out of the icy waters of grief is religion. And religious leaders are good at providing that hope. They offer it as a beacon to lost travellers on a dark sea. Above all, they know that nobody would follow a religion or belief structure if the reward was damnation rather than eternal happiness, and, in most cases, another chance at life through reincarnation or serenity under the wing of the great Creator himself. An eternity of rebirth, reincarnation, and nirvana or heaven is far more attractive than other options. The promise and hope of reward for our often-difficult years living on Earth and being a dutiful servant is easily given—and a promised outcome that cannot be disproved.

A belief structure that offers something to look forward to is obviously much more attractive than one with a miserable ending, so offering hope of something greater is vitally important.

All the world's major religions offer hope of a new start after death. Some, like Christianity, offer immediate and frequent redemption and absolution in this life through the confessing of sins. Individuals don't have to wait to die to be absolved of their sins; they can be forgiven while living by acknowledging their sins and asking for forgiveness. Catholics favour a trip to the confessional; Protestants focus more on personal prayer.

For Muslims, the process of repentance and forgiveness is also a direct, very personal request to God (referred to as *Istighfar*—asking for forgiveness*)*. Islam promises believers who practice Istighfar entry into Paradise (Jannah), described as gardens beneath which rivers flow. Muslims believe Paradise offers rewards beyond earthly imagination for all believers – men and women alike.

Some hadith traditions describe specific rewards for martyrs, including companionship in paradise, though scholars debate the literal interpretation of these descriptions. The concept of 72 virgins as a reward for martyrs, which is often inaccurately suggested, is from specific Quranic/Hadith interpretations, NOT mainstream Islamic belief. For Muslims, hope of a life in *Paradise* does not simply pertain to Istighfar; it also involves living a positive lifelong moral obligation to the teachings of Muhammad.

Although I don't feel myself drawn to Islam as a core religious belief, I would love to get better at practicing some of the more positive aspects of Muhammad's teachings—such as compassion, justice, generosity, honesty, humility, forgiveness, and equality among people.

> *My hope comes in the form of being surrounded daily by my son's energy and my memories of him, the prospect of a spiritual journey after death, and some form of reincarnation, either as a reborn soul or as energy. I'm not yet convinced of which it might be.*

Complexity

Even though few of the religions and belief systems that I review in this book are simple, I've done my best to condense the various beliefs for my own edification and for that of the reader. I'm sure most experts in the various religions covered in this book will say that my descriptions are oversimplifications, but my purpose is to provide a general, simple overview, not an in-depth study. That task is not easy, given the complexity of the language of most religions, which are full of metaphors, ritual wordings from ancient cultures and texts that have been translated.

For example, Buddhist beliefs, which are often difficult to follow, are full of mystical terms and discussions of realms of reality. In one source, I read that Buddha was born as Siddhārtha Gautama, but later, the same source states that he came into the world as Shakyamuni—another name for the same person. In another reputable source, Buddhism is described as believing in a cycle of rebirth where the soul is reborn countless times. Yet another source explains that Buddhists don't believe in the concept of a soul as such but in the doctrine of anatta (non-self) and that the mind comprises five parts called aggregates.

As a layman regarding religious doctrine, it was challenging to wade through the many interpretations by scholars on the same topics. Yet that's the purpose of this book—to simplify and clarify comparisons among the various belief structures so others don't have to spend thousands of hours trying to figure out concepts like a cycle of rebirth when there's no soul and the many other conundrums that arise when trying to grasp the basic concepts of complex religions. I have done my best, but during the writing of this book, I have often felt like a pedestrian, simply seeking some clarity of direction, only to receive multiple conflicting instructions from people who try to help.

The guidance one receives is even more challenging because preachers and spiritual teachers across faiths often use impressive words to promote somewhat simple ideas—often, I suspect, to woo listeners with the grandeur of the subject matter. To add to the complexity, the particularly hard-to-understand languages derived from Sanskrit are also full of metaphorical meanings. (I suggest explanation and interpretation by a religious scholar or teacher if you want to delve into the religions originating from Hinduism, such as Buddhism and Jainism.)

In fairness, *The Dalai Lama's Little Book of Buddhism* does point out that even a single word or expression in Tantra (religious texts) can have four levels of understanding and meaning: *literal, general, hidden,* and *ultimate*. I can reasonably ascertain the first two, but the hidden and ultimate meanings often elude me. Buddhists are not alone in the complexity of their language. Many words and expressions in the Bible—and most ancient religious texts—are open to the same four levels of interpretation.

Regardless of the many positive aspects of the major religions, I would be remiss not to share my true thoughts. The effusive language sometimes used by religious experts and preachers reminds me of the buzzwords I was taught when working on Wall Street and cold calling clients. My sales pitch was designed to impress the person I was speaking with and make the product I was offering sound more attractive. Much like *some* religions, we were selling a good product (in my case, competent financial planning). Still, the buzzwords we used definitely made the service we were offering sound as appealing as possible. In the same way, the language of religion often sounds more like a good sales pitch than meaningful prose! Here are a couple of examples:

Once again, I will quote from a book I absolutely love, *The Dalai Lama's Little Book of Buddhism*[98]. In the glossary's definition of suffering, it reads: Suffering also has been identified as the first of the Four Noble Truths. So, one can bring an end to cyclic existence *by eliminating suffering through eliminating the ignorance which grasps at the inherent existence of phenomena* by adopting the entire path of wisdom.

The underlined portion of that statement is impressive, but what does it really mean? There will likely be plenty of people with knowledgeable and informed answers to that question, suggesting the hidden and or ultimate meanings of the statement. Regardless of what they say, the phrase, when taken literally, does not make sense to me. Is it a typo, or is it designed to conjure up greater meaning? My intention is not to criticise this great little book, but to indicate the complexity of some of the statements we face when deciding on a religion that we can fall in love with.

98 Dalai Lama, *The Dalai Lama's Little Book of Buddhism.*

Interestingly, the Quran is notably simpler to read than most other religious texts. After researching why, many secular historians point out that it was compiled within 20 years of Muhammad's death, written deliberately in language the general public could easily understand. Islamic belief holds that Allah wrote the Quran directly, with Muhammad serving as the messenger through whom His words were revealed.

I think it makes sense to assume that if a literal God, such as Allah, really does exist, He probably would create a document that the masses could easily understand. It's such a shame that none of this can be verified; if so, it would be so much easier for a sceptic like me to believe. I much prefer simplicity.

One of the many reasons I enjoy reading Hemingway much more than reading religious texts is that he wrote in the simple language of the simple man. Perhaps I'm just a simple man!

(I've included a quote that is often attributed to Hemingway on *death and immortality* in the epilogue at the end of this book.)

Celebration

Nearly a year after the death of my son, I was invited at the last moment to travel to Mexico with a friend. The plan was to visit a small town called San Miguel de Allende and attend a celebration called Día de los Muertos, which translates in English as The Day of the Dead. I hadn't heard of this celebration and just happened to call this particular friend to say hi and see what she was up to. She told me of her plan to go to Mexico and invited me to join her.

That coincidental call and my visit to this charming little Mexican town were pivotal moments in a turn toward recovery and eventual acceptance of my loss. Unknown to me, when I accepted the invitation, I was about to join her in one of the most beautiful and memorable spiritual journeys of my life. For the first time since his death, I was, in a small way, able to honour my son and begin to make peace with his death by treating it familiarly, without fear and dread.

My friend and travel companion happened to be a graphic artist. On the day of our arrival, we came across a 50-foot-high pyramid being erected in one of the town squares by a Chilean artist named Tomás Burkey. His Pyramid of the Dead (Pirámide de los Muertos) was being erected to honour those artists who had died in recent years. When I explained to him why I was there and about Harrison's passion for music and history, Burkey offered to include a portrait of Harrison in the structure.

Within minutes, my travel partner created a life-size poster honouring Harrison and outlining the dangers of doctors overprescribing dangerous drugs, and we rushed off to find a quality printer.

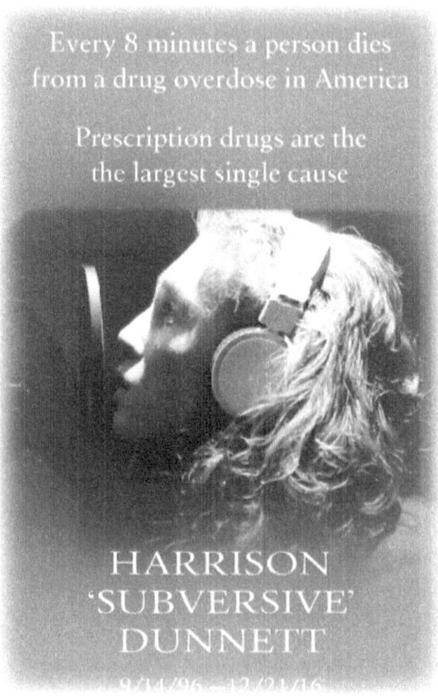

For those next three days, my son's face beamed from the top of the pyramid—above Prince and Tom Petty—within an elegant red and gold frame. Immersed in an atmosphere filled with music, dance, and colourful balloons dangling in the air, I gazed at my son's likeness. The tears began to flow, continuing until I could cry no more and started to smile… just a little. Remembering a wonderful boy and a life well lived.

According to the American author Leo Buscaglia, ancient Egyptians believed that upon death, they would be asked two questions, and their answers would determine whether they could continue their journey in the afterlife:

Did you bring joy? Did you find joy?

Sitting there, looking up at Harrison featured so prominently amongst his departed peers on Tomás Burkey's golden pyramid, I realised that my son had indeed continued his journey after death. Without doubt, he brought and found tremendous joy to the world in his short 20 years. More than I will in the entirety of mine.

It's hard to believe the coincidence that brought me to San Miguel de Allende. Día de los Muertos is a vibrant and deeply meaningful Mexican tradition that honours deceased loved ones. It was powerfully cathartic for me to spend those three days of the celebration remembering and honouring my boy and his life.

Celebrated annually on November 1st and 2nd (and sometimes longer), Día de los Muertos blends indigenous traditions with Catholic influences, creating a unique and joyous celebration of life, death, and remembrance that can be transformative, helping those who have lost loved ones face and accept what has happened. I highly recommend it to anybody who is grieving and wants to be surrounded by others in mourning to recognise and celebrate the lives of those we have lost.

There are wonderful celebrations in religions and faith-based groups all around this fantastic world of ours, and these celebrations create the bonding and fellowship that are the foundational mortar for that sense of belonging that keeps people wanting more. All the major religions and belief structures realise this and don't disappoint. Although the dates on which these celebrations differ, many of them celebrate the same events, including:

The coming of a New Year

- Christianity: New Year's Day
- Hinduism: Diwali primarily marks a Festival of Lights celebrating the victory of light over darkness which occurs in the later part of the year. Hindu New Year celebrations for most Hindus are Ugadi and Gudi Padwa.
- Islam: Islamic New Year (Hijri New Year)
- Judaism: Rosh Hashanah (Jewish New Year)
- Buddhism: Buddhist New Year (varies by region)

The coming of a New Harvest:

- Christianity: Thanksgiving (secular, primarily in the United States and Canada)
- Hinduism: Makar Sankranti, Pongal, Onam
- Judaism: Sukkot
- Buddhism: Various regional harvest festivals

Celebrations **using Lights**:

- Christianity: Christmas (celebrated with lights, although primarily religious in nature)
- Hinduism: Diwali (Festival of Lights)

- Judaism: Hanukkah (Festival of Lights)
- Buddhism: Vesak (celebrated with lights in some traditions)

Periods of **Fasting**:

- Christianity: Lent
- Islam: Ramadan
- Hinduism: Various fasting periods like Navaratri and Karva Chauth
- Judaism: Yom Kippur and Tisha B'Av

Different forms of religious **Pilgrimage**:

- Christianity: Pilgrimage to Jerusalem and Santiago de Compostela
- Islam: Hajj to Mecca
- Hinduism: Kumbh Mela, pilgrimage to Varanasi
- Buddhism: Pilgrimage to Bodh Gaya

Festivals occurring each **Springtime**:

- Christianity: Easter
- Hinduism: Holi (often called the festival of love or festival of colours)
- Judaism: Passover
- Buddhism: Various regional Spring festivals

Celebration of the Dead:

- Christianity: All Saints' Day and All Souls' Day
- Hinduism: Pitru Paksha
- Buddhism: Obon (blending Buddhist and Shinto traditions—primarily in Japan)

- Islam: Some regional traditions, though not a formalised celebration
- Indigenous traditions in Mexico blended with Catholic influences: Day of the Dead (Día de los Muertos) celebration.

Coming of Age:

- Christianity: Confirmation
- Hinduism: Upanayana (sacred thread ceremony)
- Judaism: Bar/Bat Mitzvah
- Buddhism: Shinbyu (ordination as a novice monk, primarily in Myanmar)

Day of Rest:

- Christianity: Sunday (Sabbath)
- Judaism: Shabbat (Saturday)
- Islam: Friday (Jumu'ah prayer)

Festivals relating to **Sacrifice**:

- Christianity: Easter (sacrifice and resurrection of Jesus)
- Islam: Eid al-Adha (Festival of Sacrifice)
- Judaism: Passover (commemoration of the sacrifice and liberation of enslaved Israelites)

Celebrating the **Victory of Good Over Evil**:

- Christianity: Easter (resurrection signifies victory over sin and death)
- Hinduism: Dussehra (victory of Rama over Ravana) and Diwali (victory of light over darkness)

- Judaism: Hanukkah (victory of the Maccabees over the Greeks)

> *It is refreshing to know that even given the multitude of differences and animosity amongst religious groups, there is definitely a common theme of renewal, gratitude, light, sacrifice, and community found across major world religions that help us all share the human experience and recognise common values of love and the need for community.*

References for Further Reading

1. *World Religions: The Great Faiths Explored and Explained by* John Bowker
2. *The World's Religions* by Huston Smith
3. *Religions of the World: A Comprehensive Encyclopedia of Beliefs and Practices* by J. Gordon Melton and Martin Baumann
4. Online resources such as BBC Religion, Encyclopedia Britannica, and religious organization websites

Communication from Above

A recurring theme across religions is that prophets, religious teachers, faith founders, and even authors receive visits and messages from God or his angels. It seems strange that God has decided to deliver these messages to these various people individually—and consistently without any witnesses! Why not get the message to the masses, such as through a Times Square revelation in New York? It sounds as if I am being facetious, but I am not. I really don't understand why, if these were real revelations, they would only be made to one person.

There is, of course, the adage, *God does act in mysterious ways*, and I am sure the true believer would say that the reason revelations are not presented to the masses is that God only reveals himself to those truly deserving of his grace. Nevertheless, it is unfortunate that God isn't a little bit more forthcoming and seems to only reveal himself to those wanting to promote a religion and gather followers. (Now I *am* being facetious.)

Below are some of the people who have received singular visits from above (there are many more):

Old Testament

Moses: Perhaps the most famous of all biblical figures to encounter God. According to the Book of Exodus, Moses spoke directly with God, who appeared as a burning bush. This encounter led to Moses receiving the Ten Commandments (acknowledged by both the Jewish and Christian faiths).

Abraham: As the patriarch of the Jewish, Christian, and Islamic faiths, Abraham's claimed encounters with God are pivotal in the belief structure of all three religions. In Genesis, God makes a covenant with Abraham, promising him countless descendants and a land for his people. God tested Abraham's faith by demanding that he sacrifice his son, Isaac—another significant divine interaction. (An angel intervened at the last moment, and Isaac's life was spared. It was just a test.)

Elijah: The prophet Elijah had multiple divine encounters, including being fed by ravens sent by God and, famously, contesting the prophets of Baal with fire sent from heaven, demonstrating the power of the God of Israel.

Ezekiel: Ezekiel's prophetic ministry began with a dramatic vision of God's heavenly chariot. This vision, detailed in the Book of Ezekiel, is filled with vivid imagery and complex symbols reflecting God's glory and power.

Daniel: In the Book of Daniel, he received numerous angelic visits and divine messages.

New Testament and thereafter

Paul the Apostle: Paul (formerly Saul of Tarsus) experienced a dramatic conversion on the road to Damascus and underwent one of the most powerful transformations in Christian history. According to the Acts of the Apostles, a bright light from heaven blinded him, and Jesus Christ spoke to him. This event led to his conversion from a persecutor of Christians to one of Christianity's most ardent apostles.

Muhammad: The prophet of Islam received his call to prophethood through a series of revelations from the angel Gabriel. These revelations, which occurred over approximately 23 years, were later compiled into the Quran, Islam's holy book.

More recent divine interactions include:

Rumi: The 13th-century Persian poet and Sufi mystic reported profound spiritual experiences that influenced his writings. After meeting his spiritual mentor, Shams-i-Tabrizi, Rumi embarked on a path of ecstatic love and devotion, reflected in his poetic works, most notably the *Masnavi*.

St. Francis of Assisi: Known for his profound love of nature and simplicity, Francis reported several encounters with the divine, including receiving the stigmata (the crucifixion wounds of Christ) and a vision in which he was told to repair the Christian Church.

St. Catherine of Siena: A 14th-century mystic, activist, and theologian, St. Catherine claimed to have visions from an early age, including a mystical marriage to Christ involving the exchange of hearts and stigmata. Her dialogues, prayers, and letters integrate her magical experiences with profound theological insight.

Joan of Arc: A peasant girl in medieval France, Joan of Arc claimed that saints and angels appeared to her in visions, instructing her to support Charles VII and recover France from English domination late in the Hundred Years' War. Her spiritual conviction led her to lead French troops to several important victories.

St. Teresa of Ávila: A prominent 16th-century Spanish mystic and Carmelite nun, St. Teresa experienced profound visions. She wrote extensively about her mystical encounters with Christ, most notably in her autobiography, *The Life of Teresa of Jesus,* and her earlier work, *Interior Castle.*

St. John of the Cross: A Spanish mystic and author, St. John of the Cross was a contemporary of St. Teresa. He wrote about his experiences of mystical union with God. His works, including *Dark Night of the Soul* and *Ascent of Mount Carmel,* explore the painful yet transformative journey of the soul toward God.

Guru Nanak, the founder of Sikhism, was known to have had several mystical experiences. According to Sikh tradition, he disappeared into the Bein River for three days and emerged to speak of his divine encounter, proclaiming, "There is no Hindu, there is no Muslim."

Joseph Smith: The founder of the Church of Jesus Christ of Latter-day Saints (Mormon Church), Smith reported several visions. The most significant is his First Vision, in which he claimed to see both God the Father and Jesus Christ. This is considered to be the foundational event of the LDS Church.

George Fox, the founder of the Quaker movement, experienced what he described as direct revelations from God, which led him to preach an understanding of Christ as an inward light. His self-declared experience and subsequent teachings formed the basis of the Religious Society of Friends.

Ellen G. White: White is the principal founder of the Seventh-day Adventist Church and was discussed in an earlier chapter. She reported having nearly 2,000 visions bestowed upon her by God.

Edgar Cayce: Cayce, whom I speak about in the chapter on spiritualism, was known as *the sleeping prophet*. While not a conventional prophet, he claimed to connect with the divine during trance states and offered readings that included insights into spirituality and health. His reported visions and healing advice gained him significant followers.

Paramahansa Yogananda: Yogananda was an Indian yogi and guru who introduced millions to the teachings of meditation and Kriya Yoga through his best-selling book, *Autobiography of a Yogi*. He reported experiencing several mystical experiences and visions, including encounters with the resurrected spirit of his guru.

Faustina Kowalska: a Polish nun and mystic known for her visions of the divine mercy of Jesus. Her diary, *Divine Mercy in My Soul,* details her conversations with Jesus and has become the basis for the popular Divine Mercy devotion within the Catholic Church.

More recent claims of visitations and experiences include those of Bill Johnson, founder of Bethel Church; Guillermo Maldonado, founder of a prominent megachurch in Miami; and Jesse Duplantis, author and founder of Jesse Duplantis Ministries (JDM). Duplantis has also been particularly noted for his advocacy of the prosperity gospel, which teaches that faith and donations to religious causes can increase one's material wealth—a very convenient and profitable form of theology, I'm sure.

The list goes on and on, but just about every prominent megachurch pastor and self-promoting religious visionary that I have researched declares that God has spoken to them in one form or another.

> *Millions of people throughout history have chosen to believe that these interactions with God, Jesus, angels, spirits, or other non-worldly forces were real rather than made-up. Sadly, I suspect that a significant portion of the stories may not be true.*

I don't enjoy pointing out the obvious, but there are a lot of people in this world who will do or say anything to take advantage of potential believers.

(Disclaimer—I do not suggest that any of the church leaders or visionaries I have mentioned by name have made up such stories. Each reader of this book should make those decisions for

themselves. I also have no personal knowledge or proof of impropriety by any person I have mentioned by name, nor do I intend to suggest any.)

Belief in an Afterlife

> *All major religions believe in some form of an afterlife. They wouldn't be very appealing otherwise.*

Most suggest that some aspect of ourselves exists or continues after we die, in a place similar to heaven or hell, or in some other form of existence. Some, such as Jewish followers of the Kabbalah, Hindus, and Buddhists, believe that the spirit (or, in the case of Buddhists, the karmic mindstream) is reborn and undergoes numerous cycles of rebirth and growth. It is interesting to compare them.

1. **Christianity**:
    - Belief: Christians believe in an afterlife where souls are judged by God. The righteous are granted eternal life in Heaven, while the wicked face eternal punishment in Hell.
    - Scriptural reference: The New Testament, especially in sources like John 3:16 and Revelation 21:1-4.
2. **Islam:**
    - Belief: Muslims believe in an afterlife where souls are judged by Allah. The faithful are rewarded with Paradise (Jannah), while sinners face punishment in Hell (Jahannam).

  - Scriptural reference: Quran, particularly in Surah Al-Baqarah (2:25) and Surah An-Nisa (4:56).

3. **Hinduism:**
   - Belief: Hindus believe in reincarnation (the cycle of samsara), where the soul is reborn in a new body. The cycle continues until moksha (liberation) is achieved, freeing the soul from the cycle of rebirth.
   - Scriptural reference: Bhagavad Gita, especially in chapters 2 and 6.

4. **Buddhism:**
   - Belief: Buddhists believe in a cycle of rebirth (samsara). Liberation from this cycle, known as nirvana, is achieved through enlightenment. There is no eternal soul but a continuation of consciousness.
   - Scriptural reference: The Pali Canon, particularly in texts like the Dhammapada and the Majjhima Nikaya.

5. **Judaism:**
   - Belief: Jewish beliefs about the afterlife vary. Some Jews believe in a World to Come (Olam Ha-Ba) and the resurrection of the dead (Tehiyat Ha-Metim), while others focus on the legacy left in this world.
   - Scriptural reference: The Hebrew Bible—particularly in books like Daniel 12:2 and Isaiah 26:19—and later rabbinical writings.

6. **Sikhism:**
   - Belief: Sikhs also believe in reincarnation and the cycle of birth and death. Liberation (mukti) from this cycle is

achieved through devotion to God, truthful living, and selfless service.

- Scriptural reference: The Guru Granth Sahib, especially in Japji Sahib.

7. **Jainism:**
   - Belief: Jains believe in reincarnation, in which the soul undergoes cycles of birth and death based on karma until it achieves liberation (moksha) through right belief, knowledge, and conduct.
   - Scriptural reference: The Tattvartha Sutra and other Jain texts.

8. **Mormonism**
   - Belief: Mormons believe that death is not the end but a transition to another state of existence. After death, spirits go to the spirit world, awaiting resurrection and judgment.

Injustice and Death

Often, religions give us, as a civilisation, great rules to live by. The teachings of the Ten Commandments and books such as the Quran, by and large, have helped create a populist way of life that allows communities to survive together. Simple edicts such as *Thou shalt not steal* and *Thou shalt not kill*, etc., are valuable guidelines for any group to live by. Unfortunately, religions bring with them both good and bad. Which begs the question—why do we have to accept the bad parts of religion to experience the benefits? Do we even need religion to live together ethically?

My journey in creating this book was meant to be an unbiased discovery in which I'd share the knowledge I uncovered. However, I would be remiss if I didn't also share my conclusions, not just facts. One thing I've realised is that there's a lot of good in all religions, but there is also a lot of bad. The bad in no way diminishes our ability to believe in an afterlife, but perhaps it taints the lens through which we view that conclusion.

> *I have come to realise that one doesn't need a religion that believes in a deity that oversees us or to be subjected to the negative aspects of some of these religions to accept the possibility of an afterlife or to live my life in a positive way.*

I reached the conclusion above not because of the total lack of believable facts about the origins of the significant deistic religions but more so because of the many atrocities and deaths committed in the name of religion that I can't ignore.

Sadly, millions of people have been killed in holy wars. During the nine Christian Crusades against Muslims, over 1.5 million people died (Historians debate the exact figure.) That number of deaths, represents a percentage of the world population at the time, that in today's terms would equal around 30 million people or more dead. That is a huge loss of life.

Even without considering the tragic historical loss of life in religious wars, it is impossible to ignore more recent atrocities in the form of the thousands of children who've been abused by God's representatives just in our lifetime. In 2021 an independent French commission recently released a 2,500-page report indicating that as many as 330,000 children may have been abused in France alone over the last 70 years.[99]

The Conference of Catholic Bishops in the USA also released its own report in 2004, stating that at least 5.9% of its priests (nearly 7,800) had been credibly accused of sexual abuse of children since 1950, with well over 20,000 survivors of that abuse. Studies suggest that generally, only 12% to 33% of child sexual abuse in the USA is reported, so it doesn't take a high level of math to assume that the number of children abused by clergy in the USA could easily exceed 100,000 during those 70-odd years *(My personal extrapolation).*

Obviously, throughout the centuries, hundreds of millions of people worldwide have been murdered or endured horrific suffering visited upon them by believers using religious texts to justify their actions. Nevertheless, denouncing religion outright as a fallacy having terrible consequences wouldn't be fair. Organised religions do serve a valuable purpose—bringing people together and providing a set of moral guidelines needed to create civilised communities. Also, and most importantly, we all benefit from something to believe in during dark times. If being a follower of one of the significant religions gives you comfort, go for it! Dive in and believe. Fill your heart with that belief and start the road to recovery in whatever way feels best for you. However, I hope that those who read this book will follow their chosen faith without ignoring the past and will advocate for the prevention of similar atrocities in the future.

---

99 The Associated Press, "About 333,000 Children Were Abused within France's Catholic Church, a Report Finds," NPR, October 5, 2021, https://www.npr.org/2021/10/05/1043302348/france-catholic-church-sexual-abuse-report-children.

I don't currently feel that I can dismiss all the past injustices and wholeheartedly jump headfirst into one of the major religions without some significant reservations just to be a member of a group that gives me short-term comfort.

> ***Some people who are sweet and attractive, strong and healthy, happen to die young. They are masters in disguise, teaching us about impermanence.***
>
> ~ From The Dalai Lama's Little Book of Buddhism

Motivation

One day, nearly eight years after my son's death, still finding my way, I suddenly recalled the quote above. Nothing grand—no trumpets or bolts of lightning—just a simple phrase I had read several times without allowing it to truly sink in. Eventually, my brain decided that I had to pay attention to it, I suppose, and it resurfaced, because I was listening to a book called *The Six Habits of Growth* by Brendon Burchard.[100]

As many speakers do to create a bond with the listener, Burchard starts by telling a rather long and overly dramatised story about how he'd had his heart broken as a young man (as we all have). During his recovery from this breakup, he nearly lost his life in a car accident. The experience of realising that his life might have ended in that accident gave him something he termed *Mortality Motivation*. He defines this as the pivotal

100 Brendon Burchard, The 6 Habits of Growth, Original Recording Audiobook, 2022, https://www.audible.com/pd/The-6-Habits-of-Growth-Audiobook/B0BBY76WP4.

point when we realise that life is short and decide to do something with ourselves.

Later, after listening to that story, I sat in the sun with my morning cup of tea and read a few passages from *The Dalai Lama's Little Book of Buddhism*.[101] Even though I'd read the quote at the beginning of this section several times before, when I read it this time, I was struck with clarity. Both Burchard and the Dalai Lama were saying essentially the same thing. Tragic loss or a near-fatal experience often provides us with clarity or motivation to snap us out of our regular lives and reach for something greater. Unfortunately, during the most profound grief, which often happens soon after a loss, we usually can't appreciate the significant impact that our tragic loss can have on us moving forward… if only we act on our realisation!

To me, the Mortality Motivation that arose after Burchard nearly lost his life, the Dalai Lama's lesson about impermanence through the loss of wonderful people who die too early, and the loss of my beautiful son provided powerful clarity. It emphasised that everything around us—particularly our life—can vanish at any moment. We shouldn't waste a second of our short lives dwelling on the past.

> *When grief knocks you down, if you can crawl forward just an inch, do it. No matter how slowly it goes at first, eventually, you'll be able to stand!*

Rather than being motivated by a promise of a better life after death, I find it simpler to recognise that every day is a gift. If we embrace that, hopefully the rest will follow.

---

101 Dalai Lama, *The Dalai Lama's Little Book of Buddhism*

For those who adhere to a faith and live with integrity, many religions motivate followers with the promise of eternal life and others with the promise of vestal virgins after death. We are also encouraged to do good in the world and, more often than not, to donate to our place of worship so that our souls are more likely to remain on the righteous path toward an eternal life blessed by God!

Even without promises of an afterlife and God's love, there is just a tremendous feeling of inspiration, motivation, and an uplifting of the spirit in the simple act of sitting with others and singing. People generally leave the embrace of a weekly religious service with a sense of greater community, emotional support, and love.

Grand Stories and Regalia

Fantastic Stories

One great truth about religions in general is that their origin stories are not dull! In most cases, saviours and prophets—who often have humble beginnings—suddenly become significant and emerge through dramatic revelations from above and unwitnessed interactions with angels or God. Stories describing the origins and histories of religious beliefs are frequently far-fetched, often grand, definitely impressive, and always unverifiable in any absolute sense. Depictions such as golden beams of light from above, seas parting, and miraculous healings occur in most stories about the birth of a particular religion.

As a commercial pilot for most of my life, I had to be a practical person, dealing with the dynamics of the real world, the forces of nature, and the mechanics of flight. Therefore, as such, I can't relate to many of the fanciful stories and origin tales of most religions. I have a great imagination, but I just find them hard to believe. Of course, I am cognisant of the fact that my scepticism is based on a physical world that I understand, not a world I don't understand. I therefore try to stay open-minded whenever possible.

Nevertheless, there is no denying that my personal search for a belief structure is grounded in the world I currently live in and understand. Therefore, when I consider the stories surrounding the origins of Buddhism, for example, they seem more realistic than those of most other belief systems. I have experienced feelings of enlightenment and clarity during meditation. I have experienced how painful attachment can be, and I have a constant awareness of how unfair the massive disparity between wealth and poverty is. All parts of the Buddhist thread seem very real to me.

The stories of angels and golden chariots appearing from the sky in many religions seem less compelling to me than those of Buddhism. Still, it would be unfair not to recognise that there can also be logical explanations for some of the more grandiose stories as well. For example, it is possible that:

- There may have been an earthquake, and the walls of Jericho did fall just as the Israelites blew their trumpets on the seventh day of their siege. (Joshua 6)
- Perhaps the lions were not hungry or were sick the day Daniel was thrown into the lion's den as punishment for praying to God. (Daniel 6)

- Maybe Jesus was not actually resurrected. It is very conceivable that some of his disciples removed his body and buried it to protect him from the fate of thieves or public display. Ask yourself: what would the disciples have done if, after removing the body of Jesus and returning to town with shovels in hand the following day, they saw people running around announcing that Jesus had been resurrected? Would they have admitted they had removed the body, or would they have gone along with the false narrative of his resurrection? (Yes, it would make for an excellent Monty Python skit, but it also could have actually occurred.)
- If you don't mind some risk of absolute sacrilege, dare ask yourself if there is a logical explanation for Mary becoming pregnant other than an immaculate conception?

Impressive Regalia

Rabbis, monks, priests, imams, and religious leaders from all beliefs wear some form of recognisable uniform or indication of their rank—some understated, some designed to impress. Not unlike most of our uniforms, they are often intended to signify rank or dedication to a particular pursuit. Frequently, they are designed to represent power and authority.

I will never forget how things were in the early 1980s when I was a young First Officer with Air New South Wales in Australia. As strange as it sounds, given today's hyper-security environment related to aviation, if there was a disturbance among the passengers, the First Officer was expected to put on his gold-braided pilot's hat, take his company-supplied nightstick, leave the cockpit, go to the passenger cabin, and assert some level of authority. The expectation was that he would demand the assailants return to their seats and stop their drunken behaviour.

Apart from the gold stripes on his shoulders and the wings pinned to his unimpressive uniform, the young First Officer had very little to support his supposed authority except for one very important thing. (The nightstick was meant to be hidden and only used as a last resort.) The full implication of his authority was meant to be conveyed by placing the regal pilot's hat on his head. The sight of a pilot striding down the aisle sporting gold braid on a silly hat was supposed to be enough to make inebriated Australian bushmen, rugby players, or oil workers cower and follow his command.

Fortunately, I never had to walk to the back of the plane and break up a fight! A good-looking ***hostie*** (flight attendant) is much more effective at restoring order, it seems. I would have been a total failure, having always been a bit of a smart-ass and good-looking enough to want to punch. Also, unfortunately, I am not tall enough to be scary or short enough to be an embarrassment to hit. Subsequently, I would have been the perfect target for an unruly, very drunk Aussie (as I have been several times in the pub). Australians, as a social group, don't particularly take kindly to authority, and you are more likely to get a punch or, at the very least, a "F--- off, mate" than a submissive response—or certainly that was true in those days. Now, they take you to jail for even making a snide comment to a flight attendant—and the pilots are not allowed to leave the cockpit.

Nevertheless, it was the emphasis on the hat and uniform that was supposed to be the deciding factor in controlling the crowd and commanding respect. The church, it seems, is no different in recognising the need for regalia to impress upon the congregation (passengers) the ultimate authority and importance of those who are up front (at the altar). Just look at the impressive regalia worn by leading religious figures in church ceremonies!

The Hero's Journey and Joseph Campbell

> ***I think anyone who has an experience of mystery and awe knows that there is a dimension, let's say, or a universe, that is not that which is available to his senses.***[102] ***~Joseph Campbell***

The Hero's Journey and Central Myth

After a significant loss, questions of existence, meaning, and purpose become more important to us. We have suddenly come face to face with the critical impermanence of life and look deeper within ourselves and outward for answers. Many of us, including myself, ask why we are here without our loved ones, and we try to answer that question in many different ways. These questions and our struggle with the grief we face are part of our journey toward recovery, of course.

At first, we see no way forward, but with time and the correct attitude and support, we become more open to taking a small step on our journey out of the grief and darkness that envelopes us. That forward movement won't happen until you are ready, though. As Joseph Campbell said:

102 Robert Segal, "Joseph Campbell | Biography, Books, & Facts," in *Encyclopaedia Britannica* (Encyclopaedia Britannica, Inc., March 22, 2025), https://www.britannica.com/biography/Joseph-Campbell-American-author.

"The adventure he is ready for is the adventure he gets."

For me, part of the journey forward was setting up a charity in Harrison's name called the Subversive Music Foundation (subversivefoundation.org), which sponsors underprivileged youngsters to attend a summer camp where they learn to create rap and hip-hop with a positive message. Later, I also made a website called toomuchrx.org to heighten awareness of the overuse of prescription drugs.

The questions I was forced to ask myself regarding my purpose and meaning after the loss of my son also incentivised me to try to define more closely who I am. When I was a 747 Captain flying around the world, that was easy. After I retired, I struggled to redefine myself, my purpose and meaning.

In trying to redefine myself after the loss of not only Harrison but my wife, job, father, house, and family, I finally settled on the title of *author.* After all, I had published a successful book (*Poker Wizards*) and then started writing *Dance with Angels*. Shouldn't I be able to call myself a writer?

Then I set out to write this section on Joseph Campbell, the mythology surrounding religion, our hero's journey through life, and his prolific, meaningful career as an author. I suddenly realised that trying to share a title with an actual author and philosopher such as Joseph Campbell was, at the very least, a gross misrepresentation of my abilities.

On Joseph Campbell

Campbell not only redefined my understanding of the myths we call religions, but his influence also changed my outlook on life and even the structure of this book. For those reasons, I highly recommend that people read some of Joseph Campbell's books on *The Power of Myth*, its influence on our daily journey, and how cultures and religions have been shaped and guided by myth. At the very least, check out Bill Moyers's interviews with him that are available on PBS, streaming platforms, Spotify, and on the Bill Moyers website.[103]

As demonstrated in the quote at the beginning of this section, Campbell observed that we, as thinking humans who experience the awe and wonder of the world around us, instinctively know there's something more that's much bigger than the human dimension. In the interview with Bill Moyers, he goes on to describe that we, in the West, view God as the creator of this energy and the wonderful world around us. In more ancient beliefs and cultures, God is considered the manifestation or vehicle of that energy, not its source. When asked if he was a man of faith, Campbell responded:

"I do not need faith, I have experience."

The experience he is referring to is the wonderment of being alive, of being truly aware of the world we live in and all the energy around us. The religions and beliefs I discuss in this book differ

---

103 *Ep. 6: Joseph Campbell and the Power of Myth -- "Masks of Eternity,"* Joseph Campbell and The Power of Myth, 1988, https://billmoyers.com/content/ep-6-joseph-campbell-and-the-power-of-myth-masks-of-eternity-audio/.

in their definitions of God, but the wonder we experience as part of life is communal and shared across all beliefs.

It is not just the sense of awe that connects us; there is another essential myth central to all religions, which is the most significant common theme of all. This *Central Myth* is why I have added this critical discussion about Joseph Campbell to the section on Commonality. This critically important central myth shared by all religions is called…

The Hero's Journey

The hero's journey is the term Campbell used to describe the myth that's common to all major religions and cultures. In simple terms, the hero's journey is a narrative in which a hero (such as Jesus, Buddha, Moses, or Muhammad) *undergoes a transformation through trials, death, and rebirth* (often figuratively).

> *"Life is a series of conflicts. The hero faces opposition, struggles against forces trying to stop him, and emerges transformed."* ~Joseph Campbell

Here are some examples of the hero's journey as it appears in several world religions:

Moses's experience with the burning bush and talking to God, leading his people out of Egypt, confronting Pharaoh, numerous challenges and plagues, crossing the Red Sea, and coming down from Mt. Sinai with the Ten Commandments represent the classic hero's journey stages of *departure, trials, and transformation.*

Jesus also follows a hero's journey, beginning with his *divine mission* after his baptism by John the Baptist. He later undergoes trials and transformations during his 40 days in the wilderness, and resists temptation. Eventually, he *recognises his unity with God* (The Father and I are one. – John 10:30). Jesus was then *crucified and overcame death through his resurrection.* Campbell refers to the sacrifice and resurrection as a typical motif of the hero's journey. The crucifixion represents the death of the ego, while the resurrection symbolises spiritual rebirth and transformation, bringing divine wisdom to humanity.

Buddha undergoes a similar journey, which I mentioned at the beginning of the chapter on the Buddhist religion. But it wasn't until I started to write this section that I realised how transformational it was in terms of the hero's journey that Joseph Campbell lays out!

First, there is the *call to adventure and mission* when he (Siddhārtha) leaves his life of opulence, witnesses suffering, and wants to do something about it. After discarding his wealth, Siddhārtha Gautama unsuccessfully tries to achieve spiritual liberation by spending six years as an ascetic and attempting to conquer his innate appetites for food, sex, and comfort by engaging in various yogic disciplines.

Eventually, near starvation, he takes refuge under a bodhi tree to meditate and *endures self-denial* and the *temptations* of Mara (the demon of illusion). As a result of this ordeal, he *achieves enlightenment* by realising the nature of suffering and liberation. After seven more weeks of meditation and reflection, he *embarks on a life teaching the Dharma* (truth) and guiding others toward awakening.

Prophet Muhammad also follows Joseph Campbell's hero's journey framework, undergoing key stages of departure, transformation, and return. As with the other examples, the journey often starts with someone being called to a higher purpose. Muhammad begins as a normal man, but at age 40, he retreats to the Cave of Hira for meditation. There, he receives his first *revelation* from the angel Jibril (Gabriel). After receiving the angel's message, Muhammad preaches monotheism (belief in one God) in Mecca. In Mecca, Muhammad faced persecution from his own tribe, who were polytheistic (belief in more than one god). Eventually, he was forced to move to Medina.

In Medina, Muhammad eventually faced conflicts with various Arab tribes and some of the Jewish tribes. The Jewish tribes were defeated in the significant battle of Khaybar in 628 CE. The Battle of Khaybar was a pivotal event in early Islamic history, leading to the consolidation of Muslim control in the Arabian Peninsula.

Eventually, as a victor and hero, Prophet Muhammad returns to Mecca leading an army of nearly 10,000 followers. He takes control with minimal bloodshed, destroys pagan influences and establishes the rites of the Hajj (pilgrimage to Mecca), with renewed determination to share the essence of Islam and devotion to God.

Our Personal Hero's Journey

Most popular novels and great stories feature a hero's journey similar to those found in narratives about the founding of religions. This book is effectively a depiction of my personal struggle to make sense and overcome the grief of losing a child. You are also on your own hero's journey, or you wouldn't be reading this book.

Beyond the simple comparison of the hero's journey found in most religions, whether in Christianity's resurrection, Buddhism's path to enlightenment, the struggles of Joseph Smith and Brigham Young, or Jewish struggles and persecution, Campbell identified a more profound underlying message: *The hero's journey is a metaphor for our own personal transformation.*

Central figures in most religions have undertaken this hero's journey, but you and I are undergoing it as well. Understanding this has helped me clarify that my loss and grief are a part of my personal transformation.

> ***Our grief is part of a journey of transformation, not a permanent destination.***

Fortunately, the simple but essential message that I keep realising every time I write a chapter is that, if embraced, the sense of community and belonging one can receive from all these religions is enough to pull you through adversity and grief and help you not run away—if you can form a communal belief that brings you closer to others and the energy around you. It is very gratifying to find that most religions share many more positive aspects than those that divide them.

> *Another thing I have come to learn on my own hero's journey, and while writing this book, is that I don't have to find someone else's belief to follow. I can create my own... And so can you.*

Part 2:
Scientific Theories on Life after Death

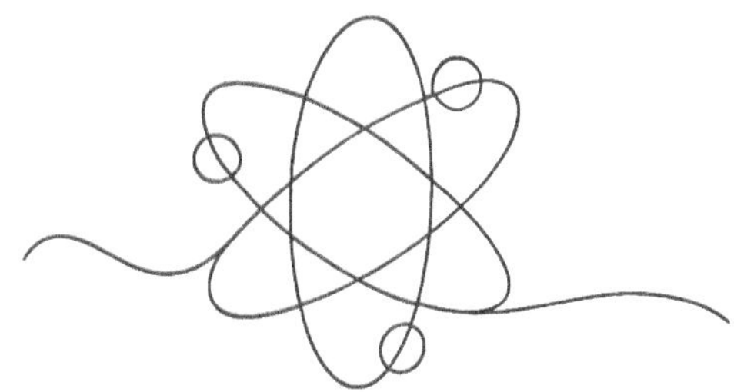

Scientific Theories

> *I regard the brain as a computer which will stop working when its components fail. There is no heaven or after-life for broken-down computers. That is a fairy story for people afraid of the dark.*
>
> ~Stephen Hawking

It is perhaps presumptuous of me to disagree with a renowned scientist who earned his doctorate studying the origins and nature of the universe at Cambridge and a bachelor's degree in physics at Oxford, but I do. Before he died in 2018, Stephen Hawking was considered by many to be one of the most highly regarded thinkers of the current century. But he was a scientist, and most scientists want verifiable proof before they will believe in anything.

Scientists, by nature and definition, are a group of people with (according to Webster's) *superior knowledge that are compelled to try and prove or disprove a scientific theory through observation and various tests before a theory can be accepted as a scientific fact.* Because of the desire to observe and obtain empirical proof before coming to those conclusions, many scientists, even the most highly regarded, have trouble acknowledging beliefs that cannot be proven by scientific methodology… or so I thought!

During my research for this book, I have been fortunate enough to cross paths with extraordinarily bright and open-minded scientists willing to consider the real possibility that there is more to life than just the physical body and brain. Perhaps it was because we crossed paths while exploring mindfulness and meditation that I met people who tended toward a sort of *confirmation bias*, I don't know. However, in my experience, I have found that there are also a significant number of highly qualified experts who are open to other possibilities and the reality of a potential for spirituality and consciousness.

One of these people is a bright woman and good friend who also has a Doctorate from Oxford—in her case, in genetic engineering—Dr Amanda Wiart. Amanda once made a simple but profound statement to me:

"We just don't know what we don't know."

Another scientist who runs the research lab at one of Australia's leading biotech firms was also open enough to say virtually the same thing based on her experiences with mindfulness meditation. In my opinion, a good scientist is aware of and open to the philosophy that even though there is no empirical proof of life after death, there is also no empirical proof that there is not.

So, is Stephen Hawking correct in assuming we just shut down like a computer being turned off? It's hard to believe there is no more to us than that! Or is the lack of belief stated in Hawking's quote just ego-speaking? Are we, as humans on this Earth, so unable or unwilling to grasp the reality of our insignificance and impermanence that we have to invent theories about an all-important consciousness or spirit within us that never dies? There must be scientific evidence somewhere suggesting that Hawking was wrong. In a book by Professor Hawking released after his death, he states the following:

There is no God. No one directs the universe.

He adds, *For centuries, it was believed that disabled people like me were living under a curse that was inflicted by God. I prefer to think that everything can be explained another way, by the laws of nature.*[104]

But then he goes on to say the following:

If you like, you can call the laws of science "God," but it wouldn't be a personal God that you could meet and ask questions.

The truth is that regardless of his brilliance, Professor Hawking is only one scientist with a personal opinion and no proof that the soul does not continue after our death. But what are the scientific facts concerning an afterlife and the existence of a soul? What is the energy within us, and what happens to it after we die?

After Dr Hawking's death, and as I was working on this book, Apple released a new product, Apple Vision Pro—fully immersive goggles that Apple touts as its first wearable spatial computer. The technology will be old by the time you read this book, of course; however, with those goggles on, I could easily watch an HD video that makes it seem as if my son is standing in front of me in the living room, performing for me, using my archive of video recordings. I have chosen not to do so just yet, but I'm not sure why. Perhaps, a fear that it will move me backward in my recovery! I recognise that my son has passed away, his body

---

104 Stephen Hawking, *Brief Answers to the Big Questions*, Reprint (New York: John Murray, 2018).

is not here anymore, and his energy and spirit have moved on. Would it be moving forward to sit in a room again with Harrison, or would it be moving backward? I don't know the answer.

Hopefully, this book will succeed and remain in print for a few years. In that case, the simple technology that allowed me to be in a room with my son when Vision Pro came out will be dated and simplistic to the reader. Still, to me, it will always be amazing that, if you choose to do so, you can sit in a room and experience in near-perfect 3D vision someone who has previously passed away. By the time you read this book, you will be able to interact with them as well!

We are living in the dawn of a new age where, with a simple movement of a finger, you will have the opportunity to experience the presence of lost loved ones. Previously, you had to look at pictures in a book or videos on a screen. Even before that, you had to look at a sketch. Now, you can experience those images in a fully immersive environment. After I die, my daughter will be able to meet and talk with me whenever she wants or needs to, if that's what she wants to do. If she is like me, I suspect that will make her sad, but I am excited that my grandchildren and their children will be able to know me in some way other than a character in a story.

In short, it is my personal view that Dr Hawking is wrong. We do not cease to exist when we die! The big question is, in what form do we exist after our body ceases to function?

One of the reasons that I embarked on this journey of discovery with a healthy level of scepticism is that I am a practical person. A lifetime of flying aircraft—first in the Australian bush and then, toward the end of my career, as the captain of a Boeing-747 piloting international flights—has made me so. As a pilot, you become programmed through practical experience to believe Isaac Newton's theory that for every action, there is an equal and opposite reaction. You push the throttle and thrust increases. You activate an aileron, which creates additional lift on a wing. If you land at the wrong speed or attitude, a most unpleasant momentum transfer occurs! Because of this knowledge, I believe in things that make sense to me in practical terms or for which there is some proof or logical explanation.

Faith is anything but practical.

To me, worshipping a specific, predefined god in a gospel or myth, or a multitude of gods, is somewhat archaic and simplistic, given the scientific advances that have occurred since these belief structures were created. This is not to say you can't define the meaning of God in your own way. From Galileo's first experiments to the birth of modern science, we have made enormous progress in physics and in our knowledge of evolution, cosmology, and the humanities. The beliefs that underpinned most faiths originated thousands of years ago and, unfortunately, are therefore no longer valid.

The surviving written texts of Hinduism date back to well before the birth of Christianity. Many other religions, such as Judaism, Egypt's ancient faith, the Greek and Roman traditions, Buddhism, Jainism, Taoism, Confucianism, and others—each carrying its own symbols—predate Christianity. Therefore, Christianity entered a world already full of religious symbolism, shared myths, and long-standing ritual traditions often formed without scientific knowledge. Typical examples include the worship of the sun as a god in many religions, including Hinduism. Or a religion such as Christianity that believes that man was created by God and was not the product of an evolutionary process.

According to some historians, Christianity borrows heavily from the imagery and stories of ancient myths and rituals that predate Christ by hundreds of years. The archaeologist and author of many published works, (D.M Murdock writing as S. Acharya), in her book, *The Christ Conspiracy,*[105] stated that the story of Jesus as portrayed in the Gospels is nearly identical in detail to that of the earlier saviour-gods Krishna and Horus.

My research showed that many mainstream scholars disagree with the claims that Jesus' story was copied directly from Krishna, Horus, or Mithras, and that these claims are not entirely true. What we do see in many earlier cultures across time is that they all wrestled with the same big questions—*suffering, justice, rebirth, and meaning*—and their myths reflect that shared human search in the very same way that I discussed in the prior chapter about *the hero's journey* and Joseph Campbell. But they were not formed based on reasonable scientific knowledge.

The bottom line is that the act of worshipping a god or gods goes back thousands of years. Of course, I am not saying that there isn't a God or that all these ancient religions were wrong! However, I am saying that the practice is simplistic compared to theories of the meta-verse or a parallel universe and our ongoing discoveries about the cosmos. That is why I think this chapter relating to scientific beliefs is so relevant to my quest for a belief structure that makes sense. I feel it should be for anybody who wants to make a rational decision involving a religious, scientific, and spiritual comparison.

---

105 Acharya S. *The Christ Conspiracy: The Greatest Story Ever Sold.* Illustrated. Kempton, Illinois: Adventures Unlimited Press, 1999.

Our Energy After We Die

As we all know, electricity is everywhere, even in the human body. Until I researched the subject for this book, I hadn't given much thought to the importance of our own energy. The electricity within us is a significant part of our survival and of what happens to us after we die. It seems that our cells are designed to conduct electrical currents because electricity is required for the nervous system to send signals throughout the body—and, especially, to and from the brain—making it possible for us to move, think, and feel.

Also, the reason our bodies do not decompose while we are alive is because of the flow of energy and blood within our bodies. This flow keeps oxygen, carbon dioxide, nutrients, and waste products moving to where they need to go. If that flow of energy, blood, and oxygen is disturbed, carbon dioxide accumulates inside our cells, making them more acidic. This leads to cell membranes breaking down and releasing enzymes that begin digesting the cell from the inside out. Subsequently, after the orderly flow of that energy and the systems within our body stop, and we die, the bacteria in our body, which are usually kept in check by our immune system, are free to multiply, roam around, and digest our tissues, a process known as putrefaction.

That's what happens to the physical body after we die, and the energy stops flowing through us, but what happens to the energy itself? We know that energy can't be created or destroyed, so what happens to it? I think the following words from author and comedian Aaron Freeman,[106] which I heard on an NPR episode of *All Things Considered*, answer that question very nicely. (I love it so much that I have asked that they be spoken at my own funeral.):

You want a physicist to speak at your funeral. You want the physicist to talk to your grieving family about the conservation of energy so they will understand that your energy has not died. You want the physicist to remind your sobbing mother about the first law of thermodynamics: that no energy gets created in the universe, and none is destroyed.

You want your mother to know that all your energy, every vibration, every BTU of heat, every wave of every particle that was her beloved child remains with her in this world. You want the physicist to tell your weeping father that amid energies of the cosmos; you gave as good as you got.

And at one point, you'd hope that the physicist would step down from the pulpit and walk to your broken hearted spouse there in the pew and tell him that all the photons that ever bounced off your face, all the particles whose paths were interrupted by your smile, by the touch of your hair, hundreds of trillions of particles, have raced off like children, their ways forever changed by you.

And as your widow rocks in the arms of a loving family, may the physicist let her know that all the photons that bounced from you were gathered in the particle detectors that are her eyes, that those photons created within her constellations of electromagnetically charged neurons whose energy will go on forever.

---

106 Freeman, Aaron. "Planning Ahead Can Make a Difference in the End." All Things Considered, June 1, 2005. https://www.npr.org/transcripts/4675953.

> *You can hope your family will examine the evidence and satisfy themselves that the science is sound and that they'll be comforted to know your energy's still around. According to the law of the conservation of energy, not a bit of you is gone; you're just less orderly.*
>
> ~ Aaron Freeman

In a scientific and easily verifiable way, everything we have done in our lives has consequences, and we live on in the effects of those actions. To me, this is the true meaning of karmic energy. Let's not forget that Buddhists believe our karma lives on after death. It is not *energy* in a scientific way, but more as a continuation of cause and effect. The words of Aaron Freeman appear to support that theory. Aaron Freeman's comments also, in my mind (not by traditional Buddhist definition), support the Buddhist concept of dependent origination.[107] You can find dependent origination fully explained in a practice guide written by Sean Oakes of Spirit Rock Meditation Center just outside San Francisco. An extract of which follows:

---

107 Sean Oakes, "Dependent Origination," Meditation center, Spirit Rock Meditation Center – Practice Guides, January 1, 2023, https://www.spiritrock.org/practice-guides/dependent-origination.

> *From ordinary discomfort to illness, mortality, the loss of those we love, and the fleeting nature of life's pleasures, the distress we feel is rooted in craving—wanting things to be different than they are. This fundamental insight depends on* ***the natural law of cause and effect called conditionality*** *in Buddhist philosophy. Though the details can get complex, the basic mechanism is straightforward: when one experience happens, a predictable subsequent one is right on its heels. The presence of the first is a necessary condition for the second.*
>
> ~ Sean Oakes

Clearly, our actions and the resultant influence on energy have an *effect*. That which is affected is changed in some way. Therefore, our actions have an effect that endures, even if we die immediately afterwards. Is that not clear and absolute proof that our karmic energy lives on? (At least metaphorically speaking.)

The scientific point of view

I love the words of Aron Freeman and the inspiring knowledge that our energy and actions affect so many of those around us, both during and after our lives. Notwithstanding the words in the Freeman quote above, from a purely scientific and verifiable point of view, we do at least know the following:

If we are buried, our bodies eventually decompose. Microorganisms break down our bodies' organic material, and, over time, this process releases energy into the environment as heat and gases such as methane, ammonia, and CO^2. This slow process of decomposition also releases warmth and nutrients into the surrounding soil, which, in turn, supports microbial life and plant growth.

If we are cremated, our bodies are exposed to intense heat, which breaks down the chemical bonds in the molecules that comprise them. The energy contained in the fat, protein, and carbohydrates of our tissues is released as heat, light, and gases into the atmosphere. Carbon-based compounds are released as CO^2 and water vapour. Bone fragments remain within the ash, which is often returned to the earth or water around us, also altering those environments.

In both methods, the body's stored energy is ultimately recycled into the environment in the form of heat, gases, and nutrients. To me, the more organic and natural way is through burial, but for some reason, we chose cremation for our son and then buried his ashes in the ground. I am not sure how much value the remaining ash provides to the soil. It seemed more spiritual in a way to have his body transformed into different forms of energy and cast directly into the atmosphere and yet still be able to bury his ashes.

Hindus cremate their dead and, when possible, cast the ashes into the Ganges River, which eventually flows into the ocean. That would have been a nice way to send Harrison's body off into the world as well. It is undoubtedly a very romantic notion.

Multiverse Theory

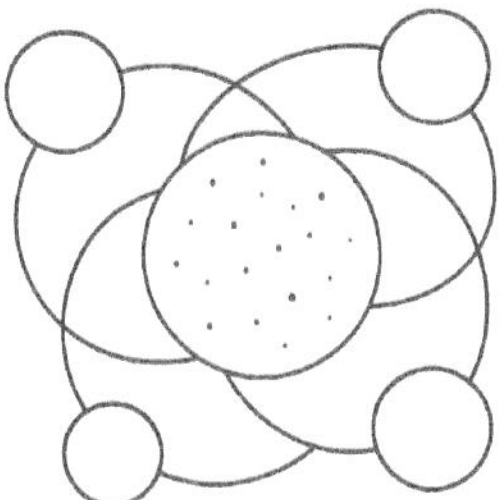

As we venture into the future, science continues to present us with a myriad of fascinating and dynamic possibilities that challenge the traditional belief structures of the old established religions. In my quest to find my personal belief structure, I thought it essential to at least take a cursory look and see if there is any objective evidence that these more recent scientific experiments rooted in quantum physics and the philosophies they inspire bring to the table.

To this end, I found myself delving into the intriguing world of topics like simulation theories (discussed later in this chapter) and, separately, multiverse[108] theory. A multiverse hypothesis states that we are only aware of our life here in our known universe and are unaware that this universe may be only one of many coexisting parallel universes in which our life—and possibly our consciousness—could be occurring simultaneously.

108 Aguirre, "Multiverse: Cosmology."

It sounds far-fetched, but some experiments in quantum physics and in areas such as the observation of cosmic microwave background radiation in our universe conducted over the last decade have given believers in multiverse and/or simulation theory more ammunition in the ongoing debate.

Perhaps I am just being creative, but it also seems possible to combine some of these scientific hypotheses, such as multiverse and simulation theories, with more surreal concepts, such as Deepak Chopra's statement that we are spiritual beings working from within a physical body and mind, or books like ***Journey of Souls,*** which describes the journey that our souls follow after the death of our physical body. Suppose either the simulation or the multiverse theory were true. Would it not be possible that our journey after death is one of our consciousness, internal code, karma, or energy of some sort moving from one of these universes to another or from one simulation to another?

Since I am extrapolating unproven theories, it could also be true that we experience an unknown, parallel state of being rather than another universe. In entertaining such concepts, I know I am allowing myself to drift well into subjective territory and being hypocritical. After all, if I dismiss fanciful religious stories and theories so quickly, it would be contradictory for me not to do the same concerning scientific theories if there is no hard evidence. Nevertheless, it is fun to imagine these sorts of other possibilities, even if there is no real proof for them.

Multiverse Theory Explained

> *The Multiverse is a natural consequence of our understanding of what happened in the early universe... that bubbles of universes just sort of pop out, and we just happened to have been one of them. It is an idea embraced by many modern astrophysicists.*[109]
>
> ~Neil deGrasse Tyson, 2022

Neil deGrasse Tyson, the American astrophysicist, writer, and TV personality, embraces the theory of a multiverse. He is a lot smarter than the author of this book, so I thought this theory was worth a general review at the very least. As is his style, Tyson, in another video, also manages to describe in layman's terms a visualisation that helps demonstrate the concept through a very simple analogy.

I paraphrase, but he suggests that you imagine you are on a ship at sea, with no modern-day technology, and you look at the horizon all around you... What you see is, to you, your whole universe. Another ship is somewhere else at sea in a totally different location. That second ship has its own horizon. (Each has its little universe and is unaware of the other that is co-existing in another location.) The people on the two ships will only see each other and be aware of the other's universe if somehow the two horizons overlap.

---

109 Does Neil deGrasse Tyson Believe in the Multiverse?, Video (YouTube, 2022), https://www.youtube.com/watch?v=B5jel0q2Ygk.

According to proponents of multiverses, our current understanding of how our universe was created supports the theory that other universes could have been created around the same time. These other universes could be similar to our universe—with minor changes due to quantum fluctuations—or, alternatively, be governed by entirely different laws of physics.

The whole concept of multiverse theory is fascinating, and it is lovely to think that my son may be alive and well in one of these alternate universes, or that when we die, our consciousness continues elsewhere. However, it is only fair to point out that this theory has also been criticised by many scientists as just speculation, or, at best, a topic better suited to the realm of philosophy rather than science because it can't be effectively and scientifically tested to prove or disprove its existence.

If you want to find out more about the different concepts and theories about this topic and won't be too threatened by terms like ***cosmological inflation***,[110] Einstein's, ***cosmological constant***,[111] ***ManyWorlds Interpretation***[112] (MWI) of quantum mechanics, equations of general relativity, Ockham's razor, string theory, and many other subjects that are too advanced and confusing

---

110 Frank H. Shu, "Cosmology - Inflation, Expansion, Big Bang," in *Encyclopaedia Britannica* (Chicago: Encyclopaedia Britannica, Inc., March 23, 2025), https://www.britannica.com/science/cosmology-astronomy/Inflation.

111 The Editors of Encyclopaedia Britannica. "Cosmological Constant | Dark Energy, Expansion & Universe." In *Encyclopaedia Britannica*. Chicago: Encyclopaedia Britannica, Inc., 2025. https://www.britannica.com/science/cosmological-constant.

112 *Learn about the Many-Worlds Picture of Quantum Mechanics*, Video (Encyclopaedia Britannica, 2025), https://www.britannica.com/video/Description-worlds-picture-quantum-mechanics/-204065.

for me to interpret without a few years of study—and probably individual tutoring from Neil deGrasse Tyson on such topics as particle physics, astrophysics, cosmology, super unification, and more—then start with the bibliographical references from Encyclopedia Britannica provided in footnotes for each topic. They are reasonably easy to understand and have further references that you can click on when you don't understand the terminology they use.

The problem with proving the multiverse theory is that we have no direct observational evidence. Therefore, any scientific experimentation and observation that currently supports these theories is indirect in nature. For example, some scientific areas of exploration—such as testing of *cosmic microwave background* (CMB) radiation[113]—offer the potential to observe variations in the temperature and density maps of the CMB in our universe and can potentially reveal patterns that some theorists suggest might be influenced by other universes interacting with our own. (Think of each universe as a bubble and those numerous bubbles floating around bumping into each other. In doing so, those collisions would be expected to leave imprints on the CMB of each universe in the form of variations in the CMB temperature map of each universe.) It is fascinating stuff, but highly theoretical and a long way from empirical proof, unfortunately.

Even though there is no specific evidence proving we are one of many co-existing universes, the possibility of multiple universes is real and logical to many scientists. If you do choose

113 Frank H. Shu, "Cosmic Microwave Background | Electromagnetic Radiation & Big Bang Theory," in *Encyclopaedia Britannica* (Chicago: Encyclopaedia Britannica, Inc., April 8, 2025), https://www.britannica.com/science/cosmic-microwave-background.

to believe one of these multiverse theories or be open to the possibility of such, one can go on to then argue that, possibly, death in our reality could be just a transition point from which our consciousness could survive or be reincarnated in a different parallel universe. These parallel existences might be a continuation of life in another universe with different life choices or distinct states of being that we cannot comprehend from our current understanding of life and awareness. In *Journey of Souls*,[114] several reincarnations occur in different worlds. Maybe these happened on worlds in a different universe. Who knows?

Remember, as my friend Dr Amanda Wiart said, "We do not know what we don't know." As a result, this type of transitional theory after death is challenging for many to conceptualise and believe without hard evidence. Given the lack of direct evidence, I can understand the possibility but not with enough clarity to fully construct a personal belief system around it.

Yoga's Quantum Theory of Oneness

It seems strange to add a section on yoga to a chapter on scientific theories. However, there are several parallels between philosophy, science, quantum mechanics, and the art of yoga. As it turns out, yoga's focus on meditation, the connection with one's inner self, and the theories of quantum mechanics—which explore the fundamental nature of matter and energy—cross paths in many ways.

One of the oldest spiritual practices is not one of the well-known religions; it is yoga, in which connecting on a deeper

114 Michael Newton, *Journey of Souls: Case Studies of Life Between Lives*, 1st ed (St. Paul, Minn: Llewellyn Publications, 1994),

level within ourselves and with that energy in the world around us is a fundamental concept. From a scientific point of view, as mentioned earlier in this chapter, one obvious possible outcome is that what happens after death is the most straightforward and most practical: our energy returns to the oneness that surrounds us. (Perhaps more of a personal philosophical interpretation than a scientific one. I like it though.) There are several other intersections as well.

Said to have originated over 5,000 years ago in northern India, yoga is irreversibly intertwined with religions that originated there as well. Buddhism and Hinduism (from which Buddhism emerged as an alternative), as well as other minor and ancient beliefs, incorporate yoga to connect with one's inner self and consciousness. As per yogic scriptures, the practice of yoga leads to the union of individual consciousness with that of universal consciousness, indicating a perfect harmony between the mind and body, man and Nature. According to modern scientists, everything in the universe is a manifestation of the same quantum field and is also connected.

Yoga's quantum theory of oneness:

Yoga's quantum *theory of oneness* proposes that all existence is interconnected at a fundamental level, aligning ancient spiritual concepts with modern quantum physics.

> *It suggests that the universe is a unified field of energy in which every particle is connected to every other. This interconnectedness is mirrored in the spiritual teachings of yoga, which advocate for the realisation of oneness with the universe.*

Core Concepts:

1. Interconnectedness:

   Quantum physics reveals that particles can be correlated with each other instantaneously over vast distances, a phenomenon known as quantum entanglement. This is similar to the yogic view that all beings are part of a single, interconnected consciousness (Capra, 1975).[115]

2. Non-Duality:

   Yoga teaches Advaita (non-dualism), which asserts that the individual self (atman) and the universal self (Brahman) are one. Quantum theory, through the principle of wave-particle duality, supports the idea that matter can exist in multiple states simultaneously, hinting at a deeper unity (Goswami, 1993).[116]

3. Observer Effect:

   In quantum mechanics, the observer effect suggests that observation affects the state of a quantum system. This resonates with yogic practices that emphasise mindfulness and awareness, suggesting that consciousness plays a crucial role in shaping reality (Zukav, 1979, *The Dancing Wu-Li Masters:*

---

115 Fritjof Capra, *The Tao of Physics: An Exploration of the Parallels between Modern Physics and Eastern Mysticism*, Reprint (Boston: Shambhala, 2010),

116 Amit Goswami, *The Self-Aware Universe: How Consciousness Creates the Material World*, Illustrated (East Rutherford: Tarcher, 1995),

An Enlightening Exploration of Quantum Physics, Eastern Philosophy and the interplay of Science and Spirituality).[117]

So… how does this shape a view of what happens after I die?

I know our energy dissipates into the world around us, and that is the simple truth. But this section has made me realise that, in all likelihood, it is far more significant than that.

> *We are all part of one interconnected world. We are, and we always will be, in one form or another. Harrison is genuinely all around me, part of me, and part of an "interconnected consciousness" that will never disappear. Our perception of that interconnected consciousness is the only thing that changes.*

Other interesting references:

Dean Radin,[118] a researcher in parapsychology, discusses potential links between quantum mechanics and consciousness in his book, *Supernormal: Science, Yoga, and the Evidence for Extraordinary Psychic Abilities.*

---

117 Zukav, Gary. *Dancing Wu Li Masters: An Enlightening Exploration of Quantum Physics, Eastern Philosophy, and the Interplay of Science and Spirituality.* Reprint. New York: HarperOne, 2009.

118 Dean I. Radin, *Supernormal: Science, Yoga, and the Path to Extraordinary Psychic Abilities*, Illustrated (New York, NY: Deepak Chopra, 2013),

Similarly, theoretical physicist Alex Hankey,[119] who trained at MIT and Trinity College, Cambridge, but now lives and teaches in India, has examined the relationships between quantum physics, Vedic sciences, energy, and matter. His conclusions are intriguing. The link in the footnotes leads to a 30-minute video of him speaking on YouTube.

It is worth noting that the work and conclusions of both men have been met with scepticism within the scientific community, and their claims remain unproven. Personally, I love the concept of oneness, and it just feels right to me.

---

119 Endowment Lecture Series Dr Alex Hankey PART 1, 2021, https://www.youtube.com/watch?v=vgfDFcriwH0.

Simulation Theory

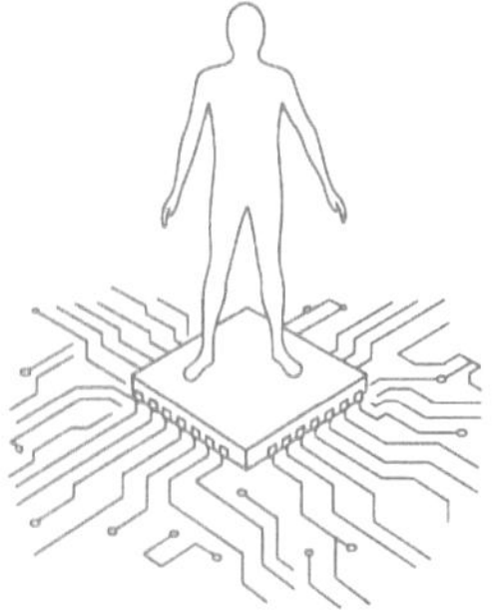

One must always listen to their child, particularly when your child is a super-smart, driven dynamo in her mid-20s!

When I lost my son, Jacqueline lost her twin brother. They were close and loved each other dearly. Twins are always bound in life in ways a father can't explain or understand, so I know she grieved deeply but differently. A part of her is gone, and she'll have to live with that loss for far more years than I will.

When they were very young, Jacqueline and her brother were inseparable. As a family, we went on many incredible adventures together, and Jacqueline's love and connection with Harrison grew stronger. During their mid-teens, as they each started to grow in independence, they had different groups of friends, and the space between them grew slightly wider. However, for the previous couple of years before Harrison's death, they were moving toward each other again. Both started to bloom as artists, and their paths and groups of friends sometimes intermingled.

In short, I'm trying to explain that Jacqueline wasn't attached at the hip to her twin brother, but they were connected in ways I'll never know. So when Jacqueline believes in something that helps her deal with the mystery of where Harrison has gone, I would naturally want to explore it. In fact, I respect her opinion so much that I dedicated a lot of time to trying to understand the whole simulation logic. Initially, it was hard to wrap my head around it, to be honest.

One day, about three quarters of the way through this book, my daughter sent me a message.

"Dad, did you know they've proven we're all just living in a simulation?"

"No, I didn't know we're all just living in a simulation!" I responded, bewildered. But it got me thinking that I should certainly be open to all possibilities when writing a book on what happens after we die—or, more specifically, my journey to find the answer to that question. So, I started looking more closely at Simulation Theory and what it was.

To research this section of the book, I first started watching YouTube videos about life on planet Earth as a simulation to see if there was even a thread of proof that this could be true. Surprisingly, there is! (Or so the simulation theorists believe.) But I must say, trying to understand the theories and research discussed is pretty daunting. Unfortunately, when I try to understand this stuff, I often look like a proverbial dog in front of a television screen—head cocked slightly to one side, eyebrows slightly raised, and mouth agape. It took a while to digest some of what I was learning and to figure out whether the theories could be verified. And it seems they can!

Simulation theory suggests that our world and everything in it, including us humans, is a computer simulation developed by an advanced civilisation. Even though this idea seems impossible, it's received much attention in recent years, capturing the imagination of scientists, scholars, and even Elon Musk. Musk has said several times that it's more likely than not that we're living in a simulation. And, of course, we now have my daughter affirming his position!

My interpretation of this theory of simulation is that there's a likely probability that the advanced civilisation that built the simulation we're now in is actually our human race at some further-developed stage, not necessarily some mysterious civilisation from outer space that created an experimental simulation of the human race. Philosophers such as the well-known scientist Nick Bostrom believe that we'll eventually become a posthuman race, and if that happens, there are three likely scenarios. (All of Bostrom's predictions seem to revolve around an extreme dystopian future for the human race as we know it!)

In his paper published in 2003, Bostrom[120] argues that at least one of the following propositions is true:

1. The human species is likely to go extinct before reaching a *posthuman* stage;

or

2. Any posthuman civilisation is highly unlikely to run a significant number of simulations of its evolutionary history (or variations thereof);

---

120 Nick Bostrom, "*The Simulation Argument*," The Philosophical Quarterly 53, no. 211 (2003): 243–55, https://www.simulation-argument.com/.

or

3. We're living in a computer simulation now.

Bostrom's core claim is not that (3) is undoubtedly true but rather that at least one of these three is almost certainly true. If his assumptions are correct, the simulation hypothesis becomes a real, live possibility rather than mere sci-fi.

All three scenarios mentioned by Bostrom[121] assume a post-human stage. What about a scenario where we humans (not posthumans) continue to develop our technology to the point that we decide to simulate our own history of development—or, for that matter, create several parallel simulations to see what would have happened if one small thing were changed? What would have happened if Bill Gates hadn't been exposed to a first-generation computer at his high school? What would have happened if Alexander Graham Bell or Adolf Hitler hadn't been born? What if the great plague of 1665 (a bubonic plague called *the Great Plague of London*) had never happened? If we were able to develop simulation technology to answer such questions, we'd undoubtedly want to know the answers, wouldn't we?

Without doubt, our technology is evolving at an exponential pace. When I was young, we used landline phones with a dial that turned. The introduction of a push-button phone in our house felt like a miracle! Now we have driverless cars, fully electric vehicles, and exciting breakthroughs in quantum physics, artificial intelligence, and video games that, with 3D technology, look incredibly real. Who's to say that in another 100 years, we

121 Nick Bostrom, *"Nick Bostrom's Home Page,"* Nick Bostrom, 2025, https://nickbostrom.com/.

won't be able to run simulations of humankind that feel totally realistic to the participants in the simulation?

If that's the case, it raises the obvious question: are we living in a reality before humanity reaches that level, or are we in a simulation created by our human race (or some other advanced race)? The latter seems to me a real possibility, at least one we should consider.

Quantum Mechanics and the Observer Effect

Simulation theory may seem like pure speculation, but some scientific findings do seem to give it some weight. One of the most critical pieces of evidence comes from quantum physics, where a phenomenon called the *observer effect* has shown that the simple act of observing electrons can change their behaviour. Some scientists say this phenomenon supports the idea of a simulated world in which the beings who created the simulation control how particles act based on what they see. Why would particles act differently when observed than if not observed if they weren't part of a predetermined program?

The following extract from a website called scienceabc.com explains it better than I can:

Quantum Mechanics[122] *is the study of how particles at the atomic and subatomic levels interact with each other and their environment. The Observer Effect is the phenomenon in which the act of observation alters the behaviour of the particles being observed. This effect is due to the wave-like nature of matter, which*

122 Venkatesh Vaidyanathan, "*What Is The Observer Effect In Quantum Mechanics?,*" ScienceABC, May 10, 2019, https://www.scienceabc.com/pure-sciences/observer-effect-quantum-mechanics.html.

means that particles can exist in multiple states simultaneously. When an observer measures a particular property of a particle, they are effectively collapsing the wave-function of that particle, causing it to assume a definite state.

Simulation theory is quite hard to accept, but it's also true that almost anything could be possible if we are actually in a computer simulation (even the foundational religious stories, which I've spent a lot of time doubting earlier in this book). Overall, simulation theory seems plausible, but when I look into the details, it becomes harder for me to digest. The thought that everything I see, smell, and touch is not real is just hard to comprehend! As a result, I find it a little bit easier to imagine my own hybrid theory somewhere between a physical science experiment and a computer simulation.

Simulation theory proponents always point to Nick Bostrom's 2003 paper to support the probability that we live in a simulation. However, when I delved deeper into Bostrom's website, I found that even though he believes the simulation argument is sound, even *Bostrom thinks that the probability that the simulation hypothesis is true is only about 20%. (*This is primarily because he feels there isn't strong evidence for any of the three options discussed in his paper.) If simulation theory is true, what does this all mean regarding life after death?

If our world is just a simulation (other than my subversive simulation theory-type of simulation proposed in the next section), it means that consciousness—or what some people may call our soul—might be an aspect of the simulation and would also, therefore, potentially be part of or live in other simulations either simultaneously or in each new subsequent simulation. Just as a character in a video game can live in different levels or worlds, does our specific thought process or individual program live outside or beyond the simulated reality we live in now? Alternatively, it could mean we cease to be... End of program!

Would either of those outcomes be so bad? I'd be okay knowing that Harrison was a character in a program… just as I am. At some point, we're out of the game, and that's it. Or maybe we're in another reality somewhere else. (It's a shame that greater minds than mine have decided the possibility of this outcome to be only around 20%. I would be okay with it!)

Subversive Simulation Theory

I'm going to have a little fun here and suggest a theory that I much prefer to the traditional simulation theory people usually talk about. I'm proposing an alternative to Nick Bostrom's possibilities, and I want to name it before some Oxford doctoral student steals the limelight and submits my hypothesis to a scientific journal. My theory is named after my son Harrison, whose stage name was Subversive. The word also fits, because by definition, it describes something that quietly overturns accepted expectations.

I call it *Subversive Simulation Theory (SST)*. It suggests the possibility of a simulation that defines the conditions under which the Big Bang occurred—not as a replacement for reality but as its origin. The concept is that an advanced intelligence would eventually, through advanced computer processing, be able to establish the initial conditions of the universe—the fundamental laws of physics, the constants governing matter and energy, and the basic conditions that allowed complexity and life to emerge. If that occurred, we could be the result of that process—and therefore genuinely living humans in a real, physical universe. Not simulated people who merely believe they are real.

If Subversive Simulation Theory was in fact a reality, we would possibly be living in a physical world that may have originated from a simulation, created by advanced intelligence. This to me sounds far more logical than the big bang being created by one single omnipotent creator.

... whether post-human, extraterrestrial, or a greater human-like intelligence. The critical point is that for this theory to be possible, the computation and advanced intelligence that initiated the Big Bang would have had to occur in a separate spacetime, not the one we now inhabit.

Another way to explain this from a different perspective is to ask you to imagine that, at some time in the future, we figure out all the required criteria and ingredients that would have created the Big Bang and the formation of the universe. This advanced/future version of us then embarks on a simulation experiment that actually implements this process. If the simulation were successful, we would be forming a new universe, totally separate and in a different spacetime from the one in which we live.

From there, three possibilities follow.

The **first** suggests a possibility of a front-loaded universe created in which the simulation ends at the moment spacetime begins. At that point, it would no longer be a simulation in any active sense—only a real universe with a simulated beginning. The universe then remains fully autonomous, with no monitoring, no intervention, and no external influence of any kind. The feelings we have and our actions are entirely ours and the consequence of natural evolution.

The **second** proposes a model of passive oversight in which the originating intelligence may observe or sustain the underlying laws of physics but never intervenes in specific events or individual lives. Love, pain, joy, and suffering are all consequences caused from within our world, not from outside it.

A **third** possibility is that reality itself is actively controlled or managed—that parts of what we experience are rendered or manipulated by the creators. This isn't a concept that sits well with me. A universe that is partly built on illusion and is constantly being managed by some outside force or intelligence isn't a world I recognise or want to be a part of.

What defines SST is not which of these options is true but what they all share: this is a real universe, and we are real within it. I'm not a professor at Oxford, and that may uniquely qualify me to ask simpler questions and suggest alternatives that don't sit neatly inside academic frameworks. If I'm asked at a party whether I believe in simulation theory, I'm going to stick with my Subversive Simulation Theory.

Popular simulation theorists often suggest we are characters inside a program, persuaded that what we see and feel is real. That idea also doesn't sit well with me. I prefer a theory in which the reality we are in is in every meaningful sense of the word real.

> ***The being behind the human is a field of pure potentiality other than something already defined.***
>
> ~Eckhart Tolle, A New Earth:
> Awakening to Your Life's Purpose

In his book, *A New Earth*,[123] Eckhart Tolle builds on the above quote to describe the *field of pure potentiality* in a few different ways. Interestingly, in one of those explanations I wrote down a few years ago when listening to his book, he refers to this field of potentiality as an energy form that lives within most human beings: *A self-advocating energy that has its own primitive intelligence not unlike that of a cunning animal whose intelligence is directed primarily at survival.*

Eckhart Tolle is a highly regarded and widely followed teacher and spiritual self-help author, but he is not a scientist. However, his definitions, which I had thought to write down long ago, in part, seem to align with some of the remarkable scientific theories I came across more recently as I was finishing this later chapter on scientific proof.

Specifically, a theory based on quantum physics commonly called the Orch-OR theory. (Orch stands for Orchestrated, and OR stands for Objective Reduction.)

---

123 Tolle, Eckhart. 2018. *A New Earth: The Life-Changing Follow up to The Power of Now. "My No.1 Guru Will Always Be Eckhart Tolle."* Chris Evans. London: Michael Joseph.

Orch-OR Theory[124]

While researching and writing this book, I did not find scientific proof of a soul's existence in the traditional religious sense; however, these relatively new theories in quantum physics offer real hope of actual evidence of a soul from a scientific perspective.

One theory rooted in quantum physics and mechanics excites me. The Orch-OR theory, which is regarded as plausible and logical by a number of scientists, suggests that not only is consciousness a quantum phenomenon present in all of the universe but that it is also rooted in quantum processes within the most minor parts of our brain.

American scientist Dr Stuart Hameroff and British physicist Sir Roger Penrose have proposed a quantum theory of consciousness that suggests our soul (some would say our consciousness) resides within structures in our brain cells called microtubules. As I interpret the information, in the simplest of terms, Dr Hameroff and Dr Penrose suggest that quantum computations within these microtubules are responsible for our awareness. The theory proposes that these *orchestrated objective reductions* (computations) in microtubules are responsible for the emergence of consciousness. They also believe that microtubules can store and

124 Stuart Hameroff, "'Orch OR' Is the Most Complete, and Most Easily Falsifiable Theory of Consciousness," Cognitive Neuroscience 12, no. 2 (2021): 74–76, https://doi.org/10.1080/17588928.2020.1839037.

process quantum information and imply that this information still exists after the death of our physical body.

The most thrilling part of their hypothesis to me is that, according to Dr Hameroff, the Orch-OR theory is capable of being proven. The falsifiability of the underlying theory is currently being examined by the Templeton World Charity Foundation.[125] Templeton has funded exploratory research examining whether aspects of Orch-OR can be empirically tested, though no conclusive results have been established.

If the basis for the theory is verified, it introduces a whole new way of viewing consciousness (which I think of as our soul) and its survivability after death.

The first set of tests was published in 2023 in the Templeton Blog.[126] According to the project lead, Jack Tuszyński, *both sets of experiments offered some support to the claims made by Orch-OR but also provided some interpretational challenges that need to be addressed in future experiments.*

As I said at the beginning of this book, I know that my son's consciousness and energy did not disappear. Orch-OR theory could eventually provide scientific proof of what many of us already believe to be true…

---

125 Templeton, "Home | Templeton World Charity Foundation, Inc.," Organizational website, Templeton World Charity Foundation, Inc., 2025, https://www.templetonworldcharity.org/.

126 Jack Tuszyński and Templeton Staff, "Is Consciousness a Quantum Phenomenon? Recent Findings Lend Some Support to Orch OR Theory," Organizational website, *Templeton World Charity Foundation Blog* (blog), June 19, 2023, https://www.templetonworldcharity.org/blog/interview-jack-tuszynski-aarat-kalra.

> *We are all part of a universal consciousness of some form or another and that we all have an individual form of soul within us that does not simply disappear when our body dies.*

It isn't easy to decipher the maze of technical terms in articles published in scientific journals, but I did my best to understand them. If you want to know more, please delve further into this fascinating theory because my explanation is somewhat simplistic. I have provided a PDF version of an article with diagrams on the Resources page at LighthouseLaneBooks.com that you can reference as a starting point. Also be sure to check out the Templeton Blog listed in the footnotes.

Psychic Spies

Remote Viewing

As part of my journey to understand if any credible scientific studies could support the belief in psychics (and where Harrison's soul might have gone), I came across a YouTube video I had seen online when I began reading this book. On the video I watched, two somewhat older men with grey hair sat in front of a fireplace, sharing stories and answering questions from a small group of believers in the paranormal. One of these men was Joe McMoneagle, whose jovial and likable qualities were enhanced somewhat by the rather rotund body of a man who has enjoyed a few too many beers. Mr McMoneagle, an ex-army officer, was, in 1978, one of the first participants in a program to assess the paranormal skill called *remote viewing*

In remote viewing, a subject—the viewer—is expected to provide information about an object, event, person, or location hidden from their physical view and located at some distance—from a neighbouring room to halfway around the world. This information is gleaned by the viewer, who physically travels to the remote location and reports on what they see, hear, etc.

Dr Edwin May, the elder of the two men, had an awkward sense of humour that perhaps had been inadvertently developed over the years to compensate for his apparent predisposition towards academia and research. Telling jokes that often fell a little flat made him likable and honest—precisely what one would expect from a man with a PhD in experimental nuclear physics.

The Stargate Program

Joe McMoneagle, the other participant in the video, was the first remote viewer inducted into what became known as the *Stargate program*. This program was initiated by the CIA and funded by various government agencies over approximately 23 years to the tune of $20-25 million. The Stanford Research Institute, which was referred to as *SRI* (a much sexier and more mysterious acronym), was one of the early investigators of remote viewing for use as a strategic tool.

Although it served other functions related to research and foreign-threat assessment, the Stargate programme was mainly established to investigate whether remote viewers could be employed effectively in actionable intelligence-gathering roles. The programme at SRI was initially commissioned in the early 1970s and was led by physicists Harold Puthoff and Russell Targ. Dr May joined the programme as the director of the research division in 1985.

Dr May stated during the YouTube interview that he had reviewed approximately 4,000 pages of peer-reviewed studies he intends to publish and that they show substantial evidence that remote viewing is effective. According to Dr May, the research was closely monitored by multiple government agencies and, as a result, reviewed by several reputable scientists. Naturally sceptical, these scientists apparently ensured the research methods used in the studies were reliable.

Over the years, various sponsors and government organisations have conducted numerous studies to assess the viability of remote viewing. In 1995, a summary evaluation[127] of these studies, authored by three esteemed scientists with PhDs, was released by the American Institute of Research. My interpretation of that report indicates that some level of remote viewing has been demonstrated. The report highlighted interesting examples of remote viewing. However, from a scientific, standardised perspective, the three scientists who prepared the report did not find remote viewing to be reliable or consistent enough to be considered a practical, ongoing intelligence-gathering tool.

The full report is also available at https://lighthouselanebooks.com

Concerning the reliability of remote viewing as a strategic, intelligence-gathering tool, the American Institute of Research concluded that...

The information provided was inconsistent, inaccurate concerning specifics, and required substantial subjective interpretation... The findings obtained in this evaluation of the intelligence applications of remote viewing lead us to the conclusion that remote viewing, as used in the present program, has limited value and was not reliable enough to be used with any significant level of certainty.

Although the researchers did not conclude there was enough specificity to use it as a reliable tool, they clearly stated that the tests showed information obtained through remote viewing was

127 Michael D Mumford, Andrew M Rose, and David A Goslin, "An Evaluation of Remote Viewing: Research and Applications" (The American Institutes for Research, September 29, 1995), https://www.amazon.co.uk/evaluation-remote-viewing-Research-applications/dp/B0006QDIRA.

more accurate than what would be expected by chance. However, the higher rate of correct responses could not be definitively attributed to the paranormal abilities of the remote viewers rather than to the traits of the judges or other aspects of the methodology. They found that it was impossible to accurately measure the influence of various biases of the review board and other factors.

To me, it sounds like scientists and judges are trying to quantify the unquantifiable. How can one define something as black or white or proved or disproved when no such definitive outcomes are possible? I suggest that you read the report and draw your own conclusions.

I was left with the impression that there is sufficient evidence to support the idea that remote viewing is possible. Maybe the results aren't entirely accurate or presented in a way that is easily defined or measurable. Nonetheless, they are certainly enough to strengthen my growing belief that dimensions and dynamics around us exist that we don't fully understand. It's possible that our soul or energy ends up in one of those unknown places after we pass away.

The full, 183-page report is freely available for download at our website: LighthouseLaneBooks.com.

Communicating with Ghosts

I, along with millions of others, have walked the haunted catacombs of Paris and gone on ghost tours in London, Salem, Savannah, and Boston. I enjoyed the scary stories offered by actors in the dungeons near the Tower of London and searched for clues along Jack the Ripper's path. I was a fan of ghost tours even before losing Harrison; before that tragedy, they were more of a fun outing. Since losing Harry, of course, I've been assessing these experiences a little more seriously, hoping for proof that spirits can really communicate with us. I wasn't entirely disappointed.

EVP Studies (Electronic Voice Phenomenon)

I, along with millions of others, have walked the haunted catacombs of Paris and gone on ghost tours in London, Salem, Savannah, and Boston. I enjoyed the scary stories offered by actors in the dungeons near the Tower of London and searched for clues along Jack the Ripper's path. I was a fan of ghost tours even before losing Harrison; before that tragedy, they were more of a fun outing. Since losing Harry, of course, I've been assessing these experiences a little more seriously, hoping for proof that spirits can really communicate with us.

A few years ago, with my partner at the time, I took a night tour of Sydney's Quarantine Station, which opened in 1832 and remained in operation until 1984, processing immigrants to Australia. Millions of new Australians were sent and often quarantined there if their ships arriving from Europe carried disease. Luggage was fumigated, and the unsuspecting voyagers were showered with carbolic acid that, within a few days, caused the two top layers of their skin to peel off as if sunburnt. Thousands died there, and parentless children went missing—some of whom are said to be buried under a little cottage that you visit.

I often wonder if this experience at Quarantine Station may be one of the reasons why Australians are such a tough lot! Perhaps not, but nevertheless, Sydney's Quarantine Station is said to be one of Australia's most haunted places. For me, the tour confirmed that in some cases, spirits and ghosts, or at least some form of representative energy of such, definitely remain with us.

At the start of the *ghost tour,* as it was billed, in the dimly lit courtyard outside the gas chamber where all arriving passengers' personal belongings were fumigated, everybody was given a personal electromagnetic field (EMF) meter, which registers changes in the surrounding EMF by detecting the changing magnetic field produced by electrical currents. More commonly used in home inspections or work environments to identify areas of high EMF exposure, they are also great fun on creepy haunted tours because ghost hunters believe they indicate paranormal activity. The little handheld device has several yellow lights that illuminate more intensely the closer you get to a source of electromagnetic activity… or as *it* gets closer to you!

Sceptics correctly point out that high readings on these devices are often attributed to electrical interference from household wiring, cell phones, and other electronic devices. You're openly told this on the tour. There were many times when the little meters registered an increase in electromagnetic exposure. Electrical wiring or power outlets may explain why the lights went crazy when we passed through the little cottage where two well-known ghosts are said to reside and where missing children may be buried underneath the floorboards. It may also explain why the lights illuminated as we tiptoed through the darkened halls of the hospital where so many died.

What I could not explain or pass off as possible random EMF emissions was an experience later in the tour when I was standing in the middle of an Aboriginal burial ground with one other person. I shudder every time I think of it even now, years later.

Late at night, far from houses and electrical currents or cell phones, on a very dark and eerie track, the walking tour eventually led us up a bush track that passes through an ancient Aboriginal burial ground. A lady who happened to be walking next to me quietly whispered, "What is that?" Nobody in the small group heard her but me, and they all kept walking. Now alone, the two of us peered at a faint white glow deep in the bush that neither of us could make out with any clarity. It was a blurry image of something light in colour about 20 feet away. It didn't move, but both of us felt it was watching us through the darkness.

I know of some ferns, mushrooms, and moss that are bioluminescent at night, and I have seen them in rainforests, so I initially assumed the glow was natural. Mesmerised, we just stood, trying to understand what we were looking at. Then, after about a minute of staring, the lights on both of our EMF meters went from nothing to full illumination! And, just as suddenly, the faint white image was gone. We both looked at each other with the same stunned expression; a chill ran through my whole body, and the hair on my neck literally stood up. We quickly turned and, without a word of prompting, both started running!

It is hard to explain such a chilling experience from that scary encounter to others, so I did not try, but my partner immediately noticed how shaken I was when I caught up with her. On that same night, she had her own encounter and was absolutely convinced that she saw the faint image of a nurse pass her in the hospital corridor.

On another ghost tour of the Aradale Mental Asylum in Ararat, Victoria, I placed two EMF meters on a ledge in a lonely holding cell and watched them simultaneously light up a few minutes later without any interaction from humans nearby. Aradale opened in 1865 and housed the state's mentally ill for over 125 years. It is reportedly the home of many poor souls that, for various reasons, have stuck around to haunt visitors. Later, I sat alone in a dark hallway of the asylum for 20 minutes, intently watching laser beams and various sensors attempting to capture passing ghosts; regrettably, I was not rewarded with a personal visit or an experience like the one from Quarantine Station in Sydney.

Aradale's abandoned asylum is made up of 64 buildings spread over more than 40 hectares, and thousands died there over the years. In the late 1800s, treatments around the world for mental illness included restraint devices, cold-water therapy, and other undesirable forms of treatment. From 1940-1950, treatments such as lobotomies became popular internationally as well as electroshock therapies. Over the years, care at Aradale improved and became more compassionate, but most people never left the facility unless they died. Some reports say that as many as 13,000 people are buried there.

The nighttime ghost tours at Aradale are fun and well-equipped with all sorts of modern tools to experience an interaction with ghosts, but, alas, even though I was a prime target sitting alone in a deserted and very dark hallway illuminated only by tiny lasers, I did not see any ghosts.

A few years later, my daughter and I went on an equally unproductive ghost tour in Jerome, an old mining town near Sedona, Arizona. Although ghosts and spirits are often elusive, these tours are always entertaining and generally full of great historical information, so we still enjoyed them. It was, however, gratifying and productive for most of the other participants, I believe, because of a phenomenon called ***apophenia***[128] (the perception of meaningful connections among unrelated things). In Jerome, we were given ***spirit boxes*** in addition to the standard handheld EMF meters. Spirit boxes, or what some people call ghost boxes, are handheld devices that rapidly scan radio frequencies to allow spirits to communicate through white noise.

Unlike the other people listening to the sounds that regularly came from our spirit boxes, I had heard these noises over a thousand times before and knew what they were. Fortunately, my prior experience was not from exposure to spirits but from nearly 40 years of flying worldwide and listening to the crackling static and background noise on very high frequency (VHF) and high frequency (HF) radios. Nowadays, new, younger pilots probably cannot even imagine a world without instantaneous satellite communication. Still, even 10 years ago, many aircraft operating in remote places around the world had to rely on HF

---

128 Kara Rogers, "Apophenia | Description, Forms, Gambler's Fallacy, & Intervention," in ***Encyclopaedia Britannica*** (Chicago: Encyclopaedia Britannica, March 13, 2025), https://www.britannica.com/topic/apophenia.

communication that bounces off the ionosphere to relay position reports to ground controllers. Often flying over remote areas and trying to reach far-off air-traffic control areas, pilots had to spend hours listening to static on radios, attempting to pick up distant voices and communications.

Depending on the type of ghost box you are using and the settings selected, the purpose of this device is to quickly scan through numerous frequencies—which creates white noise—to pick up communications from spirits. Depending on your selection, these frequencies can be HF, MF (medium frequency), or VHF.

Over and over again, people on the tour would ask a spirit a question. It is my opinion that when they heard randomised partial communication coming from the box, they would subconsciously interpret these indistinguishable sounds to satisfy their own need. To me, with thousands of hours of prior experience, the noises sounded like just a series of broken radio communications partially obscured by white noise. These radio transmissions are usually all around us, of course, but cannot generally be heard with the human ear. However, to the other people on the tour, these burps and blips within the white noise were communications directly from the other side. Their interpretation of these sounds was more likely due to apophenia, our brain's habit of finding patterns in randomised data. To explain the definition fully, I once again quote directly from Encyclopedia Britannica:

> ***Apophenia*** *is the perception of patterns or connections between unrelated or random data, objects, and ideas in situations where no such patterns exist. It is relatively common and represents a kind of cognitive bias that is perhaps most evident in the form of superstitions and similar, generally benign beliefs.*

Tools that record EVP, spirit boxes that scan radio frequencies, EMF meters, motion detectors, infrared and thermal cameras, and dowsing rods designed to move in response to spiritual energy are all widely used among paranormal explorers, ghost tour operators, and believers in haunted houses. While they provide an entertaining user experience and serve as excellent props to heighten tension and character in ghost stories and television shows exploring haunted places, I couldn't find any scientific studies demonstrating their effectiveness in paranormal investigations. I wish there were some definitive proof, at the time of this writing, I wasn't aware of any.

Return to Q-Station

Even though there seems to be no hard scientific proof that any of these gadgets work, being an epic adventurer of sorts, I could not resist the temptation to go back one more time and give the ghosts at Sydney's Quarantine Station an additional chance to prove that there is a spirit world beyond what we can see in our daily lives. Much to my surprise, I left my second visit even more convinced of the possibility than my first!

A couple of years after writing about my first visit, Q-Station (Quarantine Station) introduced a *paranormal tour* besides the *ghost tour* I took the first time. On this new (and more expensive) paranormal tour, they not only give you the standard EMF meter but also provide a plethora of the latest and coolest ghost-hunting gear. The SLS (structured light sensor) camera was the most dramatic and my favourite. Traditional SLS cameras were designed to display an infrared laser grid over the field of vision. The camera measured the depth of objects and produced a 3D image by measuring the distances between projected dots throughout the room. The technology attempts to match patterns and sometimes recognises forms that it interprets as human and presents them as stick-like figures on the screen.

Back in 2010, these cameras were initially designed as the motion-control user interface for the Xbox gaming system. Since then, the paranormal world has adopted the technology because the same screen occasionally shows stick-like figures of people when no people can be seen with the human eye. Often, those representations are generated because a table or chair in the field of vision is misinterpreted. But, at other times, seeing a figure on the screen in front of you when there is clearly no human form there or something that could be interpreted as human, is pretty exciting.

Fortunately, any amateur ghost hunter can now download an inexpensive app that accesses the newest LiDAR (light detection and ranging) technology available on many modern phones and iPads. The latest SLS cameras also project a grid of infrared light, just like the originals, but reportedly, the chipsets and sensors in newer cell phones are usually better and more advanced than those in older Kinect SLS cameras.

Using this exciting technology on the tour, my companion and I almost immediately registered a small, child-sized figure hanging from a bar in the shower block where migrants were doused with carbolic acid.

Next to the child was a more significant, prominent figure writhing as if in pain. As the four of us stood looking at the figures in shock, the words *choked,* and *daughter* suddenly pierced the air (and our psyches) from an AI-driven synthesiser app on the tour guide's phone. Her app suggests that is uses the mobile device's sensors to detect magnetic field fluctuations and then selected words from a pre-populated, AI-augmented word bank to produce unique AI-generated audio based on the chosen words. The theory is that those spirits trying to communicate can do this efficiently by manipulating energy. If you buy one, understand that they are known to produce coincidental results.

If I were reading what I have just related to you, I would assume that what I just described was part of an elaborate ruse to promote the tour and make money. As an actual participant and a sceptic by nature, I really do not think that was the case. The tour guide was a nice gal working part-time for a government-owned management company. There was very little for her to gain financially, and only three of us were on the tour. To confirm whether a false positive from the SLS camera was caused by the corrugated iron walls or door, we tested other stalls in the building with the same configuration, with no similar results. On returning to the original stall, the stick-like figures could no longer be seen on the screen, but the haunting image remained in my brain… and on my camera, luckily. The video is available at LighthouseLaneBooks.com resources page.

It is possible that the SLS camera we used misinterpreted signals from the structures themselves—the door frame, the corrugated iron, or something else—to produce the stick-like figures we saw. As I said, we could not reproduce them in other similar cubicles with an angle shot from the same height, but it is possible that there was a scientific explanation, I suppose. But not one I could find!

What is not as easily explained are the results of a much simpler device we used, which anybody can buy at a local pet shop. Surrounded by hi-tech devices, it was surprising that in the end, the most convincing was the simplest. Our guide, Mel, had a couple of small, round, clear

balls that are sold as toys for cats to play with. If moved or rolled across the floor, they produce colourful lights. They are designed not illuminate unless they detect movement or vibration.

The scary thing for us was that, on several occasions, when Mel asked the resident ghosts a question, these balls—stationary on a fixed object like a chair—would suddenly start flashing wildly!

There was no visible movement at all when the lights suddenly started flashing; I can guarantee that. I was watching them at the time and keeping an eye on our guide to make sure she was not reaching into her pocket to trigger a remote device. She was not, and I have no explanation for why these devices illuminated at critical times. It happened twice—once when a ball was placed on one of the original beds and again when another ball was placed on a chair in an old cottage known for paranormal activity. I am not easily fooled and was alert to the possibility of a scam; I am pretty sure there was no manipulation, and the interactions with our guide made me feel she was trustworthy.

> *I left the tour convinced that the possibility of some form of spiritual energy interacting with us is real.*

Although there is limited evidence to support this idea, and scientists are generally sceptical, many paranormal researchers believe that spirits may communicate with us by utilising the energy around them or that of living things. Communicating through an EVP, making lights flicker, or causing an object to move through manipulation of energy are supposedly standard capabilities of the spirits around us. They may also manipulate electromagnetic fields, heat energy, and even kinetic energy, which can manifest as changes in temperature, electrical events, or movement.

My experiences at Q-Station in Sydney were another check-mark in the *I believe in spirits* column.

Part 3:
The Afterlife

Once, very late in my mother's life, at age 93, we were sitting quietly in a lovely garden, and I asked her what she thought would happen after she died. Her vision had almost entirely deteriorated, and dementia was waging war with her senses and memory. With her eyes closed, she tilted her face toward the sun, paused for a while and said:

I think that we join up to make the atmosphere as pure as it can get, and that the atmosphere is made up of the souls of those who died before us. I don't believe in reincarnation in the traditional sense, but I do believe that my soul is kept alive in the air and will eventually be reused by someone else or an animal. Yes, our souls are reused in some way… or at least that is what I believe. I am just glad I was allowed to be a part of this wonderful life.

> *I have survived happiness and sadness, but it all works itself out in the end. Just do the best you can while you are here because our souls are here as well.*
>
> ~Leila Grace Dunnett (March 2020, age 93)

After fighting off three Covid infections, mostly blind and with failing hearing, my mother was able to celebrate her 99th birthday on Valentine's Day, 2026, just a few weeks before this book was first released. Six years after she gave me the quote. I read it to her and told her that her words of wisdom will be published for others to read for years to come. A large toothless but somehow still beautiful smile stretched across her gaunt face, and momentarily, a twinkle returned to her eyes. I think it was the best birthday present she received that day!

* * *

The first three or four years after my son's death were spent in litigation, trying to find answers and make the people responsible for my son's death pay in some way. I discovered that, initially, preoccupying myself with revenge and a need for justice, and later with a more meaningful purpose, was a way to deflect the pain. Of course, it is natural to want to avoid pain, and so after a terrible loss, we often subconsciously try to find purpose or some other preoccupation to avoid facing our deepest wounds. I sometimes wonder if focusing more on her words would have offered more solace in some ways. On rereading them during one of my final edits, I realised they were much more profound than I had first thought.

Now, much further down this journey of recovery, I have had time to sit and think about what my mother said to me in that garden years before. I also think my exploration of Buddhism, which I discussed in earlier chapters, has awakened me to the importance of finding time to sit with myself without distraction, to feel what is going on inside me, and to come to terms with grief rather than trying to avoid it. I don't know where she heard it, but my ex-wife once told me…

The quickest way around pain is through it.

It is true. Unfortunately, we do everything we can to avoid sitting with that pain. It is hard to face, and therefore, our recovery from loss takes longer.

When We Are Forced to Think About the Question of the Afterlife

Part of sitting with our grief after losing a loved one is eventually having to actually come to terms with and accept the fact that the person we have lost is gone.

I lost my son and had to accept and come to terms with death eventually. It wasn't easy, and I still struggle with it. As I was forced to acknowledge that death had entered my room, in a different but also similar way, a person with a terminal diagnosis is also forced to consider and ponder the reality of death as well, but in their case, it comes before death, not after it. The big question of whether there is an afterlife and the nature of it looms heavily over those who are about to explore the subsequent unknown, and those who have lost someone as well.

As I write this chapter, a very close female friend in Australia has been diagnosed with stage four lung cancer that has spread to other parts of her body. She is a practising Buddhist and, understandably, is devastated that she will be leaving those around her whom she loves, and she is scared. But she seems to be more at ease in some ways than I know I would be if faced with the same terrible diagnosis. She believes that her karmic presence will live on. She is less concerned about what happens after she dies and more concerned about the best way to live out the months or years she has left.

During this same time, a good old-school friend of mine, James, was diagnosed with a rare cancer that presented itself as a sizable, inoperable tumour. He was dead only a few months later. James was more agnostic than anything else, and when we spoke about the afterlife and what he expected, he said, *That's all she wrote. There is no more.* (He is in good company with Stephen Hawking, of course.) James, too, was more concerned and terrified of leaving his beloved wife and children and those who love him than about what would happen afterwards.

In both opposing views of the afterlife, the confirmation of a belief structure seemed to ease the fear and make them less concerned about that question than I would have thought. One felt that he would just be gone for good, and the other thought she would be reincarnated and live on in another life as her karmic energy. (By the way, she and James were two of the loveliest, happiest, and kindest people I have ever met, and if they, or at least their energy, did not live on, I would be very disappointed.)

A personal rumination on the afterlife

The journey I have taken writing this book has led me to conclude that, after we die, there definitely is not *nothing* (as my good friend James expected). We may not sense anything, but it is not *nothingness*. One's energy, we know, definitely folds itself back into the world around us and lives on in that way; that to me is not nothing, it is everything.

In addition to this wonderful re-entry into the world of our energy, I believe we also have a soul that continues on and embarks upon some kind of journey. Although we are not certain of the final destination, we know from reports of those who have had near-death experiences that the journey after death, for a vast majority at least, is not unpleasant. In any case, the experience after death doesn't scare me anymore. The pain associated with an unwelcome and shocking death would, of course, be anything but fun. But what happens after death may even be a relief for many in some ways.

> *I don't want to do anything to encourage death's arrival on my doorstep unnaturally. I enjoy my daughter too much, the smell of pine trees, the laughter of children, and the feeling of sunshine on my face. Nevertheless, I know I will also be free of pain after I go, and perhaps even embark on another great adventure.*

I believe the pain will disappear after I die. Hopefully, I will still be with my friends and my son or perhaps be reincarnated into a new life. If not, I will simply be part of the world around my daughter and her children as they walk on the sand, touch a tree, or dive into the water. I will always be nearby and with them.

The memories we leave behind.

When discussing the afterlife and where our soul goes, we're also confronted with the fascinating reality of creating an *afterlife* for our loved ones right here on Earth. Even as I write this, it's easy for you or me to hop online and watch numerous videos on how to build a realistic AI-generated chatbot based on anyone who has passed away. Using AI-generated imagery and software to respond through the information we've provided, our personally designed chatbot can chat with us and offer responses based on what AI believes would have been the true reply from the character we input.

My personal choice is not to create an AI-generated likeness of Harrison, as I think it would make me sad to talk to a fake replica of my son, no matter how realistic. Given the number of lyrics he wrote for his songs, his numerous journals, social media responses, and pictures and videos I have of him, I feel his (the bot's) responses would be disturbingly realistic. If that is available now, imagine what will be available to us in just a few short years!

My daughter, who is studying both computer science and graphic design at college, has assured me that if I record a series of videos and answer an extensive questionnaire for her, she will, without a doubt, be able to have conversations with me when I'm no longer here (via a computer-generated version of me). Her children would be able to talk to me if I were not around to give them advice. I am not sure if that is a good thing or not, but it is definitely going to happen in such a realistic way that it will be as though, in some ways, I haven't left at all (for those who want it).

This realisation and the opportunities it presents are truly amazing, and I may explore that in another book. For now, I have decided that my personal journey is best served by concentrating on the more traditional question of a spiritual afterlife, not the possibilities of a computer-generated one.

Reincarnation

Even Carl Sagan, atheist, lifelong critic, and sceptic of the paranormal—Once stated that young children sometimes report details of a previous life, which upon checking turn out to be accurate and which they could not have known about in any other way than reincarnation. He did not go as far as to endorse the theory, but did acknowledge that the area was deserving of more study.

* * *

The largest religious group of people that believes in reincarnation as a central belief are Hindus. If at least a billion people on Earth believe in reincarnation, perhaps it is worth investigating!

One fascinating book I recommend if you're interested in reincarnation is mentioned in the Spiritualism chapter—*Journey of Souls*. In Dr Newton's book, he shares his experience with 29 patients who underwent hypnotherapy as part of past-life regression therapy to help with behavioural changes in their current lives. While working with patients under hypnosis and hearing their stories from previous lives to help them overcome phobias, he realised he could expand this approach and have his patients describe not only how they died in their past lives but also what they experienced after death in those lives.

His book is a fascinating exposé of the progressive journey, the transition from one life to the next, and what happens in between. (To be consistently critical, I must point out that others do not corroborate what Dr Newton describes.) Absolute belief in reincarnation is an underlying premise of the book. In it, he tells the continuous journey and cycle of reincarnation, death, an after-death journey of the soul, and then subsequent reincarnation that goes on for thousands of years. The same cycle recurs on the soul's progressive journey toward enlightenment as one gets closer and closer to the source of creation. To me, in some ways, that sounds a lot like the quest of Hindus and Buddhists to reach eventual enlightenment.

If you want to take a look at what I consider to be pretty good evidence of reincarnation, some exciting case studies suggest that reincarnation is real. The University of Virginia School of Medicine has a Division of Perceptual Studies[129] that is dedicated entirely to fascinating research challenging mainstream science and philosophy that thinks all we—our thoughts, actions, and beliefs—are just byproducts of brain activity, and all that activity disappears after death. On their website, they have published numerous studies on near-death experiences, altered states of consciousness, and accounts of children who have remembered previous lives. When I last looked this up on Amazon, 15 books examined this fascinating and compelling phenomenon of young children describing people and events in their prior lives. There are also almost 50 academic studies on the same subject. I found

129 Division of Perceptual Studies, "Study of Reincarnation," UVA School of Medicine - Division of Perceptual Studies, 2025, https://med.virginia.edu/perceptual-studies/publications/books/study-of-reincarnation/.

the resources from the Division of Perceptual Studies absolutely fascinating!

Proponents of traditional simulation theory (not Subversive Simulation Theory—SST), as I first discussed in ***It's All Just a Simulation*** (Part 2), would suggest that these people's memories of prior lives are residual memories from previous simulations. Perhaps they are correct. I guess an internal code of some sort used repeatedly in a series of simulations would be a form of reincarnation, would it not? However, my gut tells me that the humanity and soulfulness within us are just too unique to be part of a simulation, thus my suggestion that SST is a more likely proposition. (But then again, I would be programmed to think that, wouldn't I?)

No matter where these memories come from, I would be surprised if, as the reader of this book, you haven't remembered special times with vivid but unexplained memories that suddenly pop into your mind, experienced déjà vu, or have knowledge that feels completely unexplainable. If your personal experiences haven't yet convinced you of memories from previous lives, read some of the fascinating stories I list below. There are many more out there.

James Leininger

The story of James Leininger, who started recalling vivid memories and reliving the life of a World War II fighter pilot named James Huston at the age of two, was studied and documented by Dr Tucker at the University of Virginia. Leininger's story was also widely distributed in a book called *Soul Survivor* [130], written by his parents. *Soul Survivor* recounts how the Leininger family pieced together what their son was communicating and provides facts about James Huston that could have only been known if he had actually experienced that prior life.

(As they would, sceptics argue that cultural reinforcement, selective memory, and parental influence may explain these cases, but I still find them very interesting and hard to dismiss.)

Shanti Devi

In the 1930s, Shanti Devi Mathur[131], who was then a small child living in India, described detailed memories of the life of a young woman named Lugdi Chaubey, who had died some two years before the girl's birth. Lugdi's family was identified from statements made by Shanti Devi, and the young girl led the way to Lugdi's house, where she recognised Lugdi's relations and displayed accurate knowledge of intimate details of Lugdi's life. The case drew the attention of Mahatma Gandhi and was extensively investigated by a committee of prominent citizens appointed by Gandhi, who accompanied Shanti Devi to the village of her past-life recollections and recorded what they witnessed. A book

---

130 Bruce Leininger and Andrea Leininger, Soul Survivor: *The Reincarnation of a World War II Fighter Pilot* (New York: Grand Central Publishing, 2010).

131 KM Wehrstein, "Shanti Devi (Reincarnation Case)," in Psi Encyclopedia (London: The Society for Psychical Research, September 15, 2021), https://psi-encyclopedia.spr.ac.uk/articles/shanti-devi-reincarnation-case.

called *I Have Lived Before*[132] was later written by Sture Lonnerstrand about Shanti Devi and tells a fascinating tale.

Sam Taylor

Sam Taylor was born 18 months after his paternal grandfather died. When he was 1-1/2 years old, Sam looked up to his father as he was changing his diaper and said, "When I was your age, I used to change your diapers." I imagine, as a father who changed a lot of diapers myself, that would be pretty unsettling! The story goes on and tells how young Sam related information that only his grandfather could have known. He could also identify his grandfather as a child and pick him out of school photos. A summary is included in this review published by the University of Virginia in 2008,[133] which also includes several other compelling examples.

Sam Taylor, amongst others who remember their past lives, is also covered in a book by J.B Tucker called ***Return to Life***[134]

---

132 Sture Lonnerstrand, I Have Lived Before: The True Story of the Reincarnation of Shanti Devi, American ed. (Huntsville, AR: Ozark Mountain Pub, 1998), https://archive.org/details/ihavelivedbefore00stur/page/n3/mode/2up.

133 Jim B. Tucker, "Children's Reports of Past-Life Memories: A Review," EXPLORE 4, no. 4 (July 2008): 244–48, https://doi.org/10.1016/j.explore.2008.04.001.

134 Jim B. Tucker, Return to Life: Extraordinary Cases of Children Who Remember Past Lives, First St. Martin's Griffin edition (New York: St. Martin's Griffin, 2015), https://med.virginia.edu/perceptual-studies/publications/books-by-dops-faculty/study-of-reincarnation/return-to-life-extraordinary-cases-of-children-who-remember-past-lives/.

The Case of P.M.

The following is an excerpt from a paper written by Dr Tucker in 2008.[135]

P.M. was a boy born with three birthmarks that appeared to match lesions on his half-brother, who had died of neuroblastoma 12 years before the birth of P.M. The illness was diagnosed after the half-brother began limping; he then suffered a pathological fracture of his left tibia. He underwent a biopsy of a nodule on his scalp above his right ear and received chemotherapy through a central line in his right external jugular vein. At the time of his death at two years of age, he was blind in his left eye. P.M. was born with a swelling 1 cm in diameter above his right ear and a dark, slanting mark on the lower right anterior surface of his neck. He also had a corneal leukoma that caused him to be virtually blind in his left eye. In addition, he limped when he learned to walk as if sparing his left leg. At around the age of 4.5 years, P.M. talked to his mother about wanting to return to the family's previous home, which he described accurately, and he also told of the scalp surgery that his half-brother had undergone.

There are hundreds of similar stories and over a dozen books on this subject available on Amazon.

These stories all but cement my belief in some form of reincarnation. Our death is not The End. It is just the start of another journey.

---

135 Tucker, "Children's Reports of Past-Life Memories."

Spiritualism

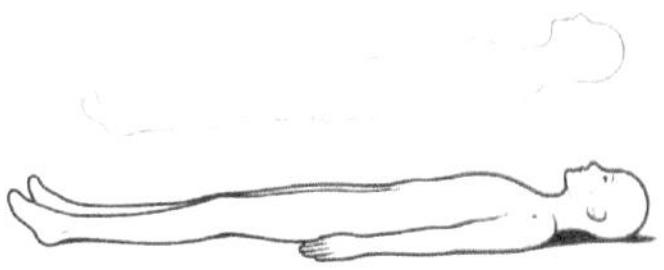

At the beginning of the Commonality chapter, I recommended a book called *Tuesdays with Morrie* by Mitch Albom[136]. Another particular observation from Morrie in the last three months of his life before finally succumbing to the autoimmune disease ALS was recognising that his body was a mere shell, like … *a container for his soul.* I mentioned experiencing this same feeling in the very beginning of this book when I described seeing my son's body for the first time after he died.

> *I viewed Harrison's body in the same way after his death. I knew instinctively it was just my beautiful boy's body, not his person, spirit, or energy. The body is a separate entity; I am sure.*

---

136 Mitch Albom, Tuesdays with Morrie (Sydney: Hachette Australia, 1998).

Spiritualism Defined

If you follow any of the main religions mentioned in this book, you believe we go somewhere after we die. If you are a Christian, Buddhist, Muslim, Hindu, Jew, Sikh, Native American, or one of many other Indigenous or tribal religions, the teachings of your faith promise continuation in some form after you die. Even Greek mythology and ancient Egyptian beliefs promoted the concept of some form of life after death. If you share the beliefs of any of these groups, your faith teaches that we go to a different place after we die or are returned to this one. In one form or another, our spirit, or a variation of it, lives on. Spiritualists believe this as well, and also that the spirit that lives on can, in many cases, communicate with people on Earth.

Spiritualism is a faith movement that emerged in the 1800s and was founded on the belief that the departed can communicate with the living through mediums. Unlike many traditional religions, Spiritualism lacks a central doctrine or sacred texts, making its claims more challenging to validate independently. However, certain aspects of Spiritualism have been subject to scientific scrutiny (and often controversy). There doesn't seem to be much empirical evidence that definitively confirms the beliefs of Spiritualism or the possibility of communicating with spirits. Still, there certainly have been many impressive displays by skilled performers who say they can.

The most significant questions remaining are… Is there any proof of the existence of another world, and, if so, do we have any way of communicating once we pass to that other world? But first, let's clarify a few terms:

Spirituality is an awareness that there is something far greater than us, something that created this universe and created life, and of which we are an authentic, important, significant part and can contribute to its evolution.

(Elizabeth Kubler-Ross from *On Life After Death*)

Spiritualism,[137] on the other hand, is a belief in spirits who have passed from this life and the cocoon of our physical bodies to inhabit a spiritual world outside the constraints of our known existence.

Spiritism[138] (the earlier version of American Spiritualism) is defined by Britannica as a specific belief system founded by French author and educator Allan Kardec in the mid-19th century. It is based on the idea that, alongside physical reality, a spirit world exists that its followers believe can be accessed through mediums. Spiritism maintains that spirits exist separately from human bodies, that humans are incarnate spirits, and that spirits undergo repeated reincarnation into the physical world in a progression toward intellectual and moral perfection.

Spiritualists believe that the soul endures beyond physical death and enters the spirit world, a non-material realm where it continues its journey. According to this view of the afterlife, we are meant to learn and undergo spiritual growth while living in

---

137 J. Gordon Melton, "Spiritualism | Religion, Beliefs, Practices, & History," in *Encyclopedia Britannica* (Chicago, IL: Encyclopædia Britannica, Inc., February 22, 2025), https://www.britannica.com/topic/spiritualism-religion.

138 Charles Preston and Dylan Shulman, "Spiritism | Beliefs, Practices, & History," in *Encyclopedia Britannica* (Chicago, IL: Encyclopædia Britannica, Inc., November 20, 2024), https://www.britannica.com/topic/Spiritism.

our current world, but souls also carry on their spiritual development in the next world. Unlike other religious traditions, Spiritualism teaches that the soul goes through several stages of moral and spiritual progress rather than relying on fixed rewards and punishments. This path may include reviewing one's past life, learning from mistakes, and progressing toward higher spiritual levels.

This belief in what happens after we die is similar to the journeys discussed in *Journey of Souls*, which I've often mentioned in this book. The description of our ongoing journey of soul development, as outlined in Dr Newton's case studies, closely resembles Spiritualism, leading me to think that Dr Newton may have researched Spiritualist beliefs and used them to craft his patients' journeys. Essentially, Newton's stories, if they are accurate, strongly support the validity of the Spiritualist storyline.

Spiritualism and European Spiritism are close enough that they are one and the same. As previously noted, spirituality is very different and centres around one being aware and trying to understand the fundamental, moral, and existential nature of self (or soul) and consideration of things like the meaning of life, the nature of our mind, our place in the world, and our belief in religion or other philosophical ways of living one's life. It is essential to draw an important distinction between these terms.

The following sections examine a few personal stories and possible evidence of spirits, which is distinct from someone being *spiritual*.

Souls on Board

I was an airline pilot for 40 years, most of which were spent flying passengers. Before every flight—just before the doors closed, the stairs were removed, and the aircraft started its journey—the flight attendant or ground representative would confirm the number of people on board by saying to me, "Souls on board," followed by the number of people.

During all those years of flying, I never gave that phrase a second thought until I was recently sitting on a plane as a passenger and heard the flight attendant say those words to the Captain. For 40 years, I had been hearing and saying a phrase that I had not even thought about until I saw Harrison's lifeless body for the first time. As I explained in the first sections of the book, I knew for sure that something was missing other than his ability to move and speak. It was as though *he*, the boy I knew as Harrison, was not even in the room.

Even though I had been using the term *souls on board* for all those years, I did not appreciate the gravity and reality of us all being souls until that day, when I was sitting in business class and heard someone else say it. I finally got it through my thick skull that we are, without a doubt, souls inhabiting a physical body, just as Deepak Chopra says.[139] In that realisation, I found one of the most fundamental stepping stones in my journey of recovery.

---

139 Deepak Chopra LLC, "Deepak Chopra - Official Website," 2025, https://www.deepakchopra.com/.

Acknowledging that it was Harrison's body that stopped living, not his soul, was like finding the first stone I could stand on to wade out of the quicksand of my emotional sadness and grief—finally, something solid to support me and move forward.

Having finally become comfortable with the fact that the soul is not necessarily destroyed when the body it inhabits dies, I had to take the next step on the path and figure out where the soul goes when it leaves the body—which leads to such questions as: Can we sometimes communicate with the soul before it moves too far into the next world? Is communication possible at all? There have always been and will always be plenty of people who say they can communicate with departed souls. Are any of them telling the truth?

Sir Arthur Conan Doyle

Who would have thought that a degree in medicine would result in two of the world's greatest novelists!

Even though he was best known for his 60 Sherlock Holmes stories, the famous author Sir Arthur Conan Doyle was also deeply intrigued by a belief system called Spiritualism. His initial interest in religion started when he was a 21-year-old student at medical school in 1880 (where, coincidentally, he also became friends with another Edinburgh student, Robert Louis Stevenson, who later authored *Treasure Island* and *Dr Jekyll and Mr Hyde*).[140]

By the time young Conan Doyle graduated with his medical degree in 1881, he had already denounced his Roman Catholic faith in favour of his alternate theories. He first wrote about his beliefs in 1887. Over the next 40 years, before his death in 1930, Conan Doyle[141] continued his interest in Spiritualism, eventually carrying out missionary work and writing four books on the subject: *The New Revolution* (1918), *The Vital Message* (1919), *The Wanderings of a Spiritualist* (1921), and *History of Spiritualism* (1926). An interesting summary of his beliefs is contained in an interview published in 1919 and available on the website *The Arthur Conan Doyle Encyclopedia.*[142]

Over his years of exploration and interest in Spiritualism, Conan Doyle interviewed and investigated many mediums. Though he was often criticised for accepting claims others found unconvincing. According to Doyle, he required proof from everyone who said they could communicate with the spirit world. Not just stating facts that the person paying for the I would know but also producing evidence that would not be known to the person paying for the service. The intention in requiring such

---

140 Marsha Perry, "Arthur Conan Doyle and Spiritualism," Conan Doyle Info, October 7, 2024, https://www.conandoyleinfo.com/life-conan-doyle/conan-doyle-and-spiritualism/.

141 Andrzej Diniejko, "Sir Arthur Conan Doyle and Victorian Spiritualism," The Victorian Web, 2013, https://victorianweb.org/authors/doyle/spiritualism.html.

142 Arthur Conan Doyle, "Life After Death: An Interview with Sir Arthur Conan Doyle," Arthur Conan Doyle Official Website, March 1919, https://www.arthur-conan-doyle.com/index.php?title=Life_after_Death.

verification when Conan Doyle went through this process was to eliminate the possibility of extra-sensory perception (ESP) and deception.

The result of Sir Conan Doyle's lengthy investigations on the subject was that he concluded that psychic phenomena were genuine. He was however accused by some, of being too believing and credulous. (There was one famous picture of fairies that he declared real, but which was later debunked, that damage his reputation.)

The Sleeping Prophet—Edgar Cayce

Life often has a habit of delivering insights when least expected—or one's subconscious does (I am unsure if it is the universe or the mind providing insights). One day, during a laborious eight-hour drive from Melbourne, Australia, to my favourite city, Sydney, life delivered one such insight. During the drive, I decided to call my Aunt Gai, certainly not doing research for this book.

Little did I know that Gai, now well into her 80s, would later provide me with a wealth of insight and reference material for my journey of discovery into the afterlife! Admittedly, one doesn't always think to consult one's favourite aunt for definitive guidance about the afterlife—but this aunt is different!

To understand why I'd include my dear auntie in this book, I'll share one of my stand-out memories from my youth when I was staying with her for a few nights. She lived in a little rustic farmhouse in rural New South Wales, and I was in my mid-20s. Gai, a nurse for most of her life, was also an avid believer in the spirit world and a power greater than ourselves. On one of the nights I spent with her, she enticed me to join her in focusing on a pea that sat alone in the centre of a large white plate for well over an hour. Our intention was to make that pea move with the power of our minds. I was so enthralled with the possibility that we might be successful in this endeavour that I didn't take much convincing. The promise of what beautiful experiences would lie ahead if I could learn to harness the power of my mind in the simple act of moving a pea was irresistible.

So there we were, on a chilly night in August, sitting in silence and mentally ganging up on this poor little pea to try to make it budge. Unfortunately, as one might expect, the pea refused to move… but the needle of my affection and admiration for my fascinating auntie did. She became my favourite relative after that memorable little experiment in Jedi training and unlocking the depths of the power within us.

It was no surprise that when I reconnected with her and mentioned the book I was working on, she told me about her experiences of being with people as they passed. Gay said that as they departed, she sometimes felt a cold breeze brush across her face. Other times, lights flickered, or she'd see a bird at the windowsill that seemed to be waiting and watching as people took their last breaths. I decided immediately that I should visit her on the farm where she now lived in Queensland as soon as possible.

Her farm was more than 500 miles from where I lived then, so I didn't know if that visit would happen. Nevertheless, about a year later, I found myself driving through that part of Australia's beautiful countryside.

Late on a summer's night in 2023, I finally found my Aunt Gai's little farm hidden along a dirt road, through a rickety metal gate, and perched on a little hill overlooking a foggy valley. I spent the night listening to her stories from years as a nurse, enjoying her infectious laugh, and leafing through her numerous books on the spirit world and beyond. Over a few glasses of wine, I felt reassured by her stories of being with the dying as their souls left their bodies.

Equally fortuitous and unexpected, among her library of books was a whole shelf devoted to the wisdom of the sleeping prophet, which immediately grabbed my attention. Suppose, for just a minute, that life's intersection of coincidences is just random. In that case, it's merely random that, just when I was writing a chapter on Spiritualism, I happened to reconnect with my Aunt Gai and come across a trove of resources on one of the most widely followed clairvoyants and faith healers in the early 1900s—Edgar Cayce. I knew in that moment that I had to include him in this book, even though few people know of him now.

Edgar Cayce

Cayce, a self-proclaimed American faith healer and psychic, was born in 1877 in Hopkinsville, Kentucky, and died in 1945 in Virginia Beach, Virginia. Unlike other clairvoyants, Cayce was unusual in that he prescribed cures and delivered messages from beyond while in a self-imposed hypnotic trance. His advice, prophecies, and dissertations when asleep were transcribed by a stenographer or, on many occasions, by his wife, Gertrude.

Cayce started performing faith healings in the 1920s when he was a Sunday school teacher. He had no formal academic or medical education, but from an early age, he read the Bible every year and was a dedicated member of the Disciples of Christ.

As mentioned previously and again later in this book, it seems to be a recurring theme in religions and among the faithful that those individuals visited by angels or who receive guidance from God or his envoys always seem to be alone! Cayce was no exception. He reported that when he was 13 years old, he was visited by a woman with wings while sitting in the woods reading his Bible.

Cayce gave his first psychic reading in 1901, when he was 24 years old, offering advice on medical issues and advocating natural remedies and homeopathic remedies. In 1925, he moved to Virginia Beach, where he later founded a hospital that focused on holistic medicine. Unfortunately, the hospital closed during the Depression, which started in 1929. In 1931, two years after the Great Crash on Wall Street, he founded the Association for Research and Enlightenment (A.R.E.), dedicated to helping people transform their lives for the better.

Even though Edgar Cayce died over 80 years ago, A.R.E. is still in operation today. Its headquarters is in the same spot as the original Cayce Hospital, and, according to the A.R.E. website,[143] the association ***provides body-mind-spirit resources for individuals to explore meditation, intuition, dream interpretation, prayer, holistic health, ancient mysteries, and philosophical concepts, such as karma, reincarnation, and the meaning of life***. (The cynic within me couldn't help notice that at the time of this writing, A.R.E. was also selling group tours of Egypt to its members. There isn't anything wrong with that I suppose.) Overall, the Association's mission statement seems sincere enough to me,

143 Edgar Cayce's A.R.E. "About Us | A.R.E. Mission Statement." Edgar Cayce's A.R.E. – Association for Research and Enlightenment, Inc., 2021. https://www.edgarcayce.org/about-us/our-mission/.

and members have access to over 14,000 original, documented readings by Mr Cayce.

My initial inclination was to classify him as a grifter and charlatan like so many other purported psychics and clairvoyants. However, on reading various biographies about Cayce, his early refusals to be paid for his work and the successes he reportedly had in treating people have swayed me a bit. As his popularity grew, people from around the world sought his guidance. Even though he apparently turned down many lucrative offers to charge for his services, he did accept some donations, which is understandable. Indeed, it seems the incentive for his work wasn't financial, and he had a genuine desire to help others. There are stories of Cayce being visited by numerous wealthy cotton merchants and receiving offers to pay for daily readings about cotton futures or propositions from treasure hunters looking for gold. All of which he apparently declined!

I should also point out that, according to the Encyclopedia Britannica, Cayce issued prophecies predicting the destruction of New York City and California. He also claimed to be able to recall former incarnations and pushed the idea that a great civilisation existed 12,000 years ago in Atlantis. So, he may not have been as clairvoyant as many of his followers thought! Nevertheless, the Association's website is worth a look, and I found reading extracts from his transcribed sessions compelling.

A description in one of the books I looked at that night at my aunt's house stuck with me for years. In it, Cayce describes deep meditation as the state closest to our soul and, therefore, to the spirit world beyond. He describes three levels of consciousness—physical (conscious), intermediate (subconscious), and spiritual (superconscious). My interpretation is that a deeper state of meditation (intermediate state) brings me closer to that spiritual realm, and, I hope, closer to my son's spirit.

The following diagram I created represents what I now imagine to be true after all my research for *Dance with Angels*.

Verifiable Evidence of Spiritualism

Communication with spirits and exploring that possibility has been central to the followers of the concept of Spiritualism—and, equally so, to the many charlatans who often take advantage of them. In America, modern Spiritualism and the first *confirmed* communication with spirits traces its beginnings to a series of apparently supernatural events at a farmhouse in Hydesville, New York, in 1848, where a young girl called Kate Fox was said to have established communication with a resident spirit.

While the movement was widely studied in the late 19th and early 20th centuries by organisations like the Society for Psychical Research (SPR), most investigations concluded that alleged spirit communication could often be explained by psychological factors such as suggestion, cold reading, or outright fraud. *Cold reading* refers to a technique that mentalists and psychics use to appear to know personal details about someone without prior knowledge by using observation, psychology, and high-probability guesses. I interviewed a mentalist called Marc Salem and wrote a chapter about him in my first book, *Poker Wizards*. I discuss those insights in the next section about poker. A fascinating book on Spiritualism is *Mediumship and Survival* (1983) by Allan Gauld.[144]

During the Spiritualist movement's greatest popularity in the late 19th and early 20th centuries, several investigations were conducted by the SPR and by figures such as Sir Arthur Conan Doyle and William James (a prominent psychologist). William James and the SPR investigated various mediums, such as Eusapia Palladino and Leonora Piper, and documented instances where they appeared to provide accurate information that was not easily explainable. James supported the possibility that these were authentic communications from the spirit world but remained cautious, acknowledging the potential for deception. The studies also garnered much criticism from the scientific community for lacking rigorous controls. A web reference about William James and his research can be found at the Harvard.edu website.[145]

Additional research was carried out on the phenomenon of cross-correspondences, a series of automatic writings produced

---

144 Gould Alan, Mediumship and Survival: A Century of Investigations (David & Charles, 1983),

145 Linda Simon, "Psychical Research and the Science of the Mind," Harvard Library, 2023, https://library.harvard.edu/sites/default/files/static/onlineexhibits/james/psychical.html.

by different mediums in various locations, purportedly dictated by the spirits of deceased members of the SPR. These writings were seen as evidence of coordinated communication from the afterlife intended to prove survival after death. However, critics argue that the complexity of the messages and the potential for subconscious influence by the mediums themselves weaken the case for their authenticity.

Researchers Sir Oliver Lodge and F.W.H. Myers were heavily involved in analysing cross-correspondences. While they considered the evidence compelling, the results remain disputed and are not widely accepted as definitive proof of the afterlife.

Clairvoyants and Poker

Even though there seem to have been several successful communications with spirits, strangely enough, I believe that the success of many less reputable clairvoyants and mediums in fooling their clients has more to do with poker than with a connection to the spirit world!

Tells in the game of poker can be a considerable advantage to an opponent. During the writing of ***Poker Wizards***, I interviewed a mentalist/body-language expert named Marc Salem.[146] My hours spent talking to Salem have made me think that often, people credited with having ESP are more likely to be individuals with an innate talent for reading people's reactions. These people can, therefore, sometimes pass themselves off as having some form of supernatural power. Salem believes that almost every thought we have manifests in some form physically. As a

146 Warwick Dunnett, Poker Wizards: Poker Strategy from the World's Top No-Limit Hold'em Players (Cardoza, 2008),

mentalist, he uses an acute sensitivity and awareness of those manifestations and micro-movements to gain unique insights into a person's thoughts. His skills are so impressive that, in 2005, the television show *60 Minutes* produced a special about him.

In modern times, we are familiar with the term *body language* and the talent some people have for reading the sometimes minuscule and often subtle forms of physical reaction displayed by individuals in response to words or other stimuli. Salem, based on his expertise in deciphering body language and reading people's micro tells, created a Broadway show called *Mind Games*. His uncanny ability to read people's subtle nonverbal cues and the secrets he shared with me make it easy to see how mediums can readily use the same techniques to manipulate their clients. If you listen to mediums, you will notice that they often start a sentence or begin to enunciate a name and then stop before continuing. They may say something like, "I see a woman…" or "Her name starts with a…" and so on. During these times, I believe they adapt what they say next based on the micro tells evinced by the client.

A San Francisco Tale

A few years after my son died, Gail went to see a popular (and expensive) clairvoyant in San Francisco. Also a sceptic, Gail went to great lengths to book anonymously by having a friend call to set the appointment so that her number or name couldn't be known beforehand. Gail offered as little personal information as possible when she arrived for the sitting. The session was recorded.

Based on the communications that Gail received from our son during the session (channelled through the medium), she was impressed by the whole experience and left feeling relieved that Harrison was in a good place and happy. Comforted and with a new, near-certain knowledge that Harrison was in a spiritual place, it was a cathartic experience for her.

One of the defining and convincing moments for her was when the clairvoyant said that Harrison wanted her to know that he was with Jordon (a camp counsellor and big brother to Harrison who died three years earlier). She didn't realise it, of course, and I didn't point it out to her, but from listening to the recording, it sounded like the medium was leading her and adapting what he said based on her reactions. For example, when naming the friend whom our son was with, he began by saying, "He is with somebody… It sounds like *Jay*—, no, *Jo*—" and various other permutations until *Jordon* was finally achieved—I assume after Gail's eyebrows were sufficiently raised.

This is not to say that all clairvoyants and mediums are charlatans, or that he was. Still, I do believe that many of the interactions that take place in such settings are based on the specific skill these people have for reading people's reactions, either subconsciously or by design. Some are probably authentic interactions with a soul or source from another dimension, reality, universe, or type of energy; unfortunately, the vast majority are not.

I could find no reports of significant, indisputable proof from the heyday of Spiritualism that confirmed communication with the spirit world. The stories and research carried out are interesting, though. If you want to delve into that period, you can readily access the two volumes of Sir Conan Doyle's *The History of Spiritualism*[147] online.

To further my growing belief that there is another, less physical world beyond our own, disconnected and not noticeable but still in existence, I would have preferred to find more scientifically tested and witnessed modern-day accounts. Unfortunately, I wasn't able to do so with any great certainty.

Journey of Souls

For many people, losing somebody they love initiates a flood of absolutely overwhelming despair. Certainly, that was the case for me. However, some people do not feel the same intense grief because they are absolutely convinced they will see their loved one again in the spirit world or after being reincarnated. To others, this sounds ridiculous. But ask yourself this question…

> *If billions of people think a God is looking over each one of us and that we will go to a mystical place called heaven, what is so far-fetched about the concept of our soul going through a process of reincarnation instead?*

I discussed communicating directly with spirits via mediums earlier in this chapter. However, there is another form of communication that lets us hear, from a first-person perspective, a soul's description of the journey and destination after a person dies. There are a few eminently qualified therapists who say they

---

147 Sir Arthur Conan Doyle, The History of Spiritualism (Vols. 1 and 2) (United States: Curious Publications, 2021).

have recorded and documented hundreds of sessions of people in deep hypnosis or other altered states of consciousness who describe their prior lives. These individuals are not only able to describe their death in those previous lives but also the experiences of their souls after they die. In this type of hypnosis, the subject speaks in the first person as the departed soul describing their journey.

Authors such as Brian L. Weiss, MD,[148] and Michael Newton, PhD, are two such professionals. Their books make for exciting reading. The journey after death they describe is undoubtedly something I would love to believe in. I am prone to favour their accounts over the other options I have examined earlier.

Michael Newton's book *Journey of Souls* has been previously mentioned in this book, but only briefly. It deserves closer attention. I highly recommend reading it as part of your exploration. In it, Dr Newton shares his experience of over a decade with 90 of his patients and provides 29 case studies of people who underwent hypnosis as part of age-regression therapy to assist with needed behaviour modifications in their current lives. He then wrote a second book detailing additional case studies.

Unfortunately, like many interactions that profess a knowledge of or contact with a spirit from the world beyond, interactions with God, descriptions from those who have experienced death, and messages on mountaintops or discussions with angels, they are often uncorroborated. You have realised by now that I am a sceptic. Therefore, I was a little disappointed that the records from the case studies don't appear to have been confirmed by anyone other than Dr Newton.

---

148 Brian Weiss, "Brian L. Weiss, M.D.," Brian Weiss, 2024, https://www.brianweiss.com/.

I love the concept and the stories that Dr Newton describes; My general impression from reading Journey of Souls was that the stories seemed real, but I also got the sense that some of the details later in the book may have involved a bit of creative license. I really don't know. I sent two requests to the Newton Institute asking if the case studies were corroborated but received no reply.

According to the *Newton Institute* website[149], Dr Newton held a PhD in counselling psychology and was professionally trained and certified in hypnotherapy. I assume, also had significant professional and personal integrity to maintain. (I wrote to the Newton Institute twice, asking for any corroborating evidence of the case studies in Dr Newton's books, but never received a response that I am aware of.) I will state again that a lack of corroboration does not necessarily mean something is untrue; I am just disappointed that recordings or notes were not directly corroborated because I would love to believe these stories. If the purpose of this book was to find something that resonates with me, *Journey of Souls* does so.

According to Newton, based on his case studies and recordings of patients under hypnosis, during the journey after death, we progress through a series of reincarnations over thousands of years, advancing through different levels of spiritual growth. Hopefully, every time our spirit returns and experiences another life, we grow in wisdom, gain new insights, increase in compassion, learn to overcome envy and bigotry, and, eventually, cope with pain and suffering in better ways. Also, during lifetimes that are less fortunate, we gain insights that help us understand

---

149 Michael Newton Institute. "Home Page." Michael Newton Institute, 2025. https://www.newtoninstitute.org.

things such as childhood trauma, perseverance, hardship, and resilience. We all have baggage, traumas, and histories that have affected us. Still, the critical takeaway is that if we, as humans, had not had these experiences, we would not have the spiritual understanding and growth we have achieved and would not be able to help others on their own spiritual journey. During the spiritual journey after death, the process that we go through helps us review and assess growth in our past life as well.

During these many cycles of reincarnation and subsequent evolution of the soul in the spirit world between lives, souls at different developmental levels are represented by different colours. From beginner to advanced, the visual representation of one's soul progresses from a white light to yellow to different shades of blue to eventually being represented by a radiant, deep-purple glow. Souls who have gone through thousands of years of development to reach this ultimate stage are called *overseers*. These souls possess great wisdom and offer guidance to others. The wiser you get over these cycles of reincarnation, the closer your soul gets to what is called:

The Source of all beings in Dr Newton's book is not described as a person but more of a collective energy that all beings and creation share.

Helping people connect more fully with their inner selves or spiritual cores is a fundamental trait of any good therapist. Understanding one's inner voice, assisting people to live a more authentic existence and dealing with demons are standard phrases used in therapy. But why do we not take these ideas seriously? Indeed, we all sense there is more to ourselves than a body and a mind! To many, that inner voice is more than just a signal from our brain or years of subliminal programming.

That voice represents the true soul within us. Like many of his peers, Dr Newton considered the act of assisting clients to reach their inner selves an essential part of his work, and he helped his patients connect with their souls through a form of deep hypnotherapy.

Throughout *Journey of Souls,* the soulful self within is revealed, and Newton explains the journey experienced after death and how the soul interacts with the mind and body of its physical form when not between lives. Toward the end, Newton describes reincarnation, when our soul is finally returned to Earth (or some other planet with intelligent life) to embark upon the process through which we select our next life. His descriptions of this subject often seem too intricate to believe, and my scepticism grew somewhat, but I remain open to the concepts he describes. Still, according to the book, as souls, we are involved in this selection process to some degree and have a certain level of knowledge that provides us with a sense of purpose regarding the further development of not just our souls but the souls of those around us as well. In short, we choose our bodies to further our learning goals for a reason.

Sometimes, we choose a body that will be damaged at some stage in the future, suffer a terrible illness, or overcome significant physical hurdles—all of which are designed to allow us to experience a learning path to hasten our soul's development. One of Newton's subjects described choosing to be crippled as a way *to gain intellectual concentration.* She *became a listener and thinker and felt guided by an internal power.* In another previous life, she reported being a Nordic man with great strength and ability who was never sick. But, as Newton explains, this is where karma enters into the equation. If a soul chooses one extreme—such as being born as a crippled child—in a future or prior reincarnation, this will be counterbalanced with an opposite choice to even out the soul's development.

To me, one of the deepest and most profound of Dr Newton's conclusions from working with hundreds of people describing their soul's journey is this:

> ***The real lessons of life are learned by recognising and coming to terms with being human. Even as victims, we are beneficiaries because it is how we stand up to failure and duress that really marks our progress in life. Sometimes, one of the most important lessons is to learn to let go of the past.***[150]

Reading this statement from *Journey of Souls* seems so accurate and appropriate for anyone who has suffered loss! Is it possible that part of one's dharma (or educational purpose of the soul) in life is to learn to grow through the deep, terrible, overwhelming darkness that overcomes you when you lose a child or other loved one? Was Harrison's soul journey explicitly designed to bring joy to me and to the thousands of other people with whom he came in contact over his 20 short years? And, at the same time, in some wondrous karmic lesson of the universe, was I given the opportunity to balance all that joy with a huge opportunity to overcome the pain of his loss and move forward to make a difference in his name? Do those who read this book have the same opportunity?

---

150 Michael Newton, Journey of Souls: Case Studies of Life Between Lives, 1st ed (St. Paul, Minn: Llewellyn Publications, 1994),

We all search for meaning to make the terrible loss we experienced more tolerable. We, as people on the other side of the death equation, can spend years tormenting ourselves with thoughts like, *Surely, his or her death was not just random!* Or, *How could such a lovely life be taken for no reason?* We look for answers, reasons, and explanations so that this tragedy can make sense. But perhaps it doesn't!

Suppose I were to fully believe the logic set out in *Journey of Souls*. In that case, I might say that my journey of experiencing the grief of losing a son was a karmic balancing of the events of a prior life that was void of such pain or a life in which I caused this same pain for the parents of others, and, therefore, it's all part of the soul's growth process. Even though I love the concept of Harrison's soul living on and undergoing the journey described in the book, the pain does not go away; it only recedes.

This is all good news, of course. Most of these case studies suggest that **when our soul leaves our physical body, we will feel a euphoric sense of freedom and brightness**. (This is similar to the majority of reports about near-death experiences that will be discussed shortly.)

> *Unlike those of us left behind, those who have recently died are not as devastated as we are because they realise there is a spirit world, and they will eventually be reunited with the people left behind.*

Unfortunately, we, the grieving ones, live in pain if we do not have a firm belief to lean on. Even if we do, we are still grieving our loss and access to the person who has passed. In doing so, are we just feeling sorry for ourselves? I think that's a question worth pondering over a good beer or two in a rowdy pub someday! Maybe when I order that pint or two, a few more years will have passed since my loss. With the beliefs I've established during my journey of writing this book, I'll eventually be able to stand up in that pub, tap my glass to get everybody's attention, announce I am buying a round for everyone in the place, and declare:

> *"This week, I finished a book I began after my son Harrison died. He lived a short but remarkable life, and his spirit continues to guide me. Please join me in raising a glass to his memory—and to the light he brought into the world. His memory, his energy and spirit live on. Of that, I'm certain."*

I am not ready to make that toast yet, but *Journey of Souls* has put me a step closer. It gives me great comfort to think that if these stories are true, my son did not undergo pain and suffering when transitioning out of this world. Instead, he experienced a peaceful transition in which his soul met a guide. That guide led him to a peaceful, majestic, infinite dimension.

Harrison went to sleep and left this life in his girlfriend's arms. He was a kind, passionate, loving boy, and his death was not traumatic, as far as we know. I expect—or certainly hope—that his transition was genuinely peaceful and lovely. In that way, at least, we were fortunate!

According to Newton's book, after we die, our soul reviews the life we just lived, our recent growth, and rejoins a group of souls similar in development and spiritual growth. These souls are met and embraced with a feeling that is like being wrapped in a bright-light blanket of love. If I had to lose my boy, this is the type of journey I would want him to have experienced when he left me.

Near-Death Experiences

In one of the very many interesting video interviews that I researched for this book, Dr Peter Fenwick, an aging but clearly intelligent gentleman, sat comfortably in what one can imagine to be a warm and somewhat quaint English country cottage. His overly long silver hair makes him look a little bit like a crackpot, but the clarity of his words quickly reverses the assumption. Additional credence, if needed, is presented as a long list of credentials that follows his name. He is a neuropsychiatrist who has studied near-death experiences (NDEs) for years and believes that consciousness is something that exists outside the brain. According to Fenwick, there is enough evidence to believe that consciousness can exist independently of the brain's functionality. Still, the big question is whether the brain creates that consciousness, or it is just a filter of sorts that interprets input from something outside itself, such as an altered reality. (At the time of this writing, a fascinating video of Dr Fenwick's interview is available on YouTube.[151])

So what do we see and think when we die, and what is the experience like?

151 *What Really Happens When You Die: End-of-Life Phenomena*. Thanatos. TV, 2018.

The near-death experience research that Dr Fenwick carried out and mentions in his book (co-authored with Elizabeth Fenwick), *The Art of Dying*[152], suggests that, in our culture, what people generally experience in a near-death episode is a journey along a tunnel of light where they meet a being of light, go into a transcendental reality of some sort, and meet dead relatives or people they have previously known. Many then come to a gate that they enter if they are going to die.

Dr Fenwick carried out a lot of personal research and discovered that it is nurses who are present for the vast majority of NDEs as well as actual deaths, not doctors. First, according to many reports by these nurses, an individual often may have a premonition that they will die soon.

A few weeks before they die, they may experience visits from relatives who have previously passed away, such as parents, siblings, or, occasionally, someone they don't know. Dr Fenwick also says that a few people (around 3%), also see spiritual beings at the door or outside a window. (Tibetan Buddhist teachings suggest that people may become aware of approaching death well in advance.)

Eventually, most people come to terms with the fact that they are going to die and will have to start giving everything up soon. People who accept that they are dying and do not resist that outcome have a much easier transition in the dying process. According to Dr Fenwick, if one does not come to terms with the fact that they must give up everything, there is a lot more struggle and conflict.

---

152 Peter Fenwick and Elizabeth Fenwick, *The Art of Dying* (London: Continuum, 2008).

(The Dalai Lama has said that we get the feeling that we will soon die, as early as two years beforehand, and our behaviour changes as a result.)

Close to the time of departure, there are often episodes of sudden lucidity in which a person who has been bedridden or even unconscious sits up in bed and says goodbye to the people around them. Interestingly, even people who have lost their memory years before may do this and recognise their relatives. Several intriguing experiences are recorded and mentioned in Dr Fenwick's book, including:

- Deathbed visions of people appearing who are not there.
- A bright light appearing to people in the room just after the moment of death. Thirty-five per cent of nurses interviewed by Dr Fenwick reported having seen this light. Sometimes, one or more people in the room at the time see it, and others do not. (My Aunt Gay experienced the same light).
- Shapes leaving the body, like smoke rising or a mirage.
- A clock and/or watches stopping.
- Cats or other animals howling at the time of death.
- Birds appearing at the windowsill.

I was struck by the insight from Dr Fenwick and others' research on consciousness, which shows that those nearing death who can let go of their attachment to the self often go through a stage of awakening. During this, they shed their previous life narrative and stay in the present instead of dwelling on the past or future. (This closely resembles the Buddhist idea of not attaching to the ego.) As they approach death, they tend to become increasingly content and reach a transcendent state of non-duality. Non-duality is a concept common in major religions, describing a blissful state where one loses the sense of *I* as a separate entity and instead feels one with the surrounding world, not apart from it. According to Dr Fenwick, the more self-centred a person has been throughout their life, the harder it is for them to relinquish everything and accept the dying process peacefully. (I know a few people who may find this transition challenging, unfortunately.)

After we die, he points out the fascinating fact that NDEs in different cultures vary significantly. The journey of the Japanese generally involves reaching a dark river and finding a boatman to cross it. The NDEs of hunter-gatherers often involve a journey down a river to an island. In the West, NDEs frequently include tunnels and a bright light. Dr Fenwick says these differences result from a combination of cultural upbringing and worldview.

> *If there is a path that we all follow after we die, why would people's NDEs from different nationalities be so different from one another. Shouldn't they all be the same?*

At first, I thought this difference in experience supported the more scientific theory that most of the phenomena we experience during the dying process are generated by our brain. If our bodies and brains are wired to provide a version of reality that makes the journey comfortable, then these differing experiences across cultures would make sense and support that theory.

But having said that, if, as many scientists suggest, the white light and tunnel that Westerners see is actually caused by influences on the brain, such as oxygen deprivation and/or disruptions in the visual cortex and optic nerve, shouldn't exactly the same experience take place in all humans, regardless of location and culture? (To make this more confusing, the following section discusses another study by Dr Pim van Lommel, a medical doctor and researcher, that actually emphasises more cross-cultural similarities than Dr Fenwick.) In either case, Neuroscientists would probably answer that question by saying the raw neurological effects are similar, but the brain interprets them differently due to cultural programming.

> *My totally unqualified opinion is that these differences in cultural experiences after we die suggest that a purely scientific explanation of what we experience is less likely. To me, they support the argument that there are, in fact, more spiritual influences at work.*

~

I initially went to Amazon to find books dealing with near-death experiences. My search produced well over 200 books on the subject, which was daunting. Fortunately, there is no shortage of people who have had these experiences and want to share them nor of authors who wish to summarise some of the thousands of accounts by people who have come back from death (or thought they had).

In seeking clarity from a peer-reviewed scientific journal instead, one of the first articles I uncovered was in the *Annals of the New York Academy of Sciences*. It was written by Dr Pim van Lommel, a Dutch author, cardiologist, and researcher in near-death studies. The following opening statement in the article struck me:

There are good reasons to assume that our consciousness, with the continuous experience of self, does not always coincide with the functioning of our brain: enhanced or nonlocal consciousness, with unaltered self-identity, apparently can be experienced independently from the lifeless body.[153]

Pim van Lommel's well-researched article explores NDEs in survivors of cardiac arrest and challenges the conventional belief that consciousness is solely a product of brain activity. Differing slightly from Dr Fenwick's view, Pim van Lommel's article reports that research shows NDEs occur globally and share common elements, including out-of-body experiences (OBEs), visions of tunnels, bright lights, life reviews, and encounters with deceased relatives.

Dr Lommel was part of a Dutch research team that studied 344 cardiac-arrest patients from 1988 to 1992. The researchers found that 18% reported NDEs; yet no medical explanation (oxygen deprivation, drugs, or brain damage) could account for why some experienced them while others did not. Notably, some patients vividly described their surroundings even during periods when measurable brain activity was absent (they had a flat EEG—electroencephalogram), raising questions about whether consciousness can exist independently of the brain.

Near-death experiences profoundly transform the individual, often resulting in a reduced fear of death, increased belief in an afterlife, and heightened empathy.

---

153 Pim van Lommel, "Near-Death Experiences: The Experience of the Self as Real and Not as an Illusion," Annals of the New York Academy of Sciences 1234, no. 1 (October 2011): 19–28, https://doi.org/10.1111/j.1749-6632.2011.06080.x.

What actually happens in our brains as we die?

Of course, as they would, scientists and doctors who have trouble imagining the possibility of a nontangible soul and life after death suggest that these experiences reported by people who have physically died and returned to life are simply imagined. Some scientists suggest that many of our near-death experiences are generated from the parts of the brain near the brain stem. The supposition is that, along with other explanations such as oxygen deprivation and a sudden increase in brain activity, chemicals are released into our system at the time of death to help make the experience of death less traumatic and harrowing.

In my continuing investigations into the nature of NDEs, the first article I will reference was published in *Scientific American* in 2011 by Charles Q. Choi. It simplifies the research of neuroscientist Dean Mobbs at the University of Cambridge's Medical Research Council Cognition and Brain Sciences Unit. Mobbs, along with Caroline Watt at the University of Edinburgh, detailed this research in an online publication dated August 17, 2011, in *Trends in Cognitive Sciences.*[154] The article points to previous research showing that many perceptions—such as the OBEs that many people report during NDEs—can be reproduced by stimulating different parts of the brain. I found the results of this research compelling in their explanation of what occurs during an NDE. But unfortunately, I am not a scientist, and my interpretation of the reports I read does not seem conclusive enough to rule out anything else going on that may be spiritual.

---

154 Dean Mobbs and Caroline Watt, "There Is Nothing Paranormal About Near-Death Experiences," Trends in Cognitive Science 15, no. 10 (October 2011): 447–49, https://doi.org/10.1016/j.tics.2011.07.010.

If scientists believe that chemicals and brain activity produce all the experiences described by those who survive NDEs, it seems surprising that there is not more evidence for these scientific theories. The only proof we have about what happens after the body dies seems to come from the first-hand experiences of those who have returned to us after clinical death. That's why, to me, learning from the thousands of NDEs is so critical to understanding what happens next.

Fortunately, some recent evidence opens a new window into the brain's activity as we die. A result released in 2022 was obtained accidentally when an 87-year-old patient undergoing an ECG died from a heart attack. An EEG (electroencephalogram) was in progress at the same time, recording 900 seconds of brain activity before, during, and immediately after his death. The results provide insights into the brainwave activity that took place during those 15 minutes. According to an original research article published in *Frontiers in Aging Neuroscience*[155] in February 2022 and then later summarised in a more easily accessible press release to Scimex,[156] the organiser of the study, Dr Ajmal Zemmar, concluded the following:

Something we may learn from this research is: although our loved ones have their eyes closed and are ready to leave us to rest, their brains may be replaying some of the nicest moments they experienced in their lives.

---

155 Raul Vicente et al., "Enhanced Interplay of Neuronal Coherence and Coupling in the Dying Human Brain," Frontiers in Aging Neuroscience 14 (February 22, 2022): 813531, https://doi.org/10.3389/fnagi.2022.813531.

156 Frontiers Media Release, "Does Our Life Flash before Our Eyes during Death?," Scimex, February 22, 2022, https://www.scimex.org/newsfeed/does-our-life-flash-before-our-eyes-during-death.

The original report, simplified in terminology I could understand, shows that the brain may coordinate a therapeutically beneficial response during the dying process. This may help explain why people who have NDEs often remember vivid details from their current or past lives. The fluctuations seen, especially in the gamma band, might be the brain's last attempts to retrieve memories and recreate essential events from the person's life right before they die. This finding calls into question what people thought they knew about when life ends and supports the recollections that so many survivors of NDEs have relayed to us.

These are very credible and interesting conclusions. It is nice to know that when we die, the transition to death is not an unpleasant one. But those same very comforting conclusions do not, in my mind, undermine my support for the belief that our souls undergo a journey after we die and might live on. This may indeed be the case, but it seems likely that the first part of the journey that survivors of NDEs have described is likely (as scientists suggest) more because of physical stimulation or reactivity of the brain than a total body experience separated from the earthly body (and brain) that the soul inhabits.

It's worth noting that the same study also alerts us to some ethical implications for medicine—especially regarding organ donation—when we now know that the brain continues to show activity for a while after we die. (Unfortunately, I selected *Organ Donor* on my latest driver's license renewal!)

On Life After Death: Elisabeth Kubler-Ross

To further explore the insights from those who have left our world or been pronounced clinically dead and returned, I turned to another of the hundreds of books on this subject: ***On Life After Death***[157] by Elisabeth Kubler-Ross. Dr Kubler-Ross and her associates claimed that they investigated over 20,000 near-death experiences, both of those who returned from being dead and those experiencing the process of death who then died. The results contained data from around the world. The circumstances of death were varied, with nearly half the NDEs resulting from a sudden loss of life, many on the operating table and others who were murdered or took their own life. Although many knew they were going to die and others did not, the consistency in the recollection of what happened during the dying process and after was remarkably consistent.

Dr Kubler-Ross and her team concluded that there were many common denominators among those subjects who recalled what happened during their period of death. (Not everyone who has an NDE recalls what happened to them; Kubler-Ross likens this to the fact that we all have dreams, but only some of us recall them.) The narratives she describes, both those she experienced personally and through her research of recorded instances around the world, are so moving and precise that I am fully convinced that her conclusions are in all probability what I expect to experience when I die and what my son experienced during his last moments in the arms of his girlfriend before his heart stopped.

157 Elisabeth Kübler-Ross, On Life After Death (Berkeley: Celestial Arts, 1991)

Whether the following sequence of events actually happens, or if we just think and feel they happen, makes no difference to me. I believe this is the experience of death... and it is not bad. Among those who were able to recall their dying and death, the majority had strikingly similar experiences. For this reason, Dr Kubler-Ross stated that she firmly believes this is what happens:

1. At the time of death, we all will experience a separation from the physical body of an ethereal being or spirit—what many describe as having an out-of-body experience
2. When we leave the physical body, there is an absence of fear, anxiety, or dread.
3. We feel whole in ourselves and have total awareness of the environment around us from the point of view of an observer. (There are thousands of documented experiences in which people have returned to life and describe in great detail what was taking place at the time of their death as seen from a distance, providing specifics that could not possibly have been known to them. Most of what they remembered occurred at a time when there was no measurable brain activity. Even blind subjects have been able to describe such details.)
4. During this out-of-body journey, we experience people around us to guide us and help with the transition. In short—we are never alone when we transition through death.

I found it refreshing that a scientist such as Dr Kubler-Ross directly acknowledged how difficult it is for any of us to conceptualise a realm beyond the traditional three-dimensional world that we experience daily. I do not have a PhD, but my way of expressing this is to repeat Dr Amanda Wiart's quote—***We don't know what we don't know.*** A professor named Mark Mumby, with whom I was on a retreat recently and who *does* have a PhD, had a much more intricate way of saying the same thing:

> *Our mind is a contextual engine that can't understand things that it can't put into context from the knowledge base it already has.*
>
> ~ Mark Mumby, PhD

Yes, it is hard to put into context and believe the findings and conclusions of the experts cited in this chapter and throughout this book, but if you are able to think outside the perception of the world as we know it and be open to the possibilities, you can really start to feel a lot better about the process of death and what happens to us afterwards.

It is fascinating to me that although there are cultural differences in some cases regarding our initial experiences while dying, what has been reported as happening next is overwhelmingly similar from many different accounts and sources. Apparently, after we die and are greeted by our guide, friend, or previously lost family member, most report passing through a gate, a tunnel, or a valley with a bright light beyond. Many believe this bright light is God, a definition that varies by region and personal beliefs.

According to Kubler-Ross (as in *Journey of Souls*), after our guides and guardian angels meet us, we pass through a symbolic transition. Often, people describe this transition as a beautiful white brightness at the end of a tunnel with the sensation of approaching something grand and all-encompassing. Kubler-Ross, in her near-death experience, passed through a beautiful valley filled with colourful flowers.

Although I have been accused of having a substantial ego, if given the chance, I will do my best to leave that ego behind, accept this transition, and embark on what I believe is another journey ahead of me—one which, fortunately, may involve seeing my son again. Or at least his soul and energy.

* * *

One Sunday morning, about seven years after Harrison's death, I found myself listening to a moving song by Mazzy Star called *Fade into You*. I was driving home after a night with a woman, and I knew the relationship would not last. Unexpectedly, tears started to flow from my eyes and down my cheeks. It wasn't because I was ending a relationship with that particular person; that was instinctively the right move. For some other reason, I was suddenly overcome with deep sadness and didn't understand exactly why. It is still hard not to cry when a feeling of emptiness rises out of the blue, even eight years after losing my son. Fortunately, it is just on occasion now, and most of my feelings no longer evoke that sense of profound emptiness and loss.

Luckily, just as my eyes started to tear up, my beautiful daughter texted me to say she was listening to our favourite song, *Cold Heart*, by Elton John and Dua Lipa. Her message woke me from my sadness and reminded me of the many things I am glad of, even after losing my son. (I know that our favourite song is about breaking up, but it's also about calm after loss, detaching from the grief a little, and moving on. It actually wouldn't matter what the lyrics say; it is our joint song, and it reminds me that I enjoy my daughter's love.)

> *If you are ever feeling down, play Cold Heart or another song you love, and dance around the room with abandon. You will cry as I do, but with any luck, the tears of sadness will be mixed with a healthy dose of happiness.*

Was the grief that suddenly hit me on that drive home the result of a lapse in judgment caused by a desire to fill my personal *existential void* that was created from the loss of my son? I don't know… but I realise that when these feelings overwhelm me, I should embrace and acknowledge the sadness rather than run from it. My daughter's well-timed text not only saved me in that moment, but it also reminded me to appreciate the good things—like 20 great years with Harrison and 28 with my lovely daughter. Even though we have suffered a loss, it helps sometimes to list the things we are grateful for and not to focus on what we no longer have. It is part of survival and recovery… I hope!

* * *

As stated before, there are so many near-death experiences and books written about them that the premise of our going to another place and having some sort of spiritual journey speaks for itself. The only other proof we could expect would be undeniable communication from the other side that we could rely on. I could not find any such evidence.

However, I did find a couple of books with titles that suggested such proof, so I took a look at them.

Life after death: Is there evidence?

In my search for an answer to that question, I started looking for popular books that offered an answer and could present actual proof. One of the most popular books out there has over 600 reviews on Amazon and uses the word *evidence* in the title. I could not wait to read it. Unfortunately, my enthusiasm vanished when I read the Introduction. The whole premise of this book seemed to be that if there is no life after death, there is no meaning to our lives on Earth, and we can therefore only feel despair! (Ergo, there must be life after death for there to be meaning to our lives here.) Wouldn't it be nice if such simplistic reasoning were justification that there must be more to our existence? (I deleted the title from this section because I don't want to speak ill of another author's book.)

Even if, during the writing of this book, I have not found sufficient evidence that we actually go to another place, I need a better premise than the one the author laid out in his Introduction. I need some reasoning that actually makes sense to me, so the hope I have that my son's soul lives on seems practical to me. The author's premise did not provide that reasoning. As is the case with all the authors and speakers who try to justify a belief in Christianity or other major religions, the basic premise seems very flawed.

It really upsets me to think that there are people out there who preach that for our life to have meaning here on earth, we must believe in a God greater than ourselves. There is nothing wrong with choosing to believe in God, but doing so because you are told that life is meaningless without God doesn't sit well with me. Nor do I think it is appropriate to consider your loved one's life meaningless or that he or she didn't go to Heaven if you don't believe in God. It took me a few years to start to gain a bit of clarity after my cloud of grief. Eventually, I began to realise that even though we are in pain and looking for answers, or feel like we are not whole and possibly believe life is not worth living

> *It's better to not give up on the memory and knowledge of how beautiful you are inside and how lovely and wondrous life is on this Earth—or was before you lost that special person! That strength inside us is still there; the world is extraordinary and full of opportunities. It is hard for us to see this when we are grieving, but it is all still there.*

Proof of Heaven by Dr Eben Alexander

Unlike the first book I found in my quest to prove life after death that I mentioned above, *Proof of Heaven*[158], by neurosurgeon Eben Alexander , was a much more enjoyable journey into the subject of an afterlife. At one point in his life, Dr Alexander became critically ill from a severe and rare form of meningitis that effectively shut down his neocortex (the part of the brain that creates thoughts and makes us human). During his illness, Dr Alexander was in a coma for close to a week.

While in the coma, he had an NDE. There are hundreds of thousands of accounts of NDE's going back hundreds of years, but what is significant and different about Eben Alexander's experience is that it could not be explained as most near-death experiences have been. The big difference in Alexander's case

158 Eben Alexander, *Proof of Heaven: A Neurosurgeon's Journey into the Afterlife* (New York: Simon & Schuster, 2012).

is that it was not his death that created his after-death journey; he was alive.

Alexander's experience included common NDE phenomena such as seeing a bright light, travelling with a guide, and entering different levels of consciousness that he thought represented heaven or another universe. He described this as something more than the experience we have in the world when we focus on the physical body and the mental aspects of our brain. Because his neocortex was effectively shut down, he postulates in the book that the journey he took would only have been possible if our consciousness is separate from our physical body and brain. The opinions of other neurosurgeons in the book confirm his premise. (Doctors that I know who have read the book also feel his assumptions are valid, but other neurologists dispute whether his assumptions are entirely valid.)

Before his coma, Alexander, like most people in the medical profession, focused on the body and the mind, which can be explained through science. Dr Alexander's perspective changed after his NDE while in a coma. According to *Proof of Heaven*, one of his biggest takeaways was that he realised the universe is much larger than it appears when we look only at its immediately visible parts. In the book, he states:

> *Each of us is intricately, irremovably connected to a larger universe. It is our true home, and thinking that the physical world is all that matters is like shutting oneself up in a small closet and imagining that there is nothing else beyond it.*
>
> ~ Dr Eben Alexander

I found Dr Alexander's realisation compelling. It is similar to Deepak Chopra's premise, which I have mentioned previously. Chopra believes…

We are spiritual beings having a human experience. Not physical beings who occasionally have spiritual experiences.

I now agree.

Souls Among Us

When I first started writing this brief section on December 19th, 2023, the seventh anniversary of Harrison's passing was approaching; he died on the morning of December 31st, 2016. Writing just a few hundred words each day has given me the emotional confidence to think I might actually finish a reasonable book someday. I guess you, as the reader, will let me know if I was successful! If you have found this book helpful in any way, please drop a review wherever you bought it, hopefully at LighthouseLaneBooks.com. But if not, a review on Amazon would be greatly appreciated. Reviews and referrals really matter to an author.

Far more important than reviews and selling books has been the achievement of moving forward after a tragedy, finding purpose after loss and putting my feelings out there, which has given me hope that perhaps I will have one less regret on my deathbed. The more profound unspoken hope is that perhaps I reach a more meaningful level of achievement in this life if I can help even one person through the terrible time after losing someone close. I don't wish the terrible darkness of losing a child on anybody else. If, through this book, I can hold someone's hand and help them out of that darkness, the thousand hours or so spent writing it will have been worthwhile.

Almost exactly two years later, on December 21st 2025, on a third rewrite of this book, I revisited this chapter. With a hot cup of my morning brew, I picked *Classical Mix* on a streaming service and sat at my computer once again. The music seemed fitting for a cold, rainy day, sitting on my lovely little floating home looking out across Richardson Bay, just north of San Francisco. A beautiful piano solo, ***Habito***, performed by Lupe Sinsonte, began. Looking out across the bay at the misty hills and fog drifting down through the valleys of Mt. Tamalpais and across the heavy traffic of a distant highway, I was struck by the beauty of life. The simplicity of my tiny perch, gazing across a glassy bay, watching waterbirds and raindrops and listening to this beautiful music, was in total contrast to the energy of people passing by on that road that disappears into the mist. I don't think I would have felt the same way two years prior!

Had it really taken me nine years to get back to this state of ephemeral admiration for the beauty around us and the lives we navigate within it? Of course, I still miss and grieve for Harrison, but I know his spirit surrounds me and always will—his smile is always in my thoughts and his laughter a part of me. Yes, I shed a tear while writing this, as I'm sure you still do when thinking about the beauty of the person you lost and how they aren't here to share this moment with you. But now, certainly, when revisiting this chapter, I have grown to believe they are here and always will be if you love them. They are not truly lost to us; their soul and energies have simply moved on. But we get to keep the feeling of their presence—I absolutely believe that death isn't the end, but where is the proof that a soul continues, and the ability to interact with us?

Personal Stories

A Communication from Harrison

Light snow crawled across the windscreen as beams of ragged yellow light illuminated a white road against a gloomy, grey night. Red brake lights from the car ahead of us appeared and then disappeared as our car slowly made its way up a mountain highway toward Lake Tahoe, deep in a snowstorm, with 10-mph traffic. I sat in the front passenger seat, my ex-wife, Gail, was driving, and our lovely daughter Jacqueline was in the back.

It was our annual pilgrimage of a sort, around three years after Harrison's death and another attempt to be together and support each other around the difficult time between Christmas and New Year's when Harrison was killed. Together, late at night, stuck in a car, in a worsening snowstorm, we started to listen to some of Harrison's songs. Amazing lyrics that opened a door to his heart and soul filled our senses. A tear and an occasional smile were the only outward expressions that interrupted our self-imposed silence. Sadly, lyrics that I hadn't spent enough time truly listening to when he was alive had much more meaning now that he was gone. We listened to Harrison's songs for at least 30 minutes and absorbed often cryptic but always heartfelt lyrics like these from his many songs:

> ***With passion and love, I'm going to speak my mind till my passion is done.***
>
> ***In these verbs, I keep a piece of my soul, a piece of my heart.***

If you can't rock with it, then you can't feel my art.

Speak My Mind[159], Harrison Subversive Dunnett

* * *

I'm painting pictures of hope. If I died today, I wouldn't even care. If you're doing what you love, they're going to feel it everywhere.

From the Bay[159] , Harrison Subversive Dunnett

* * *

I have been thinking about my life and what it could have been .

If I would have made the right decisions and should have did, been a little bit smarter or less impulsive.

I aint realised till I pushed my fam away, and it's repulsive,

Because sometimes the ones we love most are the ones who don't care,

and the ones we trust are the ones who aint there.

So play this when you are lonely, I can be your homey.

---

159 Harrison Subvers!ve Dunnett, *Speak My Mind, From the Bay, and Grindin*, Subversive Music, https://linktr.ee/subversivemusic.

If you stressin, learn your lesson, life a blessin, I be phoney.

Grindin[159], Harrison Subversive Dunnett

It seemed so appropriate that the three of us together should pay homage to Harrison and his lyrics in this way, and we all felt closer to him as a result. So rarely do we have the opportunity to sit in concentrated effort and connect with Harrison. It was a great thing, and I don't recall us ever doing it together for so long or in an environment with virtually no distractions. Nevertheless, after a while, Jacqueline started to feel sad and asked if we could change the music. Gail obliged and changed the input from her phone to the car radio.

A new song started to play on the FM station, and the mood lifted for about 30 seconds. And then, mid-song, the car's input changed back to the Bluetooth connection, and one of Harrison's songs started to play. Jacqueline and I looked at each other and then at Gail, smiling, assuming she had changed it using one of the media buttons on the wheel. She just looked at us in return with a serious and clearly surprised expression and gave an almost imperceptible sideways nod without saying a word. The message was clear: the change didn't come from her, and she swears to this day that she did nothing to initiate any music input back to Bluetooth.

Being a natural sceptic, I would have dismissed it as a random hiccup in the audio system if it hadn't happened two more times in quick succession. On the latter two, I watched Gail and her hands very closely. She did nothing to make the music change back to Harrison's on either occasion. After the third time that a song on the radio was interrupted, we were all thoroughly convinced that Harrison, or the universe, in some way had just sent us a message. We had summoned this connection unintentionally, I suppose, through our combined thoughtfulness and concentration on Harrison's wonderful songs and the memories they brought.

We were rewarded with what was my only direct connection to what I believe to be Harrison's energy after he died. It was a chilling experience for all three of us and was instrumental in my desire to understand further the possibilities that our soul, or some form of energy resulting from it, lives on after the death of our body.

Vasco

These little stories are anecdotal at best, but we all have them. I'm sure you have some or know of friends who do. As I was telling the story about what happened to Gail, Jacqueline, and me in the car to a friend of mine, Paul, he didn't even let me finish before his enthusiasm to share his personal encounter took over. His encounter was so inexplicable and impactful to him that he still recalls it 15 years later. He was almost on the edge of his seat wanting to share it with me. He had a couple of great stories, and this is the first:

"*Vasco is happy about the way you are taking care of your mother*" were the chilling words he heard over the phone one evening 20 years ago that have found a place so vividly in the recesses of his memory. They were chilling because Vasco was the name of his father, who had died a few years before the call. And Paul was, in fact, looking after his mother and making sure the last few months of her life were as comfortable as a loving son could make them.

Hearing the words would have made sense if the word *would* were injected into the sentence, and it were spoken by his wife, Lyn. But the sentence wasn't *Vasco would be happy you are looking after your mother*, and the words had not come from his wife or a sibling to comfort him and say thank you. They were spoken by his nephew over the phone, whom he hardly ever talked to and who had called him out of the blue with a message from beyond.

As it turns out, Vascos' brother's son, James, who lives in San Jose, miles away, and was only encountered on the rare annual family get-togethers, had a girlfriend, Lisa, who was away somewhere travelling with her high school team. One of the other girls' mothers, who was travelling with all the girls as a chaperone, happened to be a medium of some renown who had appeared on several late-night TV shows and had decided to entertain all the girls with a I in the motel room they were staying in. This mother knew Lisa and that she had a boyfriend named Danny but had no connection with Danny and indeed no known knowledge of his uncle, my friend Paul, who lived far away.

As the six or so girls huddled together on the twin beds of a dimly lit room in the Motel 6, far removed from Paul, the mother asked them all to join hands and be silent. Then, without any semblance of logical explanation, the mother who was leading the I said, "Before we start, there is a spirit here who won't even allow me to begin unless I say something. I don't know if it will mean anything to anybody, but I am going to say it so we can move on." *Vasco is happy about the way Paul is taking care of his Mother.*

It did, in fact, mean something to Lisa, who vaguely remembered being told by her boyfriend that his uncle owned a restaurant called Vasco's somewhere in San Francisco. Immediately after the past life reading that night, Lisa called Danny and told him what had happened, asking if his uncle, who owned the restaurant, was named Paul. Danny, in turn, called his Uncle Paul and passed on the message!

Calls like the one Paul received that evening from his nephew are not easily forgotten. I can understand why Paul was so keen to share it. Occurrences like that cannot be coincidental, and to those willing to recognise it, they impress upon our memories the clear message that there is a lot more to our lives than we are aware.

Do we all have proof of an afterlife in stories like these? Probably not. But to me, they are definitely proof of something greater than ourselves. If not an afterlife or an adjoining world of soulful existence, then certainly the sheer number of these statistically improbable coincidences indicates some form of interconnectedness that we do not understand.

On one extreme, I sometimes laugh and wonder if some kid or form of AI injected a code for levity into the simulation in which we all live. My heart and more emotional brain hope for the soulful world theory, but in any case…

I am thoroughly convinced that we do not cease to exist when we die. There is definitely something beyond the plane of our simplistic understanding. There are way too many inexplicable things that go on in our lives for there not to be something else happening beyond our understanding of rational thought.

Divine Intervention

As humans, we operate, talk, walk, and interact physically. We react to input, form independent thought, and act on it. Simple, inherent flight-or-fight responses developed over thousands of years of evolution protect our bodies and influence how we work and feel. Our brains react to stimuli and signal feelings of pleasure or pain by triggering the release of chemical compounds and hormones. Endorphins relax and relieve pain; serotonin (amongst other things) creates a sense of well-being and happiness; and dopamine, oxytocin, and other compounds stimulate pleasant mental or physical sensations. But many of us believe there is more to our sense of being human than the actions of a body stimulated by chemical compounds and the thoughts generated by an evolutionary brain.

The well-known author and speaker, Deepak Chopra,[160] is fond of reminding us that…

160 Deepak Chopra LLC, "Deepak Chopra — Official Website," 2025, https://www.deepakchopra.com/.

> ***You're a spiritual being having a human experience. You're not a human being having a spiritual experience.***
>
> (Popularised by Chopra, but originated from the French philosopher/priest ~Pierre Teilhard de Chardin)

Have you ever thought, *that person came into my life for a reason*? In *Journey of Souls* (discussed in the prior section), Dr Newton explains that our earthly, soulful experience isn't just a single event but part of a larger play in which souls (within our earthly bodies) inevitably interact with each other to undertake the ongoing karmic lessons necessary for spiritual growth. This view of our life experience makes sense when considering the impact of the unique people you've encountered. Besides the obvious influence of family members who are or were a significant part of your life, most of us have met at least one person who has profoundly affected us.

I recall one such interaction vividly, and it had a profound impact on me. The following section, titled *Meeting Max and Recovery*, describes what I now feel, after years of reflection, was more of a preordained divine intervention than anything else. I seriously doubt it was a coincidence. The experience was such a pivotal moment in my life and recovery journey that I wanted to share it with you. In my mind, it also strongly supports the theory that there are souls and guardian angels that appear when needed.

Meeting Max

Did I receive divine intervention from a ***guardian angel***, or was it just another soul that helped me through the most challenging time of my life? I am not sure. We seem to become more open to the people we need in times of crisis, but I also suspect some universal force may send them. Certainly, I have been fortunate that they often seem to appear when needed the most!

On a moonlit night, only weeks after my son's death, I escaped to the hot mineral springs of the Esalen Institute on the coast of California to be alone and literally figure out if I wanted to live or die. On my first night there, I immersed myself in a dark pool of hot mineral water, poised under a star-ridden sky, and listened to the sound of crashing Pacific Ocean waves on the cliff below me; at first, I was alone, but then the silhouette of another person slipped into the pool. We started to talk in the shadows; that's when I met the soul that saved me.

* * *

Immediately after you lose someone important, you are in shock and just trying to survive. On the outside, you may look like you are coping, but inside, you are in turmoil, shock, and a state of denial.

Reading books on recovery just isn't on your radar initially, so I wasn't thinking about things like which *stage* of grief I might be in. I was just confused and in pain. A year or so later, though, I did read a book by Elizabeth Kubler-Ross and David Kessler, called *On Grief and Grieving*[161] . In the book, the authors discuss five stages of dealing with death…denial, anger, bargaining, depression, and acceptance, and then apply those same stages to the grieving process.

I didn't realize it at the time, but about three weeks after Harrison's death, I was somewhere past the initial impulse of denial yet still feeling confused and avoiding the truth of it all; the lack of access to my son's body and visual confirmation certainly extended my period of denial.

For the first few days after the terrible news, Harrison's mother, my daughter, and I stayed together in the family home. Friends came over to visit, and the days were mainly spent at the kitchen table in a cloud of confusion, pain, and denial, organising the memorial and funeral service, piecing together what

161 Elisabeth Kübler-Ross, David Kessler, and Maria Shriver, *On Grief and Grieving: Finding the Meaning of Grief Through the Five Stages of Loss* (New York: Scribner, 2014).

happened, trying to understand this terrible, devastating tragedy. Small facts started to emerge. Harrison was put on a bunch of medications… But why? He was treated as a heroin addict when he had never had heroin! He had been clean and sober, not drinking for over a month… why would he be put on numerous medications at all? And why would the heart of a perfectly healthy 20-year-old boy suddenly stop in the middle of the night when under the *care* of a rehab where he had gone to give up drinking and Xanax? He had been tested almost every day for over a month and had been clean and sober.

While seeking answers, days were also filled with tasks like sifting through 20 years of pictures to create a memorial, all the planning, and the candlelight vigil in the town square, much of which helped to avoid what had happened. Eventually, after the memorial and many tears with friends, the days started to blur into one another, and those around us returned to their own lives. Other, more distant friends called initially but didn't anymore, possibly because they didn't know what to say or do and weren't equipped to share that pain with us. Perhaps people and the support fade because they don't want to face the reality that the same thing can happen to them, or maybe they need to get back to their lives.

I have now come to realise that after the loss of a child, even though you may have a great support network, ultimately, the grief and pain are yours to own. Asking others to bear that pain for you is not fair or realistic.

Within a few weeks, the memorial was over; friends had drifted away; and I was forced, amongst the silence, to spend more time facing the reality of what had happened. An escape was needed from the feeling of tragedy, ongoing questions, pain, confusion, and despair.

> *There are only two choices when you lose someone who is a part of you: either figure out how to move forward with your life or go on living in perpetual pain. I needed to make a big decision...*

I knew I didn't and couldn't live with the sadness, so I needed to figure out how to move forward. Some friends suggested escaping to a popular retreat down the California coast called The Esalen Institute, which has plenty of room to be alone in Nature, optional meditation and yoga classes, and warm hot springs to warm you while reflecting and hiding the tears. If there was ever a time to start healing, this was it, so I booked a week of reflection, meditation, and retreat to help me try and clear the cloud surrounding me.

Esalen was advertised as the perfect retreat for internal exploration, unlimited meditation, yoga, and spiritual enlightenment, which sounded like the place for me. I just needed to escape—mainly, not talk to anybody— get away from the noise, and see if I could reconnect with myself again to figure out if the pain could be managed. You don't have to go to some expensive retreat to sit amongst trees and commune with your thoughts. If no woods are nearby, you can simply find a field or a riverbank to sit in silence. Perhaps with your face upward, trying to focus on the warmth of the sun on your skin or the feeling of the breeze in your hair, your breath... anything but the pain you have been going through! Yes, it is essential to acknowledge the grief and despair, but I think it is equally important to give yourself some escape from it.

After some delays in setting off, a stunning purple-and-deep-orange sunset accompanied me on my drive to Big Sur. It was comforting to see through the fog of my own grief and enjoy a bit of that splendour, even if only for a few moments. I pulled over several times to gaze out over the Pacific Ocean at the crimson sky as it gradually darkened to deep purple. In the quiet of my thoughts, and sometimes to Harrison's music when I could bear the tears, I watched the majestic sky unfold. The chance to stop and reflect on my own lack of will to live seemed like a scene from a surreal movie I had suddenly become a part of. As a result, I didn't reach Esalen and check in until well after dinner.

That was fine with me. The lavish terraced hot springs at Esalen are clothing optional, which means that when in the cliff-side pools of warm water, it is more of a clothes-off environment. I was slightly uncomfortable with the prospect of taking off my clothes and settling into a public hot spring with strangers, so I was okay with the late arrival. Something about the vulnerability of it all, a sense that perhaps it would be a bit creepy or something, held me back. Maybe that is why I was in no rush to get there during daylight. I am not sure, but I did know that in my current state of mind, I didn't want to join a party in a hot spring with a bunch of naked people when I arrived. I was looking for solace—nothing else.

After settling into my cabin on a bluff overlooking the ocean and grabbing a little food that was still available, it seemed late enough to minimise the interaction with others, so I set off on the short hike down the hill from my accommodation to the baths. A greater than healthy dose of cynicism combined with emotional overload didn't endear me to the thought of having a conversation about the fundamentals of Buddhism, Zen meditation, or astral projection with another naked person I didn't know! Or that's what I thought would be the conversations in a place like this. Over time, I learned that my expectations and prejudices can often be unproductive, but it is hard for us to eliminate judgment and bias from our thoughts! I am improving as time passes, but I was way off base on that occasion.

The warm, inviting, subtly lit mineral baths at Esalen are set on a cliff overlooking the Pacific where waves break like an orchestra of white foam over the boulders below. Cloudy water over 110 deg., constantly replenished from the springs above, flows down the cliff, through the baths, and eventually into the cold ocean below. When I finally did arrive, there were still a few people scattered around the four mineral pools, but luckily, not many. Since it was midweek and late, most people were up around the fire pit at the retreat a few hundred yards away.

I was alone at last, to find myself or lose myself, I wasn't sure which. Quietly, I discarded my clothes and surreptitiously waded into one of the dimly lit mineral pools. There I sat, looking up at the sky, ignoring the other couple of people who wandered in or out, and enjoying my silence and solitude.

When Max first appeared in the shadows across from me, she was just another silhouette in the dark night. A communal feeling results in those pools late at night but one where people generally respect each other's space and need for reflection. The two of us continued sitting silently, looking up at the stars, feeling the natural mineral water's warm, healing beauty, and a silent night, covered in immense darkness lit by tiny white lights above. The rhythmic sound of waves crashing below and the soothing bubbling of the spring was more than enough to fill the silence. The company of an additional shadow or two, enjoying the same experience, was enough to allow some solitude while keeping the personal loneliness from taking over. I was thankful for the occasional shapes around me, but, over time, they meandered away, except for one person.

Eventually, the other silhouette moved to change their view of the stars and, as a result, came and sat nearer to me. Far enough away to be respectable but close enough for me to make out the outline of a woman, hair pulled back with defined shapes of a neck and chiselled jaw. I expect I was just an outline with features that were equally unclear to her.

When we finally did exchange pleasantries, there was a captivating kindness and a silk-like tenderness in her voice. After speaking for a while, I remember thinking how strange it was to be so close to another person you can hardly see, naked, communicating and connecting with the power of words alone! No ego, sexual drive, or shyness… just purely an emotional and intellectual connection so rare to experience when our immediate judgments are usually based on many external factors like looks, clothes, or facial expression. Initially, there was none of that with Max: just kind, soothing conversation. That conversation weaved into a story that lasted months and still affects me all these years later.

A few minutes of conversation turned into hours under that unforgettable sky. Those few hours turned into a night lying together talking, then weeks and a journey together to try and help refugees arriving in Lesvos (Greece) from Turkey in 2017. After spending cold weeks together in a futile attempt to overcome Greek bureaucratic red tape, we eventually gave up. We travelled instead on a romantic trip to the beautiful island of Santorini, where some warmth started to slowly feed my soul and badly broken heart. But that story of some level of renewal all started with a calming, soft voice from a shadow in the middle of the night… and her first few words telling me she was a doctor who had spent over a decade working at a hospice facility, interacting daily with the journey of death and helping people with that grief.

Even though a longer-term relationship wasn't meant to be, Max was the perfect person to be my bridge forward during that time of loss. Without realising it, I needed love to help compensate for my pain, and understanding from a person in a world which few can understand. She gave me a little happiness to fill the void where all happiness used to live, a hand to hold, a smile to enjoy, hope, and a reminder that life can go on. The universe, God, or fate decided to provide that to me, and I will forever be grateful.

Was it the universe or some divine force that provided her to me, or was it just a coincidence? I don't know, but I do know she gave me the support and hope to live, love, survive, and hopefully do some good in the world. If the universe doesn't provide for you the way it did for me, perhaps you must find that partner from within! It's a challenging task, I know. I am eternally grateful that I may have met the one person in the world who was perfectly equipped to help me that fateful night. But one thing is sure during your grief: support from within and from others can be a huge aid in your recovery.

Part 4:
Recovery

Is Proof Necessary, or Is Just Faith Enough?

One lucky morning, I was sitting in business class on a plane en route from Honolulu to Sydney, Australia. Just as we were rolling down the runway and about to lift off, the lady sitting across from me grabbed her husband's hand and, with her other hand, motioned over her chest in the sign of the cross and mumbled a prayer.

I am not sure if her prayer was answered or if fate, a sound aircraft, and skilful piloting kept me alive; however, it's nice that I am sitting at my desk, years later, trying to finish this book, so something worked. I am sure, however, that after the flight, she probably thanked God for preserving her life. Her faith is all that matters to her and is very real, and that's what matters really.

I, on the other hand, during take-off, was rejoicing inside—not because God had decided not to kill me but because I was given, once more, the wonderful experience of flight as we lifted off the runway like a majestic, giant bird leaping into the air! Perhaps I should say that God had given me that opportunity as a gift. I would say that if I believed in a God who hands out pleasure, reward, and punishment like a dealer at a poker table, but I don't. Nevertheless, I acknowledge the possibility of some ultimate power that creates our world and universe, be it a software program, a collective energy, a gift of evolution that plots its path, or, as many imagine, an ultimate creator who looks over all of us. I just gave thanks for being here.

On the previous leg, from San Francisco to Honolulu, I sat next to a man named Roy. He and I began to chat, and I shared that I had recently lost my son. Roy, a big, strapping guy somewhere in his 50s, was from the Midwest and owned a car dealership or two. He was pleasant enough to talk to, seemed empathetic, and was what I had always imagined my vision of the stereotypical hardworking, effusive, American car salesman would be. He had recently lost a good friend to cancer and needed somebody to chat to. Another fellow ***road warrior*** of sorts. At his suggestion, I agreed to meet with him later for a steak at his favourite restaurant in Honolulu.

Apparently, the hour or so Roy spent in his room before meeting me (which may have included a drink or two) allowed him to meet with God. During the two hours we were apart, it seems God had instructed him to pray for me. Roy was sincere and well-meaning when we met that evening, but within a few minutes and another drink at the bar, he proceeded to preach to me as one would to a gospel congregation. His demeanour changed, and, speaking in what sounded to me like rhymes, he began to tell me that my son was still alive.

"He has not died," said Roy. "He is with God because God is with him as He is within us." Therefore, Harrison was still with me because God is inside me, and Harrison was with God. Roy assured me that *Jesus, our saviour, would never take my son from me, and he will be with me forever.*

Dumbfounded by the sudden transition in our conversation and these revelations, I was not sure how to respond. I managed to nod my head to indicate my gratitude and mumbled words of confirmation that, unfortunately, encouraged him to continue.

When I asked him, with sincerity, how he knew it was God who instructed him to pray for me and not just his moral code of ethics or his internal empathy generating this kind response, he proceeded to embark on a word soup of phrases that he had presumably heard from preachers over the years. Nevertheless, his delivery was full of conviction, and I am sure that Roy believed his words were original thoughts.

According to Roy, our thinking is not generated by our mind but by God. His earnestness was so impressive that it made me consider the following:

> *Belief, in itself and because of its strength, creates for many the same assurance as a proven fact. Do we even need proof, or is a firm enough belief structure enough to give us confidence in what we are told is true?*

I was amazed at how deeply he believed what he was saying. His beliefs were clearly unshakeable, and it was as though he expected his words to transform me through a sudden epiphany. His sermon at the bar and the words that followed did provide me with insight, but what came to me was not belief in what he was saying but, instead, the realisation that millions of seemingly normal people have been indoctrinated so consistently and deeply by religions of one form or another that they morph into a believer, a follower, or a self-proclaimed guru. Perhaps the transformation occurs when certain keywords they have heard thousands of times at church or read in their holy texts—words like *faith*, *loss*, *heaven*, and so on—are triggered. Perhaps it is just that people find profound contentment, safety, and empowerment in their deep belief. It is their touchstone, and that is why they feel required to help those around them by sharing those beliefs.

Now, after years of work on this book and my numerous, not-so-subtle criticisms of established religions, I believe that deep belief, in itself, is its own justification. To the believer, there is no need for proof of its origins or the credibility of its stories. This is, of course, what *Dance with Angels* has been all about for me—finding a belief structure that I resonate with, something I can believe in wholeheartedly to help me through this terrible time of recovery. I have found this resonance in my research and writing, and I have come to a greater understanding of the importance of simply believing. Yes, I admit, I started this journey being critical of and, in most cases, dismissing any religion or faith that could not be proven or is followed by those with what is commonly called blind faith. Looking back at my writing, I realise now that being so dismissive of others' deep faith is an arrogance of which I am not proud.

After years of thought, research, and reflection in writing *Dance with Angels* (and perhaps less anger), I am now far less likely to dismiss the empowerment and solace that people find in their faith. Even if, in my opinion, there is no underlying proof of their chosen religion and it lacks credibility, that doesn't necessarily negate its benefits.

> *I have now concluded that belief is more important than proof when searching for recovery.*

As a critical thinker, I tend to question what I read or hear more than many people do, but I am wrong to hold others to the same standard. For me, Buddhism is the structure that I seem to be drawn to of late—that and the belief that my son's energy and karma are, undoubtedly, all around me. But I do not think that others must believe this as well.

As long as someone is not being taken advantage of financially or emotionally by their religious affiliation, and it enables them to find family, a belief that feels right in their core, makes them feel loved, and gives them hope, that is much more important than finding one with credible origins. I have found that none of the world's religions completely makes sense from a practical or historically proven perspective. What is more important is finding a belief that satisfies our soul and does good for ourselves and those around us. That faith can be one we create ourselves, from the threads of numerous religions, if that's what feels better.

I aim to take the best from the religions I have studied and remove anything I find harmful. That is the belief system I wish to follow. Maybe extracting the good and discarding the bad will form the basis of a new religion and be the subject of my next book. If I go ahead with it, I might call it something like *The Book of Holos*, which comes from a Greek word meaning totality and completeness. (My *Book of Holos* will exclude the bad and the ugly and the doctrine, though.)

Positive Avoidance or Cowardice?

A philosophical discussion

Time passes, and they say it heals… But does it really, or do we just get better at ignoring the facts? It took me about five years after Harrison's passing before I could go several days without feeling pain. One evening, roughly at that five-year point, I recall being on the deck of my floating home, enjoying a sunset across the bay, standing at my BBQ alone, cooking and enjoying a balmy breeze. I remember thinking, "It's such a shame that Harrison isn't here!"

But on this occasion, the question seemed to come from an observer within me that I had not met before. I particularly remember asking this internal observer if I was starting to react a little bit more rationally to his loss this time. It certainly felt more emotionally removed from the observation but didn't understand why.

Thinking about it, I realised I had been slowly accustomed to ignoring that he isn't with me in real terms. Focusing on my memories of him and the warmth they provide sustains me now. He's gone in body, but, over time, I've somehow managed to push that thought farther into the depths of my mind and imagine he's still with me. He is, and yet he isn't! Is it avoidance or cowardice to do this? I don't know. But I do know that it seems to work for me. He is just… *with me*, and I try to avoid dwelling on the death and loss. It is as though my body and mind have decided that there is just no more room for that pain inside me.

If you have a therapist, ask them if it's okay to try this strategy. I'm not sure if it's good long-term to ignore these realities, but I know it makes my days better just to set the tragedy of his loss well aside and focus on his energy and great memories. But it does beg the question… Am I fooling myself into feeling like he is still alive by ignoring his death? I hope a therapist buys this book and decides to answer that question. I can't, but I can say that I feel a lot better now that I have moved into this new state of being.

Is faith a way of avoiding the realisation that life may be just a singular and finite existence?

The thought has occurred to me, of course, that by pretending at times that Harrison isn't dead may be just subconsciously a way of avoiding the possible reality of a singular existence and that there may be no afterlife. On this journey of discovery, I've also asked myself if the need to believe in a greater power is another way of deceiving myself. Even though they are not mutually exclusive, aren't we better off having belief and faith in ourselves first, and then a greater power if we choose to do so? Beyond the obvious reasons of needing a sense of belonging and community, I wonder why we so often want something to believe in beyond ourselves. Is that also just a way of avoiding the stark reality of a finite and solitary existence?

Is our desire to imagine something greater than ourselves, such as a creator, driven simply by a need to escape what we perceive as the limits of our average lives? For many, it's hard to deal with our struggles alone, and faith gives us the support we need. For others, it's just a way to avoid facing the possibility that we are all there is.

I've lived a fortunate life in many ways; I've avoided a tedious job by being a pilot and doing something I have loved. But for those who believe they'll never overcome their economic and emotional struggles, it's challenging to face the harsh realities of life without the hope that there's something more. Many people face the challenge of simple survival, often feeling chained to the rules and limitations that society imposes on them. It's no coincidence that across the world, poorer populations tend to report being more religious than richer ones. Is that because the ultra-poor need more hope? In my case, my desire to find a belief in something greater than myself is because of my loss, not poverty, but the desire is there. Nonetheless, in my case, I am painfully aware that a need for faith may be a deception of my own making.

It may not be your reason for believing in an afterlife, and you don't have to be poor to want to believe in God. Still, many of us do seek something more than our subconsciously disappointing existence by imagining a creator greater than ourselves, offering a new dimension of hope to enjoy on our journey through life and after it. Believing in something greater than ourselves helps us deal with the reality of our lives (or how we perceive that reality).

Regardless of anything I have said above, it is just very hard to accept a concept that life simply ends with death … that there is nothing more! It certainly isn't what I'm hoping for. I would really like to believe there's something more, but I don't think that my belief in an afterlife stems from an inability to accept that perhaps we are meaningless without that belief. It really comes from my own experience that I mentioned earlier in the book when I saw Harrison's body and knew instinctively it wasn't him. It was just his body. That, and all the cumulative examples of circumstantial evidence that I have mentioned in this book, are pretty compelling to me when I add them all together. There *is* something more!

Time to Recover

The reality is that you will grieve forever. You will not get over the loss of a loved one; you will learn to live with it.

~ Elisabeth Kübler-Ross and David Kessler, On Grief and Grieving[162]

They say time heals, and it does. In the section of this book on Buddhism, I wrote about Joe Biden's sentiment that we will someday smile at a memory of the people we have lost rather than cry. It is true, but it can be an arduous journey getting to that stage. If you are reading this book, you have been down or are looking down the same difficult road. Unfortunately, we all have to face the path through grief at some stage during our lives. It's really a question of when and under what circumstances we have to deal with grief, and that determines how long it takes to fulfil Biden's promise that someday you will smile a lot more.

For a year or two after Harrison's death, my solution for avoiding my grief and not moving down that road was drinking enough to feel numb. Often, when I sat alone in the evenings in my floating home, the beauty of that experience seemed only to deepen the feeling of loneliness and grief. Drinking three or four gin and tonics—or, occasionally, a bottle of wine—helped

162 Elisabeth Kübler-Ross, David Kessler, and Maria Shriver, *On Grief and Grieving: Finding the Meaning of Grief Through the Five Stages of Loss* (New York: Scribner, 2014).

me avoid thinking about Harrison's lost life and the future he would never get to live.

Obviously, that sort of behaviour is not the ultimate escape. It is the ultimate trap—and luckily, I managed to listen to enough self-help meditation tapes, go to enough therapy, and read enough books to avoid sliding further down into the abyss of alcoholism and pity. Perhaps starting to write this book helped me avoid that trap door. I don't know.

By late 2023, a day before my 68th birthday and three days before the seventh anniversary of Harrison's death, I had progressively managed to cut back on my alcohol intake over the preceding two years and was only having a glass or two of alcohol a week. Also, around this time, I started to have unusual, subtle ruminations on the potential for a fulfilling, exciting life ahead of me. These were only whispers coming from deep inside me when in my youth, they had been loud voices. But at least I was having those stirrings again.

I tell you this because it is true that time will help you heal and start to rebuild some of the *you* that was lost with the death of that person so close to you. I loved my boy so much that when he died, I felt I had lost most of myself. Children and those we love can occupy a huge part of our being, and when they are gone, we think we have lost that part of us as well.

But that absence within ourselves can be filled again. Eventually, we can start to feel *almost* whole and able to move forward. Certainly, in my case, I began to imagine the possibility of an exciting future. I slowly regained the self-confidence that I lost after losing my son and had to rebuild myself. Being aware that we have broken through to the beginning of some happiness and potential again is a great feeling when it finally happens. Unfortunately, it is not a straight road.

A couple of days after my birthday, I awoke around 1:30 am on the 31st of December. This was about the time my son took his last breath. I visited the bathroom and stumbled back to bed. The next morning, as I was having a coffee, I looked at my phone to find a photo of a memory candle that Harrison's mother had lit to remember our lovely boy on this auspicious anniversary of his death.

> *Sadly, I had totally forgotten that this was the morning my son died.*

As if asking for forgiveness in some way, I lit a candle, listened to some of his wonderful songs, and watched a video of him dancing and singing. Unfortunately, doing so toppled me into a full day of regret. It was not so much listening to his songs and remembering him but more that I had forgotten to acknowledge the anniversary of his death! Just when I thought I had finally broken out of the cycle of grief, I was shoved into the murky shadows of sadness again.

You would now expect me to say that I started drinking and my recovery took a huge downturn. Fortunately, that wasn't the case. As a result of the passage of time, my writing, reading, and my having developed a beginner's ability to observe my thoughts from an external perspective (perhaps as a result of meditation) helped me avoid the trap of an easy drink. Maybe the building of my personal belief strategy in this book had also helped. Fortunately, by that evening, with some rest, good food, and good company, I snapped back into a more *normal* self.

However, reflecting on that particularly sad day reminds me of how growth is never a straight line. It's like a graph of the stock market's long-term activity. It rises for a number of days or weeks, then has a short-term reversal before resuming the uptrend. (I really hope that the crash of 1929 is not just around the corner in my recovery, for now I seem to be continuing a trend upward over time.)

What I have found is that…

The more I invest in myself and believe in myself, the steeper my trajectory and growth out of grief toward happiness seems to be.

(At least this has been the case with me so far.)

<u>My personal tip for acknowledging yet working my way through periods of sadness:</u>

To get myself out of a slump—or what some may call depression—I find it helpful to begin my day with a routine that includes a shower and listening to an informative and/or motivational audiobook or podcast. The simple act of listening to somebody else's guidance gets me out of my head and into a mindset of future possibilities and dreams, or at least a glimpse of a path forward.

Also, when I slip back into grief, a period of malaise, or general unmotivation, I try to force myself to take just a couple of steps forward and complete a few things that are good for my soul, like meditating, getting exercise, and so on. Educating myself in the shower or on a walk is one of these activities.

Widening the Lens

Some therapists use an exercise called *Widening the Lens*; others call it *Context vs Content*, and most call it *The Dot Exercise*. Whatever it's called, it really helped me when I was in my darkest, most singular place early on. If you have a trained therapist, ask them whether it would be helpful for you to do it regularly.

The exercise goes something like this. Take a blank sheet of white paper and draw a small black circle about the size of a coin in the middle of the page. Now, fill in that circle, and make sure it is all black. After doing so, take a look at that piece of paper and try to grasp the reality that, because of your pain and grieving, you are in a myopic state, surrounded by darkness. Your darkness is that black dot, and you are inside it in the deepest early stages of grief. Just have faith that, eventually, you will see some light outside that black circle. Hopefully, over time, you will break out of it entirely and expand into the white part of the page—the wondrous world around you, full of possibilities, personal potential, and happiness. If I can make it out of that black circle, you can, too. (There are times I pop back into the grey boundaries of it, but I certainly see a lot more light and hope than I did in those first terrible periods of grief.)

Finding Purpose

Viktor Frankl, in *Man's Search for Meaning*, which I have mentioned already numerous times, stated that happiness is directly related to one's sense of purpose (which gives us meaning). Although he was a religious man, Frankl did not state that we must also believe in the afterlife or in a God to pursue a life of happiness. My takeaway was that…

> *We are far more likely to find joy again if we can find purpose as well.*

With my analogy of being taken by a shark in an earlier chapter, I tried to explain that I loved my boy so much that when he died, I felt I'd lost most of myself. Children and those we love and to whom we dedicate our lives can occupy a considerable part of our being, so much so that when they are gone, we feel we lose that part of us as well. But what we feel we have lost is not gone, and eventually we can start to feel whole and able to move forward. We can begin to imagine the possibility of a happy future and slowly regain the self-confidence that often disappears when we lose a loved one and have to rebuild. It is hard, but it happens.

Finding some purpose in writing this book, which I hope may help others, and in creating The Subversive Foundation (Subversivefoundation.org) has helped me. This may be why so many others who are going through grief try to help others and form charities. Purpose can really help regain some of the joy that's lost when grieving. That purpose can be as simple as sharing your experience on TikTok or reaching out to others who are suffering. I have just started trying to do more of this myself on TikTok @Warwick.Dunnett. If you want to, please follow and share your experience, and I'll do my best to respond.

Beautiful Sunsets

I am sensitive to the fact that beautiful sunsets used to make me cry, and you may be going through that stage of grief as well. If that is the case, understand that I know how terrible it feels. Even though you can't, at this stage, believe that you could ever be happy again, there is hope, I promise.

Around seven or eight years after my son's death, I decided to foster a dog so I would not feel so alone. I ended up with a beautiful, 120-pound Cane Corso (Italian Mastiff) that nobody else wanted called Sister. The poor dog had been sitting in the shelter for nearly a year! We connected immediately. After a month, we were so close that she sensed my sadness whenever I was feeling down and wouldn't leave my side. Often I sat on my sofa watching the day's end with Sister's 20-pound, massive head on my lap. The sun moved behind Mt. Tamalpais across a slowly greying bay. The sight was breathtaking, and I felt I had been given a gift to be able to watch it.

One of the regular benefits of living on the water and facing southwest is that I often get these spectacular unencumbered views of orange light beams cutting through a mist that hangs over a little town called Mill Valley. In the foreground, the houseboat where *Sitting on the Dock of the Bay* was reportedly written swayed slightly on purple water that grew darker every time I looked up. A Spotify playlist called *Peaceful Piano* was flowing out of the speaker like a wave of comfort, and a Roku gin and tonic was in my hand. An hour before, I was tense, in emotional pain, and short of breath. Suddenly, I felt better and appreciative of life.

Yes, it could have been the one gin and tonic (my limit now), or the lovely music, or the comfort of a dog! Still, feeling pleasure at last—and not tears or guilt—from such an incredible sunset made me realise I was recovering, albeit slowly. Of course, my opinion is based on the limited experience of my own recovery; however, I would like to hope that with time and enough introspection, this can happen to all of us who find or build a belief structure, find purpose, and who embrace the journey of grief rather than avoid it.

I have also been able to feel better by sitting at my keyboard and sharing how I feel with others who may have also dealt with the feeling of being distraught, lost, lonely, or in emotional pain as I was. You obviously don't have to write a book to share your thoughts and your pain though. Even if you don't have an audience, the simple act of internally verbalising your grief and allowing it to flow through you and onto a page is hugely comforting.

Indeed, in my case, it has been facing my feelings of loss and loneliness head-on that has healed me the most. A sense of community and support is also imperative, but the personal challenge of facing and acknowledging your pain internally is, in my opinion, paramount. It was finally sitting with myself and letting my pain run through me and into this manuscript that has been my most potent medicine.

Alternate Outcomes

Ever since Harrison died, there has been a thought lurking in the back of my mind, unwilling to surface for fear of being pushed back into the dark and hidden for good. It's a whisper that I don't want to speak, much less put on paper, because it somehow insinuates that the tragic death of my son was for the best… which is, in so many ways, unthinkable. It is a rationalisation that feels like a crime, like a betrayal or sacrilege. But if I am going to share honest feelings and truths, it has to be said.

Typing what I am about to say, onto my keyboard as part of this memoir now seems even worse… as if I might be in some way glad that my son had died! Obviously, I will never be glad that he is gone, but there is a possible alternate outcome that I think is important to acknowledge as part of our recovery. Eventually, after all these years, I have summoned enough fortitude to come face to face with the question…

What would really have happened if Harrison had not died? Would he have necessarily experienced a good and wonderful life?

We assume a wonderful life and future that has been taken away. I often imagine him standing on a stage, the crowd dancing, his beautiful smile like a beacon reaching across the crowd, making everybody else smile as well. Was that future assured, or could he have lived a tortured life of addiction, lost love, failure, and died alone, homeless, cold and lonely under a bridge? Or worse yet, jumped off that same bridge in an act of desperation and anguish! This type of alternate potential reality is less relevant to those who lost somebody living a well-balanced and everyday routine. That was not my son's life. He lived on the edge of any situation and emotion, not in the middle. If that does not describe the person you have lost, then skip this section because the potential for a less wonderful outcome would be less likely, I'm sure.

The pain of imagining and verbalising something so terrible as a negative outcome for Harrison is hard. However, to stay true to myself and to you, the reader, it's just as important to consider the possibility of a worse life ahead if they had lived, rather than the perfect picture we hope for and imagine. Could that have been a possible outcome? I would hope I could have helped him avoid that darker path, but I wasn't effective enough as a father to stop him from dying in an unimpressive rehab, so it's possible I wouldn't have.

Sadly, it would be wrong of me not to acknowledge that his painless death in his lover's arms might be better in some way than the future that awaited him. If I believed in God as a person who looks over us and guides our lives, I might say, "God wanted him to die painlessly in the arms of a woman he loved for a reason." I can't say that, even though many would. In many ways, I envy the blind faith that would allow them to believe such a statement. It must be very liberating to believe something like that absolutely. I can, however, recognise that there would have been a lot worse ways to die. I just wish that death had occurred about 60 years later.

Once you recognise and acknowledge these alternative possible outcomes, if you are a person of faith in a traditional religion, you may find it soothing to think, *It was all part of God's plan.* That doesn't work for me, unfortunately, because I have come to discover that I am agnostic at best. Nevertheless, that phrase and others like it, such as, *He is in a better place*, have provided solace to millions of people, including my sister's children and husband. Acknowledging alternative outcomes that are not all roses and happiness was beneficial to me in some ways, but I honestly think everything would have turned out okay for him if he had lived.

No matter how painful the process is, you may want to take a few minutes to visualise some more balanced alternative outcomes. We imagine that they missed out on a great life ahead, but sadly, that may not have been the case. It seems to rewire the brain in some way to acknowledge these alternative realities. I suggest you take a few minutes and live the pain of what may have been in a worst-case scenario, even if you would never have wished it, try to be a realist and balance out the image you have of an inevitable, wonderful future that was *taken away.* In reality, that future may not have been great. We don't really know. I feel a bit disloyal even thinking these thoughts, though. I think Harrison would have made it and been great. But I really don't know.

Jack London, and Quality vs Length

It took me a long time even to consider a future for myself and look forward, rather than dwelling on the past or trying to deal with my current loss. Reflecting on your *current life* and the *past life* of the person you have lost is part of recovery, though. I had to do this as part of my journey in writing this book, and doing so gave me a new appreciation of how we value a person. As a result…

> *I have found it valuable to consider the quality of a person's life, not just its length.*

Since my son's death and my stark realisation that every breath we take and everything we do can end so quickly, I have tried to take it to heart. Harrison's loss has added a sense of urgency to my own future and the way I will pursue it. Although his life was cut short, Harrison unknowingly exemplified Jack London's classic credo that follows. Jack London died at the age of 40, but he has left an enduring legacy. (You can find the following quotes, framed and posted on the wall of The Jack London Lodge in Glen Ellen, California.)

(The Jack London Credo)

I would rather be ashes than dust.

I would rather my spark should burn out than
it should be stifled by dry rot.

I would rather be a superb mentor,
every atom of me in magnificent glow,
than a sleepy permanent planet.

The proper function of man is to live, not to exist.

I shall not waste my days trying to prolong them.

I shall use my time.

Manifesting a better future

As is so often the case, when writing this section on recovery, the world once again displayed its seemingly endless desire to provide another serendipitously uncanny road sign. I had been in Australia for a few months and had just returned to my cute floating home in Sausalito, California. My tenant, who had been renting my home while I was away, had left me a gift: A book called *Mind Magic*[163] sat beside my bed, with a lovely inscription inside.

To Warwick, the best landlord
a girl could ever hope for.

I gained a friend who changed my life with her sweet gesture and the gift of an excellent book. Strangely, for several months before this gift, in Australia, I had, without any specific intention, been imagining the possibility of once again being in love. As it turned out, there is clearly some truth to the philosophy of visualising and manifesting what you want, because I later fell in love with the same girl who wrote me that note, and although we didn't end up together, I found a good friend (and was given a great book).

Mind Magic by Dr James R. Roy is not simply a book about the incredible power of visualising and manifesting a more positive future. As a neuroscientist, the author is uniquely qualified to explain how successfully embedding your intentions in your

---

163 James R. Doty, Mind Magic: The Neuroscience of Manifestation and How It Changes Everything, 1st ed. (New York: Avery, 2024),

subconscious sets in motion a scientifically sound process that activates brain networks associated with goal orientation.

In short, our inner, often subconscious intentions, once formed, can activate and unlock some of our brain's unused resources. We often find ourselves working toward our goals without even being fully aware of the reasons we do so.

Yes...visualising material wealth, having dream boards of your beautiful car and house that you will own someday, or imagining a piece of paper with a seven-figure bank account balance can reprogram subconscious actions. We have all heard of this from motivational speakers, and it is referred to as *the law of attraction*. However, those goals seem so wrong to me now. *Mind Magic* is the first book I have read that focuses on the power of manifesting a positive future, not a materialistic one, and provides a pathway to help those of us whose perspective and rationalisation of life has been turned on its head because of tragedy and loss.

Dr Roy describes his view of manifesting as, *at its heart, a practice of well-being, engagement with the world, and living a great life.* Which, to me, was very refreshing. It certainly is the type of future I think we all deserve after suffering through the grieving process and seeking a new beginning and a way forward.

What is also so very important is the book's discussion of trauma and how, when we suffer from an emotional injury (such as suddenly losing a child, partner, or parent, that emotionally traumatic experience takes on an *exaggerated authority* in our minds that is even powerful enough to alter our own genes, and certainly alters how we view the world and react to it.

What is vitally essential is reprogramming our subconscious and creating positive intentions that can override and repair the negative experience of our loss and pain from grief.

An excellent daily practice I follow is revisiting what I want to create for myself moving forward. I have compiled a list of things that would make me happy, and I try to review it daily. I see myself healthy, holding hands with a woman who loves me and I can trust. I see my daughter, healthy and happy. And I envisage myself standing on a stage helping people in some way.

I know it is hard to visualise yourself being happy and feeling loved. Particularly when we feel so shattered internally, it isn't easy. Still, if my experience is true for others, it seems there will come a time when you slowly start to imagine a positive future again, one full of happiness. It is not out of reach. Don't give up.

Dealing with Guilt

I touched on guilt earlier in the book in the chapter titled, *It Doesn't Really Matter, Tim*. In that section, I was speaking about the guilt that we feel when, after losing a child or loved one, we experience pleasure. They have lost their life, and you feel like you have lost a part of your soul. It just doesn't seem right to look at a beautiful sunset with a lover and feel contentment, happiness, or even hope. For me, it took years to get past that.

But there is another type of guilt that, for me, has not disappeared as quickly. It is not guilt born of a sense of unfairness nor guilt that fades with time. It is the guilt that I carry for not being there to protect Harrison when I should have been.

The undeniable fact is that I decided to go to Australia to be with a lover and also take my mother somewhere for Christmas instead of being there for Harrison. That can be excused because I thought he would be safe in a rehab, and I had no idea of the dark underbelly of that industry or that he would be bartered off and fall prey to unscrupulous players, putting him at risk. Nevertheless, the feeling of guilt remains.

As part of this book, I haven't spent a lot of time explaining the circumstances that led up to my beautiful boy finally falling into the hands of the nefarious owner of a rehab and medical professionals who cared more about money than health. However, as part of the tragic story, there was a stage where an agent (often referred to as a *body broker* in the industry) offered Harrison money to leave the first rehab we had vetted and to attend another that we had not. The reason this happened was that a recovering addict with insurance coverage can be worth well over $100,000 in billing to a rehab. I didn't know that at the time, but I did sense that something wasn't right. I should have jumped on a plane to make sure he was safe, but I didn't. If I had, he would still be alive.

With that knowledge comes a great deal of regret and guilt that I struggle to avoid. I know, people always say you shouldn't beat yourself up by saying, "If I hadn't done *this*, or if I had done *that*, he would still be alive." But it's undeniable that you will carry this sort of guilt on your shoulders. If not consciously then subconsciously, there will always be a little voice wondering if things could have been different if…?

So, how is the best way to deal with guilt? Western religions often see guilt over wrongdoing as a spiritual condition that can be absolved by God through confession and making amends. To me, receiving absolution from God through confession seems too easy and convenient. Although it would be a great solution if I could do that, my research for this book has led me away from the belief in a singular god, so it wouldn't seem fair to acknowledge one to receive absolution.

Eastern traditions primarily view guilt as a form of disharmony with one's dharma that can be rectified through right action. Taoism takes a slightly different approach, seeing little benefit in guilt at all as long as one does their best to return to harmony with the natural flow of the Tao. Buddhists tend to redefine guilt as regret.

I am glad to say, at least, across all these different religious views, they all seem to treat guilt as something that is resolved through realignment rather than through punishment. For me, there was definitely a part of me that felt like I deserved some form of punishment for letting this happen to Harrison. Realignment is a much better way to release guilt! Achieving this realignment and avoiding guilt is tough, though.

If, like me, you don't feel a priest can magically absolve you of guilt, talking to a therapist is an integral part of recovery. Not only is it beneficial to be able to share one's feelings of guilt with someone, but they will also be able to suggest and guide you through techniques such as practising self-compassion and, in many cases, using behavioural therapy to challenge and avoid guilt traps and help you reframe the responsibility that you feel and can't get rid of.

In other ways, rituals of release can also be very helpful in letting go, such as writing a letter to the person you have lost and expressing your apologies. Journaling and putting your feelings on paper are very helpful. Writing this book has been immensely cathartic.

In short, all the resources I have found suggest that guilt should be acknowledged, acted upon if necessary, and then released; and it is best dealt with through compassion, reframing, and letting go. Finding the right person and the techniques to help achieve these goals is really important. I am still on that journey and don't want to suggest I have found all the answers. Ridding yourself of guilt and moving forward after loss is difficult. Time and writing this book have probably been my biggest saviours.

End Parts

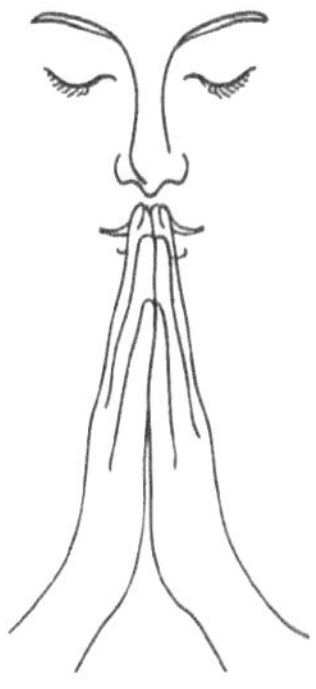

The religion that can make your beauty most known will win your greatest respect.[164]

Hafiz – Ancient Persian Poet

In the chapter on similarities among religions, I touched on the sense of community that all the world's religions offer as their main drawcard. It is, after all, a great feeling to be with a group of like-minded friends and companions. Not many of us would prefer to be alone in this world—especially if we're poor, hungry, suffering, or grieving. This is often why it is easy to be attracted to the warm, supportive atmosphere of a religious group. Along with the sense of community, all belief systems have teachings about what happens to you after you die, which in turn provides hope and solace.

---

164 Daniel Ladinsky, A Year with Hafiz: Daily Contemplations (New York: Penguin Publishing Group, 2011),

However, feelings of increased strength, confidence, and community are not only available in a place of worship; they can occur in any setting wherever there is support, love, and respect—a village where the residents all look after each other in old age, an Alcoholics Anonymous meeting, an Al-Anon meeting, a Facebook group, or even simply in a cozy room with a therapist or counsellor. Not everybody has the money to pay for a therapist, of course, or access to these sorts of communities. Hence, the easiest option for many is to rely on groups such as religious communities to feed us with those great feelings. After all, every town has several churches!

Dance with Angels has been a transformational journey in many ways. I started writing it as a critical sceptic, ready to totally disregard each religion immediately if it was not verifiable or believable to me. However…

> *Undeniably, I have been forced to acknowledge and embrace the fact that, despite the lack of proof, the beautiful sense of community and a multitude of other benefits that derive from a supportive religion can be a massive help to those in need.*

Those benefits are particularly evident and helpful after the loss of a loved one. Simply put, the emotional support and sense of a like-minded community that a religion offers are even more critical in some ways than the after-death belief it teaches.

As I have said on several occasions, I don't want to present myself as an expert; clearly, I am not. This book has just been a documentation of my journey and a fact-finding mission to try to find a belief that works for me. I share my conclusions, not as ultimate answers to repair your heartbreak, only as support while you repair yourself. With that in mind, I offer the following remedy that has worked for me:

> *I haven't found a way to overcome my grief completely. I know it will always be with me. But facing it all the time would be too painful. I often put the pain aside and try to ignore it to allow myself some personal compassion and relief.*

When I can handle it, or when a song or an unexpected memory triggers it, I allow myself to confront the pain fully, letting tears come or a desire to die and be with him. Then, when I can't bear it anymore, I put that feeling away again. Each time I go through this process, it becomes a little bit easier to face anew.

Each time the overwhelming grief has been conquered, I support my daily existence, carrying Harrison still in my heart, in my thoughts, and memories, knowing that his energy definitely surrounds me as it was released back into the world and didn't disappear. An integral part of this personal way of transformation out of grief for me comes from facing my deepest fear—the pain and loss I feel when fully acknow*ledging my son is dead.* Perhaps it is different for others. I don't know, but for me, it is just incredibly overwhelming to recognise and come to terms with his loss head-on. That is why I only deal with it in small bursts and then put it away,

Joseph Campbell once said:

> ***The cave you fear to enter holds the treasure you seek.***

There is no doubt that working my way through grief, entering that cave, and forcing myself to come to terms with the loss of my son has eventually helped me see some light at the other end of that tunnel again.

The Light

Paris 2025 (Nine years after my son's death)

Without realising it, in tackling this book and undergoing the process of recovery and dealing with the fact of my loss directly, I was in fact entering my own *cave* of sorts. The tendency to want to ignore or avoid the terrible grief you feel after loss is substantial. We all have to find our way of facing grief; for me, it was through this book. It took years to write, and when I thought I was close to finishing, I just wanted to get it done and move on. In an attempt to do precisely that, I made the obvious choice and decided to move to Paris for a while!

In the summer of 2025, nearly nine years after Harrison's death, I rented out my floating home in Sausalito and used the money to help me move to Paris for a month, living as a struggling author with only two goals. I reasoned that, at least, following in the footsteps of writers like Hemingway, Fitzgerald, and James Joyce might inspire me to finish this multi-year project. When not writing, I could fulfil my second goal and meander through romantic streets and museums, reflecting on my next direction in life.

Almost as quickly as the decision was made, I found myself sitting in a charming little apartment in the heart of Paris, only a few blocks from the Louvre. In my small, one-bedroom apartment, the 13-foot ornate ceilings embraced tall, classic windows decorated with elaborate wrought-iron balconies through which I watched pigeons playing on zinc-clad, sloped roofs across a cobblestone lane. It was perfect!

What made Paris even more special was the pleasure of having Jacqueline with me for a week of my stay. Together we meandered the back streets, looking up at sneering gargoyles, romantic spires, and classic Parisian homes. We looked sideways to avoid the ever-increasing threat of speeding ebikes, scooters, or electric cars and down at the large stones on which we walked that were hundreds of years old. We enjoyed a few days of a lovely Parisian summer together, eating baguettes in grassy parks and sitting outside restaurants drinking coffee and tea, talking about how we could quickly learn French, and people-watching.

I was happy again! Our joint loss of Harrison was embraced and acknowledged, and he was there with us in our love and memories of him. We thought of him often and mentioned his name without pain. As part of meandering around with Jacqueline, I practised the art of observing, being more acutely aware of my surroundings and of the smaller parts of life. In doing so, not surprisingly, I let go and was less burdened by the bigger struggles of life. Being more present is challenging in our modern age. The French have been improving the art for hundreds of years and even have a name for it. If you are good at it, you are referred to as a *flâneur.*

My primary goal concerning the book was to edit and make changes where required to get it published. However, Paris is too beautiful a city not to be inspired and creative, to love, recover, and gain more than just a time for editing a manuscript. And, as if handed a revelation, Paris gave me what I believe is the perfect conclusion for this book—a fitting end to this leg of my journey on this planet.

One day, while trying to introduce my wonderful daughter to the art of *flânerie*, we wandered through an entrance to a beautiful square and park contained within the walls of the Palais-Royal, not far from where we were staying. In that entranceway, the Passage des Quatre-Fontaines, there is a bronze sculpture by the artist Jean-Michel Alberola. On the floor beneath the sculpture, there is a plate with the following inscription from a poem by André Malraux:

… L'homme que l' on trouvera ici, c'est celui s' accord aux questions que la mort pose à la signification du monde.

As a condition of my newly found pursuit of stopping and taking time to observe the minor parts of life that are often overlooked, I took the time needed to translate this unobtrusive little quote just beyond our feet. In doing so, to my complete surprise, I unearthed the profound realisation that I had reached the end of the manuscript you have just read. The English translation of the quote is…

… The man we find here is one who is in tune with the questions that death poses and about the meaning of the world.

As I read the translation out loud to my daughter, we both looked at each other in surprise, simultaneously realising how significant it was to my journey and how remarkable it was that we would find ourselves standing here, above that quote, just as I was finishing this book.

It occurred to me that I was now that man. The journey of this book has led me to an understanding that, for me, the meaning of the world is one in which we are connected to others, as I am to the memory of my son and my daughter. That love will not change just because my son's physical body was separated from his soul. He remains with me always, as I will stay with my daughter Jacqueline after my body gives up its time of living.

I have also faced and answered, at least in my mind, the questions that death poses, such as the meaning of a life well lived. To me, it is one in which one explores one's potential and has received and given as much love as possible.

I think I have found the man I was looking for; he is the man from the André Malraux quote, and he is within me.

Epilogue

It is said that with beer in hand, Earnest Hemingway once declared...

Every man has two deaths: when he is buried in the ground, and the last time someone says his name. In some ways, men can be immortal.

To those who have lost someone very dear, my personal reflection and words to help are as follows:

> *After a few years, you will only cry once or twice a week, not every day. The love will never go away but will become stronger. You will not lose it. Some memories may fade but will be replaced by new ones. You will always see their smiles and laughter in your dreams. You can hold them in your mind and never let them go. They are a part of you and always will be. They are not gone.*

Only people who have suffered your kind of loss can understand the terrible, deep darkness and anguish you are going through. Will the terrible heaviness ever disappear entirely? I don't know, but, for me it is becoming more hidden as the years go by… Yet I know it is always with me, and there is a part of me that doesn't want to let it go entirely either.

> *Somehow, you will eventually celebrate your time together rather than lament the time you did not have. I guarantee that your memory of them will often trigger a smile and not tears.*

Not... The End.

For Jacqueline and Harrison

Having now completed this book, I cannot help feeling regret at being so engrossed in my pain at the time of my son's death and in my suffering over the first few years that I never gave enough thought to how terrible and damaging it must have been for Jacqueline to be faced with that stark and emotionally crippling encounter with death when we first saw Harrison in that room after he died.

It was so early in a budding and beautiful life.... She must have felt heart-wrenching pain at the loss of her brother. Still, I had not previously thought how traumatising it must have been to suddenly be torn away from the seemingly blissful life of a teenager starting her life away from home and then being thrown into the cold realisation at that moment of how deeply life can hurt us.

Part of the reason I overlooked her pain more than I should have is that Jacqueline did not seem to be grieving the way I expected during the first few months and even a couple of years after Harrison's death. We spoke about it at the time because I had read a book or two about how important it is not to hide from grief. But, as it turns out, I think her process was the better one. She is a tough girl and always has been. She decided that she would not let our tragedy ruin her first years away from home, exploring independence at university, making new friends, and living a happy life. The time when children first leave home is a beautiful moment in their lives, and I am proud of her for deciding to move on and be happy.

Eventually, her pain came through, but she maintained her self-preservation and chose not to lose that part of her life. Harrison would not have wanted to rob her of that. We can all learn from her decision.

> *We can carry the pain and love within—or on our sleeve if we like—and decide if we will let it ruin or strengthen us. We can live a life of sadness or a life of joy, where we start anew, remembering the beautiful times we shared with those we've lost and who continue to accompany us on our journey, or we can choose to stay in the old chapter and never move forward.*

Jacqueline: You and Harrison will always be the warmest part of my heart and soul and are the meaning in my life. After I am gone, I think we will meet again someday. If not, I certainly know that, at the very least, my energy will go back into the Earth. I will be walking with you, one way or another, and I know that I came to understand the true meaning of life when I had you and watched you both grow up.

Love, Dad

End Note

In closing… I don't know if an actual God has Harrison in Heaven, or if *God* is just a collective energy that embraces him. Whatever the case, I do believe he is in a spiritual place, and I will connect with him again. Until then, he will be in my heart every day and night.

I started this book by acknowledging TobyMac's song, *21 Years*. I will close with lines from this song that are so relevant to the loss of my 20-year-old son. I find them tremendously soothing. I am 69 years old as I finish this book, and it won't be long before I embark on my next adventure. When that happens, I will be the one running into my son's arms. When we die, I believe we are given or manifest what we want most. Being greeted by Harrison, or his energy in some form, is what I want most in this life and the next.

Are you singing with angels?
Are you happy where you are?
Well, until this show is over
And you have run into my arms
God has you in Heaven
But I have you in my heart
I have you in my heart

(From TobyMac's song, 21 Years)

Appendix: Notes by Religion

In the first five or so years of writing *Dance with Angels*, I relied primarily on traditional libraries and independent research using publicly available sources. In 2025, I began using AI tools such as ChatGPT [165] to assist in locating background material and summarising commonly accepted perspectives, which I then checked manually before incorporating information into the book.

Wherever possible, AI-generated content has been excluded from the main manuscript and is presented here only in this appendix as supplementary reference material. The following notes reflect a combination of traditional sources, historical references, and AI-assisted summaries. Readers are encouraged to independently verify quotations and citations. Where interpretations or scholarly debates exist, I have attempted to note that explicitly.

This appendix is intended as a high-level comparative reference, not as a definitive theological or scholarly treatment. Interpretations vary widely within each tradition.

---

165 OpenAI, ChatGPT (large language model), San Francisco: OpenAI, 2025, https://chat.openai.com.

Christianity

Primary authority or reference material: The Bible

(The *New International Version* is currently the most widely purchased.)

A reference made up of 66 books written by different people at various times in history about God, his son, Jesus, and how we should interpret and interact with God. (The Protestant Bible is made up of 66 books; the Catholic Bibles include 73 books, with seven additional deuterocanonical books.)

- **Central Figure**: Jesus of Nazareth (born in the first century CE
- Christianity started as a sect of the Jewish religion. Its followers believe that there is only one God, and that God created the universe and everything in it. The faith is centred around the belief in the teachings, life, and resurrection of Jesus, who Christians believe was the Son of God.
- Christians believe in the same God as the Jewish religion and Islam. These three faiths stem from Abraham, who is mentioned in the holy books of all three religions. For this reason, these belief systems are called *Abrahamic* religions.
- Christianity has over 2.2 billion followers worldwide. It's the religion that has more avowed followers than any other. Over 70% of Americans identify as Christian.
- Christianity is often divided into the three main branches: Orthodox, Catholicism, and Protestantism. Within those branches are additional denominations. The most significant component is Catholicism, representing roughly half of

the world's Christians, who acknowledge the Pope as their spiritual leader.

Primary rules and moral code: These were set out in what's most widely referred to as the Ten Commandments. According to Moses and passages from the Old Testament, the finger of God himself inscribed these directives.

(Unfortunately, Moses received them directly from God with no witness' present – WD)

It's a common theme among most religions to provide guidance for the masses. The Ten Commandments, which serve as primary rules of behaviour for Christians, differ slightly in their order and wording depending on the version of the translation. The following are the general precepts that God (according to Moses) wants his followers to understand (summarised from passages found in Exodus 20:2-17 and Deuteronomy 5:6-21):

1. I am the Lord thy God.
2. Thou shalt have no other gods before me.
3. Thou shalt not take the name of the Lord thy God in vain.
4. Remember the Sabbath day and keep it holy.
5. Honour thy father and mother.
6. Thou shalt not murder.
7. Thou shalt not commit adultery.
8. Thou shalt not steal.
9. Thou shalt not bear false witness against your neighbour.
10. Thou shalt not covet.

Many Christians believe that God created the world in six days, resting on the seventh, as described in Genesis. This contrasts with the scientific consensus, which supports the Big Bang theory and a universe billions of years old.

Islam

Islamic beliefs about the afterlife are rooted in the Quran and Hadith (sayings and actions of the Prophet Muhammad). They are fundamental to Islamic theology, serving as a moral and ethical framework for Muslims, guiding their actions and conduct in this life in preparation for the hereafter. Here's a summary of critical Islamic beliefs regarding the afterlife, with direct references:

- **Allah** – the Arabic word used for God in Islam; the singular, all-powerful divine being.
- **Resurrection and Accountability:** Muslims believe in the Day of Judgment, when all individuals will be resurrected, and their deeds will be accounted for. The Quran states, *Then indeed you, on the Day of Resurrection, will be resurrected.* (Quran, Surah Al-Mu'minun, 23:16).
- **Heaven (Jannah) and Hell (Jahannam)**: Muslims believe in the existence of Heaven (Jannah) as a reward for righteous deeds and Hell (Jahannam) as a punishment for wrongdoing. The Quran describes both in detail, detailing the pleasures of Paradise and the torments of Hell.
- **Balance of Deeds**: Islamic belief holds that one's good and bad deeds will be weighed on a scale on the Day of Judgment. Those with more good deeds will enter Paradise, while those with more bad deeds are destined for Hell. The Quran says, *So whoever does an atom's weight of good will see it,*

and whoever does an atom's weight of evil will see it. (Quran, Surah Al-Zalzalah, 99:7-8)

- **Intercession**: Muslims believe in the possibility of intercession by the Prophet Muhammad and other righteous individuals on the Day of Judgment. This intervention can help reduce the punishment for some believers.
- **Eternal Life**: In Islamic belief, one's existence in the afterlife is eternal. Those admitted to Paradise will enjoy everlasting bliss, while those in Hell will endure eternal punishment. (Some scholars hold that punishment is not always *eternal. WD*)
- **Belief and Good Deeds**: The importance of faith in Allah and good deeds is central to Islamic belief in the afterlife. Salvation is attainable through sincere belief and righteous actions. The Quran emphasises this: *But whoever does righteousness, whether male or female, while he is a believer—those will enter Paradise.* (Quran, Surah Al-Nahl, 16:97)
- **Resurrection of the Body**: Muslims believe in bodily resurrection, in which individuals will be raised with their physical bodies on the Day of Judgment.

Hinduism

Hinduism is, without a doubt, one of the world's oldest and most diverse religions, with a rich tapestry of traditions and philosophies. Here are some verified facts about Hinduism:

- **Origins and Development**: Hinduism has no single founder and represents a synthesis of various Indian cultures and traditions. It developed over a period of more than 3,000 years, with roots stretching back to prehistoric times in the Indian subcontinent.

- **Sacred Texts**: Hinduism boasts a vast body of scriptures, divided broadly into two categories: Śruti (*that which is heard*) and Smriti (*that which is remembered*). The Vedas and Upanishads are part of the Śruti and are considered divinely revealed. Other important texts include the Mahabharata and Ramayana epics, the Bhagavad Gita, and the Puranas.
- **Belief in a Supreme Being:** Hinduism is henotheistic (which means it recognises the supremacy of a single deity without denying the existence of others) and is inclusive of various deities and spiritual ideas. The concept of Brahman (the ultimate reality or universal consciousness) is central in Hindu philosophy. (Not to be confused with *Brahma,* considered to be the creator god. WD)
- **Diverse Deities:** There are many deities worshipped in Hinduism, with the Trimurti (trinity) of Brahma (the creator), Vishnu (the preserver), and Shiva (the destroyer) being prominent. Goddesses such as Lakshmi, Saraswati, and Parvati also play significant roles.
- **Karma and Reincarnation:** Hinduism introduces the law of karma, where the actions of an individual influence their future lives. The soul (atman) undergoes a cycle of birth, death, and rebirth (samsara) until it achieves liberation (moksha).
- **Dharma:** This is a key concept referring to duty, righteousness, and moral order. One's dharma varies according to class (varna), stage of life (ashrama), and individual characteristics.

- **Yoga and Meditation:** Practices such as yoga and meditation are integral to Hinduism, aiding in spiritual growth and self-realisation. The Yoga Sutras of Patanjali are a key text outlining the philosophy and practice of Yoga.
- **Festivals and Rituals:** Hinduism features a rich array of festivals and rituals that vary regionally and according to tradition. Notable festivals include Diwali, Holi, Navaratri, and Kumbh Mela.
- **Caste System:** Historically, Hindu society has been organized into a complex caste system comprising different social groups (varnas) with assigned roles and duties. This system has been subject to criticism and reform in modern times.
- **Philosophical Schools**: Hinduism encompasses several philosophical schools, each with its own interpretation of texts and beliefs. Major schools include Vedanta, Mimamsa, Nyaya, Samkhya, Yoga, and Vaisheshika.
- **Historical and Archaeological Evidence**
  - » Indus Valley Civilisation: The roots of Hinduism can be traced back to the Indus Valley Civilisation (circa 3300–1300 BCE). Archaeological discoveries, including artifacts, sculptures, and the urban layout of towns suggest early forms of Hindu worship. Notably, the Pashupati Seal depicts a figure resembling Shiva, one of the principal deities in Hinduism (Marshall, 1931).[166]

166 Sir John Marshall, ed., *Mohenjo-Daro and the Indus Civilization: Being an Official Account of Archæological Excavations at Mohenjo-Daro Carried Out by the Government of India Between the Years 1922 AD 1927*, vol. 1 (London: A. Probsthain, 1931), https://archive.org/details/in.ernet.dli.2015.722.

   » Vedic Period: The Vedic texts, composed between 1500–500 BCE, form the foundation of Hindu philosophy and rituals. The Rigveda, the oldest of these texts, contains hymns that reflect early Hindu religious practices. Linguistic and textual analyses place the composition of these texts in ancient India, which is supported by archaeological findings of contemporaneous cultures (Witzel, 1995).

- **Textual Evidence**
   » Epics and Puranas: The Mahabharata and the Ramayana, the epic narratives central to Hindu culture, provide insights into the socio-religious fabric of ancient India. While their historical veracity is debated, certain locations and events described have been linked to actual places and traditions in India. For instance, the city of Dwarka, associated with Krishna in the Mahabharata, has been excavated, revealing an ancient settlement (Rao, 1999).[167]

- **Scientific and Medical Contributions**
   » Ayurveda: Hinduism's contributions to ancient science and medicine, particularly through Ayurveda, are well-documented. Texts like the Charaka Samhita and Sushruta Samhita, dated to the first millennium BCE, detail surgical procedures, herbal treatments, and medical ethics. These texts have been studied and validated

---

167 Shikaripur Ranganatha Rao, *Lost City of Dvaraka* (New Delhi: Aditya Prakashan, 1999)

by modern scholars for their advanced understanding of health and medicine (Meulenbeld, 1999).[168]

– **Philosophical and Metaphysical Insights**

Yoga and Meditation: Hindu practices such as yoga and meditation have gained global recognition for their benefits to mental and physical health. The Yoga Sutras of Patanjali, an ancient text, outlines the principles of yoga, which have been corroborated by modern scientific research showing the positive effects of these practices on stress reduction, mental clarity, and overall well-being (Sherman, 2001).

– **Comparative Studies and Influence**

Cultural Influence: Hinduism's influence on art, literature, and culture is substantial. Temples such as those in Khajuraho and Hampi exhibit advanced architectural and artistic skills, reflecting the sophisticated aesthetic sensibilities of ancient Hindu society. These cultural artifacts are studied by historians and archaeologists for their intricate designs and religious significance (Dehejia, 1997).[169]

– **Modern Relevance**

Contemporary Studies: Modern research continues to explore the impact of Hinduism on society and culture. Studies on the sustainability of traditional Hindu practices, such as the ecological management of sacred groves and water bodies, highlight

---

168 Gerrit Jan Meulenbeld, *A History of Indian Medical Literature*, vol. 1, part 2, 5 volumes, 3 parts (1A, 1B, 2A, 2B, 3) vols., Groningen Oriental Studies (Groningen: E. Forsten, 1999), https://archive.org/details/Meulenbeld-HIML/HIML%201A%20/.

169 Vidya Dehejia, *Indian Art*, Paperback (London / New York: Phaidon Press, 1997)

the religion's deep connection to environmental stewardship (Gadgil & Vartak, 1976).[170]

- **Key references about the afterlife**
  - **Vedic Texts:** The Vedas, particularly the Upanishads, are foundational texts that discuss the cycle of birth, death, and rebirth. The Bhagavad Gita, which is part of the Mahabharata, expounds on the concept of the immortal soul (atman) that transmigrates from one body to another based on Karma (actions in past lives). The dialogue between Krishna and Arjuna in the Bhagavad Gita offers detailed philosophical insights into reincarnation (Bhagavad Gita, Chapter 2, Verses 12-13).[171]
  - **Brihadaranyaka Upanishad:** As one of the principal Upanishads, this text discusses the journey of the soul after death. The soul's actions determine its future births, aligning with the law of Karma (Brihadaranyaka Upanishad, Chapter 4, Section 4).[172]
- **Historical and Anecdotal Evidence**

---

170 Madhav Gadgil and V. D. Vartak, "Studies on Sacred Groves along Western Ghats in Maharashtra and Goa: Role of Belief and Folklores," in *Glimpses of Indian Ethnobotany*, ed. S. K. Jain (Bombay, India: Oxford University Press, 1981), 272–78, https://portals.iucn.org/library/node/26468.

171 Swami Mukundananda, "Chapter 2: Sānkhya Yog | Verse 22-23," in *Bhagavad Gita - The Song of God* (Jagadguru Kripaluji Yog, 2014), https://www.holy-bhagavad-gita.org/chapter/2.

172 Swami Krishnananda, "Chapter IV, Section 4 - Fourth Brahmana: The Soul of the Unrealised After Death," in *The Brihadaranyaka Upanishad* (Rishikesh, India: The Divine Life Society, 1983), https://www.swami-krishnananda.org/brdup/brhad_IV-04.html.

» **Cultural Practices:** Hindu funeral rites, which aim to aid the departed soul in its journey to the next life, provide cultural evidence of belief in life after death. The practice of shraddha (rituals for the deceased) is meant to ensure the soul's peaceful transition and favourable rebirth. These rituals are described in texts like the Garuda Purana, which details the afterlife and the soul's journey (Garuda Purana, Preta Khanda).[173]

» **Case Studies of Reincarnation:** Ian Stevenson, a prominent psychiatrist, documented cases of children who claimed to remember past lives. His research, particularly in India, presented detailed accounts of individuals recalling previous incarnations with verifiable details. While controversial, these studies have intrigued many scholars (Stevenson, 1974).[174]

– **Philosophical and Metaphysical Insights**

» **Yoga and Meditation:** Practices like yoga and meditation are believed to provide a deeper understanding and experiences of the soul's immortality.

» **Patanjali's Yoga Sutras** describe the attainment of spiritual knowledge through disciplined practice, potentially

173 Kausiki Books, *Garuda Purana: Pretha Khanda: English Translation Only without Slokas*, vol. 3 (Kausiki Books, 2021).

174 Ian Stevenson, *Twenty Cases Suggestive of Reincarnation*, 2nd ed. (Charlottesville: University Press of Virginia, 1974)

offering personal insights into the nature of life after death (Yoga Sutras, Chapter 3, Vibhuti Pada).[175]

- **Scientific Studies and Theories**
  - **Near-Death Experiences** (NDEs): Some modern studies on NDEs draw parallels to Hindu beliefs. Individuals experiencing NDEs often describe encounters with a bright light, a sense of peace, and seeing deceased relatives—experiences similar to descriptions found in Hindu scriptures. While not conclusive proof, these studies contribute to the discourse on life after death (Greyson, 2000).[176] (There are a number of connecting discussions about NDEs throughout the journey of this book)
- **Comparative Religious Studies**
  - **Influence on Other Cultures:** Hindu concepts of reincarnation and karma have had a profound influence on other religious and philosophical systems, including Buddhism and Jainism, which also incorporate these ideas. Comparative studies highlight similarities and

---

175 Patañjali, "Chapter 3: Vibhūti Pāda," in *The Yoga Sūtras of Patañjali*, trans. Edwin F. Bryant, 1st ed. (New York: Farrar, Straus and Giroux, 2015), 672, https://patanjaliyogasutra.in/vibhooti-pada-3-55/.

176 Bruce Greyson, "Near-Death Experiences," in *Varieties of Anomalous Experience: Examining the Scientific Evidence*, ed. Etzel Cardeña, Steven J. Lynn, and Stanley Krippner, 2nd ed. (Washington, DC: American Psychological Association, 2014), 333–67, https://doi.org/10.1037/14258-012.

differences, emphasising the widespread acceptance and adaptation of these beliefs (Harvey, 1990).[177]

– **Common concepts about life after death**.

Hinduism encompasses a wide range of beliefs about life after death that vary among its different traditions and texts. However, some key concepts are commonly found across many interpretations:

» **Reincarnation (cycle of samsara):** A fundamental belief in Hinduism is the concept of reincarnation, where the soul (atman) is reborn into different physical forms after death. The nature of one's next life is determined by one's actions, thoughts, and deeds in the current life, a concept known as karma.

» **Karma:** Karma refers to the actions performed by individuals and the consequences they bring. Virtuous actions lead to positive karma and potentially a better rebirth, while non-virtuous actions lead to negative karma and a less favourable rebirth.

» **Moksha (liberation):** The ultimate goal in Hinduism is moksha, which is liberation from the cycle of birth and death. Achieving moksha means the soul is united with the divine, often conceptualised as merging with Brahma, the ultimate reality or universal soul. This state is characterised by eternal bliss and freedom from all worldly suffering.

---

177 Peter Harvey, An Introduction to Buddhism: Teachings, History and Practices, 1st ed., Introduction to Religion (Cambridge, UK: Cambridge University Press, 1990), https://www.goodreads.com/book/show/418423.An_Introduction_to_Buddhism.

» **Punarjanma (rebirth):** Before achieving moksha, souls are believed to undergo a cycle of rebirth. The nature of the next life is influenced by the soul's accumulated karma.

– **The Role of Rituals and Ceremonies:**

After death, various rituals and ceremonies are performed for the deceased, believed to aid the soul in its journey to the next life or toward moksha. These rituals also provide solace and closure for the living.

» **Different Paths to Moksha:** Hinduism recognises different paths (such as Bhakti, Jnana, and Karma Yoga) to achieve liberation, emphasising that individuals can choose their path based on their disposition and circumstances.

It's important to note that these beliefs can vary widely, and individual Hindus might interpret or prioritise these concepts differently based on their personal beliefs, regional practices, and specific sects within Hinduism.

Buddhism

Buddhism is a major world religion and philosophy that originated in ancient India. Its foundational concepts were created and taught by Siddhārtha, known as the Buddha, in the 6th to 4th century BCE. It is a complex and diverse tradition with a rich history and philosophy. His teachings were adopted by his followers as a spiritual path and later called Buddhism after his death. During his lifetime, Siddhārtha Gautama referred to his teachings as *the Dharma* (the way). Here are some known and verified facts about Buddhism:

- **Historical Foundations:** Siddhārtha Gautama, who became known as the Buddha or the *Enlightened One*, was a prince in ancient India. He lived between the 6th and 4th centuries BCE. His teachings form the foundation of Buddhism.
- **Four Noble Truths:** Central to Buddhist teaching are the Four Noble Truths:

1. The truth of suffering (dukkha),
2. The truth of the cause of suffering (samudaya),
3. The truth of the end of suffering (nirodha), and
4. The truth of the path that frees us from suffering (magga).

- **Noble Eightfold Path:** The Noble Eightfold Path provides a set of guidelines for ethical and mental development with the goal of freeing individuals from attachments and delusions; it includes:
    - right understanding,
    - right intent,
    - right speech,
    - right action,
    - right livelihood,
    - right effort,
    - right mindfulness, and
    - right concentration.
- **Concept of Karma:** In Buddhism, karma refers to action driven by intention, which leads to future consequences.

Good intentions and actions often lead to positive future outcomes, while bad intentions and actions typically result in negative outcomes.

- **Rebirth and Samsara:** Buddhists believe in the cycle of rebirth (samsara), in which individuals are reborn after they die. This cycle is viewed as a continuous process of birth, death, and rebirth and is influenced by one's actions and consequences (karma).
- **Nirvana:** The ultimate goal of Buddhism is nirvana, which is a state of liberation and freedom from suffering and the cycle of rebirth. This is achieved through the practice and development of morality, meditation, and wisdom.
- **Branches of Buddhism:** The three major branches of Buddhism are
    - Theravada (practiced mainly in Sri Lanka, Thailand, Myanmar, Laos, and Cambodia),
    - Mahayana (practiced in East Asia, including China, Korea, Japan, and Vietnam), and
    - Vajrayana (practiced in Tibet, Mongolia, and parts of Russia and China).
- **Scriptures and Texts:** Buddhist scriptures and texts vary among different schools but primarily include the Tipitaka or Pali Canon in Theravada Buddhism and the Mahayana Sutras in Mahayana Buddhism.
- **Monastic Life:** Monasticism is a vital practice in many forms of Buddhism, where monks and nuns adopt a lifestyle of poverty, celibacy, and meditation. The Sangha, or community of monks and nuns, is considered one of the Three Jewels of Buddhism, alongside the Buddha and the Dharma

(teachings). (Sangha traditionally refers to the monastic community, though in some modern or Western interpretations it may include lay followers.)

- **Spread and Cultural Influence:** Buddhism spread from India to various parts of Asia and has significantly influenced the culture, art, philosophy, and social structure of countries such as Tibet, Thailand, Nepal, Japan, Korea, and others.

Judaism

Judaism is one of the oldest monotheistic religions. While the concept of proof in a religious context is complex, the origins of Judaism are supported by some historical, archaeological, and textual evidence.

Verifiable Evidence of the Jewish Religion

- **Historical and Archaeological Evidence**
  - **The Exodus and Early Israelites:**

  Evidence: While the historicity of the Exodus remains debated, some evidence points to the presence of a Semitic group in Egypt during the Late Bronze Age, possibly linked to the Israelites. The Merneptah Stele, dated to around 1208 BCE, is one of the earliest references to Israel outside the Bible and suggests that a group known as *Israel* existed in Canaan during this period (Redford, 1992).[178]

---

178 Donald B. Redford, ***Egypt, Canaan, and Israel in Ancient Times***, 1st Princeton Paperback Printing (Princeton, N.J.: Princeton University Press, 1992), https://archive.org/details/egyptcanaanisrae00redf.

- **King David and the United Monarchy:**
    - Evidence: The Tel Dan Stele, discovered in northern Israel, dates back to the 9th century BCE. It mentions the House of David and provides evidence for the historical existence of King David and his dynasty. This inscription supports the biblical account of a united monarchy under David and Solomon (Biran, 1994).[179]
- **The Babylonian Exile:**
    - Evidence: The Babylonian Exile, a pivotal event in Jewish history, is well-documented both in the Bible and by external sources. Babylonian records, such as the Nebuchadnezzar Chronicle, describe the conquest of Jerusalem and the exile of its elite, corroborating the biblical narrative (Liverani, 2005).[180]
- **The Dead Sea Scrolls:**
    - Evidence: The Dead Sea Scrolls, discovered between 1947 and 1956, are ancient Jewish texts that include parts of the Hebrew Bible, sectarian writings, and other religious documents. Dating from the 3rd century BCE to the 1st century CE, these scrolls provide critical insights into

---

179 Avraham Biran, ***Biblical Dan*** (Jerusalem: Hebrew Union College, 1994), https://www.goodreads.com/book/show/5957331.

180 Mario Liverani, *Israel's History and the History of Israel* (London; Oakville, CT: Equinox, 2005), https://archive.org/details/israelshistoryhi0000live/page/n3/mode/2up.

Jewish religious practices, beliefs, and the development of the Hebrew Bible (Vermes, 2011).[181]

- **Textual Evidence**
  - » **The Hebrew Bible (Tanakh):**

Evidence: The Hebrew Bible is central to Judaism and contains a wealth of historical, legal, and theological material. While its religious content is a matter of faith, the Bible also includes descriptions of real historical events and places. Many of these accounts are supported by archaeological discoveries such as the Tel Dan Stele and the Siloam Inscription (Finkelstein & Silberman, 2001).[182]

- **Cultural and Legal Influence**
  - » **Jewish Law (Halakha):**

Evidence: The continuity and influence of Jewish law (halakha) through millennia is evidence of Judaism's enduring legacy. The Talmud, a key text in halakha, has been studied and applied by Jewish communities worldwide for over 1,500 years, demonstrating the religion's influence on Jewish culture and identity (Neusner, 1994).[183]

---

181 Geza Vermes, *The Complete Dead Sea Scrolls in English*, 7th ed. (London, United Kingdom: Penguin Books Ltd, 2011), https://www.kennys.ie/mind-body-and-spirit/the-complete-dead-sea-scrolls-in-english-7th-edition-penguin-classics.

182 Israel Finkelstein and Neil Asher Silberman, *The Bible Unearthed: Archaeology's New Vision of Ancient Israel and the Origin of Its Sacred Texts*, Paperback (New York: Free Press, 2002)

183 Jacob Neusner, *The Talmud: A Close Encounter* (Minneapolis, MN: Augsburg Fortress, 1992), https://www.abebooks.com/Talmud-Close-Encounter-Neusner-Jacob-Augsburg/31876679941/bd.

- **Modern Evidence**
  - » **Archaeological Sites:**

    Evidence: Numerous archaeological sites in Israel and surrounding regions provide tangible evidence of ancient Jewish life and worship. Sites like the Western Wall in Jerusalem, Masada, and the ancient synagogues of Galilee are physical testaments to Jewish religious practices and community life over millennia (Levine, 2000).[184]

Mormonism

A few extra interesting points about Mormon belief (a branch of Christianity) worth mentioning:

- **Godhead** - Mormons believe in what they call the *Godhead*, which consists of God the Father, Jesus Christ, and the Holy Ghost. These three entities are seen as distinct but united in purpose.
- **Core Scriptures** - In addition to the King James version of the Bible, the LDS Church considers its core scriptures to be: (1) Book of Mormon, (2) Doctrine and Covenants, and (3) Pearl of Great Price (which, according to the LDS website, includes two lost books of the Bible, a translation of the Gospel of Matthew, Joseph Smith's history, and the Articles of Faith.)
- **Joseph Smith** - Mormons believe that the fullness of the gospel of Jesus Christ was lost after his death and that of his

---

184 Lee I. Levine, *Jerusalem: Portrait of the City in the Second Temple Period (BCE–70 CE)*, Illustrated (Philadelphia: Jewish Publication Society, 2002)

apostles until it was finally fully restored through Joseph Smith in 1830.

- **A Prophet-President** – The modern-day LDS Church is led by a *Prophet-President* and a Quorum of the Twelve, following the pattern of the early Christian church.
- **Polygamy** – At one time, some Mormons practised polygamy, but that was officially discontinued in 1890. Today, the mainstream LDS Church no longer tolerates polygamy and takes disciplinary action against members who engage in it.

Verifiable Evidence of the Mormon Religion[185]

The Church of Jesus Christ of Latter-day Saints (LDS Church), commonly known as Mormonism, is a relatively recent religious movement founded in the early 19th century by Joseph Smith. The religion's foundational texts and historical claims have been the subject of much scrutiny.

Below are key aspects of Mormonism that have been subjected to historical and textual analysis.

Book of Mormon

- Origin and translation:
  - Evidence: Joseph Smith claimed to have translated the Book of Mormon from golden plates revealed to him by an angel named Moroni. Smith stated that he translated

185 OpenAI Team. "OpenAI. (2024). ChatGPT [Large Language Model]." Web-based, Python. ChatGPT. San Francisco, California: OpenAI, March 2023. https://chat.openai.com.

the text using divine instruments called the Urim and Thummim. Critics argue that there's no physical evidence of the golden plates, and the translation process, as described by Smith, lacks verifiable proof (Bushman, 2005).[186]

- Notable Study: Some scholars have examined the linguistic and cultural references in the Book of Mormon, noting similarities to 19th-century American culture and biblical texts rather than ancient American civilisations. However, these analyses are interpretative and don't provide conclusive proof regarding the book's divine origin (Givens, 2002).[187]

Archaeological Evidence

Ancient American Civilisations:

- Evidence: Book of Mormon describes advanced civilisations in the Americas, such as the Nephites and Lamanites, who allegedly lived from around 600 BCE to 400 CE. Archaeologists haven't found definitive evidence to support the existence of the civilisations described in the text. While there are significant ancient cultures in the Americas, such

---

186 Richard Lyman Bushman, ***Joseph Smith: Rough Stone Rolling***, Illustrated, Reprint, Vintage (New York: Knopf Doubleday Publishing Group, 2005)

187 Terryl Givens, *By the Hand of Mormon: The American Scripture That Launched a New World Religion*, Paperback (Oxford; New York: Oxford University Press, 2002), https://archive.org/details/byhandofmormonam0000give_g9i5.

as the Maya and Aztecs, their histories don't align with the narrative in the Book of Mormon (Sorenson, 1985).[188]

- Notable Study: Some Mormon scholars, like John L. Sorenson, have proposed theories that attempt to reconcile the Book of Mormon with archaeological findings in Mesoamerica. However, these theories remain speculative and aren't widely accepted by the broader archaeological community (Sorenson, 1985).[189]

Historical Documentation

Joseph Smith's Life and Claims:

- Evidence: The historical record of Joseph Smith's life, including court documents and contemporaneous accounts, does provide a certain amount of detailed information about the founder of Mormonism. Unfortunately, his earlier life does not help lend him a lot of credibility. For instance, it is a fact of record that he was tried in 1826 for *glass-looking*, a practice of claiming to find buried treasure using a seer stone—a practice he later claimed helped him translate the Book of Mormon (Quinn, 1998).

  (I found it interesting that Smith had a history of folk magic practices and treasure-seeking prior to founding the church. The founder of Scientology, L. Ron Hubbard, was previously a published science fiction writer. It seems that both were notably creative in their endeavours prior to starting churches. WD)

---

188 John L. Sorenson, *An Ancient American Setting for the Book of Mormon* (Salt Lake City: Deseret Book Company, 1996)

189 Sorenson, John L. An Ancient American Setting for the Book of Mormon. Salt Lake City: Deseret Book Company, 1996.

– Notable Study: Richard L. Bushman's biography, ***Joseph Smith: Rough Stone Rolling***, explores Smith's life and acknowledges both the faith claims and the challenges posed by historical evidence. While Smith's personal history is well documented, it doesn't provide verifiable proof of the divine origins of his revelations (Bushman, 2005).[190]

Contemporary Analysis

DNA Studies:

– Evidence: Modern DNA analysis has been used to test the claim in the Book of Mormon that Native Americans are descended from Israelites. Studies show that Native American populations primarily share ancestry with East Asian groups, not Middle Eastern populations, which challenges the historical claims of the Book of Mormon (Southerton, 2004).[191]

– Notable Study: Simon G. Southerton, a former LDS Church member and scientist, published a book titled Losing a Lost Tribe: Native Americans, DNA, and the Mormon Church (2004), which discusses the implications of DNA evidence for the Book of Mormon's historical claims. This has led to significant debate within and outside the LDS community.

---

190 Bushman, Richard Lyman. ***Joseph Smith: Rough Stone Rolling.*** Illustrated, Reprint. Vintage. New York: Knopf Doubleday Publishing Group, 2005.

191 Simon G. Southerton, ***Losing a Lost Tribe: Native Americans, DNA, and the Mormon Church***, Paperback (Salt Lake City, Utah: Signature Books, 2004).

Conclusion

In summary, Mormonism is a well-documented religious movement with a significant number of followers and a substantial historical and cultural impact. However, the verifiable evidence supporting its foundational claims—such as the divine origin of the Book of Mormon and the historical existence of its described civilisations—remains inconclusive. The movement's core beliefs are primarily based on faith, and historical and scientific studies often challenge its literal claims.

Unfortunately, there is no factual evidence that would make a belief in Mormonism a credible option for me. As with all religions, there appear to be positive aspects to Mormonism, but it is my conclusion that the foundations are not credible. (WD)

References

Bushman, R. L. (2005). *Joseph Smith: Rough Stone Rolling.*

Givens, T. L. (2002). *By the Hand of Mormon: The American Scripture that Launched a New World Religion.*

Sorenson, J. L. (1985). *An Ancient American Setting for the Book of Mormon.*

Quinn, D. M. (1998). *Early Mormonism and the Magic World View.*

• Southerton, S. G. (2004). *Losing a Lost Tribe: Native Americans, DNA, and the Mormon Church.*

Sikhism

While the core beliefs of Sikhism are rooted in spiritual teachings, there's substantial verifiable evidence of the religion's historical development, sacred texts, and cultural impact. From the preserved manuscripts of The Guru Granth Sahib to the historical accounts of the Sikh gurus and the enduring legacy of Sikh practices, there's a solid foundation for understanding the tangible aspects of Sikhism. As in other religions, there is no specific evidence for the afterlife or the existence of God. There is the following:

- **Textual Evidence**
  - **The Guru Granth Sahib:**
    - Evidence: The Guru Granth Sahib, the central religious scripture of Sikhism, was compiled by Guru Arjan in 1604 and later finalised by Guru Gobind Singh. It contains the teachings of the Sikh Gurus as well as writings from various saints and poets from different religious backgrounds, reflecting the inclusive nature of Sikhism. The original manuscripts, including the Kartarpur Bir (1604), are preserved and have been studied extensively by historians and scholars, providing verifiable evidence of the text's authenticity and its role in Sikh religious practices (Mann, 2001).[192]
- **Historical Gurdwaras: (Sikh temples)**

---

192 Gurinder Singh Mann, *The Making of Sikh Scripture*, 1st ed. (New York: Oxford University Press, 2001), https://global.oup.com/academic/product/the-making-of-sikh-scripture-9780195130249?cc=pk&lang=en&.

  - » Evidence: Numerous historical gurdwaras are associated with the lives of the Sikh gurus, serving as physical evidence of Sikhism's historical presence and continuity. For instance, the Harmandir Sahib (Golden Temple) in Amritsar, established by Guru Arjan in 1581, is a significant religious and cultural site for Sikhs worldwide. Its construction, architecture, and continued use as a place of worship provide tangible proof of Sikhism's enduring legacy (Fenech and McLeod, 2014).[193]
- **Sikhism's Cultural and Social Impact** on Punjab and Beyond:
  - » Evidence: Sikhism's influence on the culture, politics, and social structure of Punjab is well-documented. The religion's emphasis on equality, community service (Seva), and resistance to oppression has shaped the region's history, particularly during periods of Mughal and British rule. Sikh military and political movements, such as the establishment of the Sikh empire under Maharaja Ranjit Singh, further demonstrate the tangible impact of Sikhism on regional and global history (Singh, 2006).

Taoism

As with other ancient religions, Taoism's core concepts, such as the Tao and wu wei, are primarily philosophical and therefore do not offer empirical proof. However, the religion's historical texts, archaeological sites, and influence on Chinese culture

193 Louis E. Fenech and W. H. McLeod, *Historical Dictionary of Sikhism*, Historical Dictionaries of Religions, Philosophies, and Movements (Lanham: Rowman & Littlefield Publishers, 2014)

and medicine provide substantial, verifiable evidence of its long-standing presence and significance.

- **Tao Historical and Textual Evidence**
  - **Lao-Tzu and the Tao Te Ching:**
    - Evidence: Taoism is traditionally attributed to Lao-Tzu (also spelled Laozi), a semi-legendary figure believed to have lived around the 6th century BCE. The foundational text of Taoism, the Tao Te Ching (Dao De Jing), is attributed to Lao-Tzu and outlines the core teachings of Taoism. The Tao Te Ching emphasises the Tao (the Way) and the principle of Wu Wei (non-action or effortless action). Although the historical existence of Lao-Tzu is debated, the Tao Te Ching is a well-documented ancient text. Manuscripts such as the Mawangdui Silk Texts (discovered in the 1970s), which date to the 2nd century BCE, provide verifiable evidence of their antiquity (Henricks, 1989).[194]
- **Zhuangzi:**
  - Evidence: Another significant Taoist text is the Zhuangzi, attributed to Zhuang Zhou (also known as Zhuangzi), a 4th- century BCE philosopher. This text expands on Taoist themes and offers a mix of philosophy, humour, and parables. The historical figure of Zhuangzi is better documented than Lao-Tzu, and this text has been

194 Laozi, *Lao-Tzu: Te-Tao Ching: A New Translation Based on the Recently Discovered Ma-Wang-Tui Texts*, trans. Robert G. Henricks (New York: Ballantine Books, 1989), https://archive.org/details/laotzutetaoching0000laoz/mode/2up.

widely studied and preserved through various historical manuscripts, reinforcing its authenticity and influence in Chinese thought (Graham, 1981).[195]

- **Taoist Temples and Sites:**
  - Evidence: Numerous archaeological sites and temples throughout China attest to the long-standing presence of Taoist practices. The Wudang Mountains, for example, are a renowned Taoist centre with temples and monasteries dating back to the Tang Dynasty (618–907 CE). These sites are part of the UNESCO World Heritage and provide tangible evidence of Taoism's historical and cultural significance (Huang, 2012).[196]
- **Traditional Chinese Medicine (TCM):**
  - Evidence: Taoist principles are deeply intertwined with the development of Traditional Chinese Medicine. Concepts such as the balance of yin and yang, the flow of qi (vital energy), and the importance of harmony with Nature are foundational to both Taoism and TCM. Ancient texts like the Huangdi Neijing (Yellow Emperor's Inner Canon), which dates to the 3rd century BCE, illustrate the integration of Taoist philosophy into medical practice. These texts have been studied and used in Chinese medicine for centuries, providing verifiable

---

195 Zhuangzi and Chuang-Tzu, *Chuang-Tzu: The Inner Chapters*, trans. A. C. Graham, reprint, revised, Hackett Classics (Indianapolis: Hackett Publishing Company, Inc., 2001).

196 Yuanji Huang, *Tao Te Ching: The Science of Life*, trans. Thomas Cleary, vol. 1, 2020, https://archive.org/details/tao-te-ching-huang-yuanji/page/7/mode/2up.

> links between Taoism and health practices that remain relevant today (Unschuld, 2003).[197]

The Tao Te Ching and Zhuangzi remain central to Taoist thought, with historical manuscripts and archaeological findings supporting their authenticity and impact. Unfortunately, once again, there's no tangible and verifiable proof of what happens after you die.

---

197 Paul U. Unschuld, *Huang Di Nei Jing Su Wen: Nature, Knowledge, Imagery in an Ancient Chinese Medical Text*, 1st ed. (Berkeley: University of California Press, 2003), https://doi.org/10.1525/california/9780520233225.001.0001.

Bibliography

Aguirre, Anthony. "Multiverse: Cosmology." In *Encyclopaedia Britannica*, March 27, 2025. https://www.britannica.com/science/multiverse.

Alan, Gould. *Mediumship and Survival: A Century of Investigations*. David & Charles, 1983.

Albom, Mitch. *Tuesdays with Morrie*. 1st ed. Sydney: Hachette Australia, 1998.

Aśvaghoṣa. *Buddhacarita, or, Acts of the Buddha: Complete Sanskrit Text with English Translation*. New enl. ed. 1984, Repr. Delhi: Motilal Banarsidass, 2004. https://archive.org/details/buddhacaritaorac0000asva.

Alexander, Eben. *Proof of Heaven: A Neurosurgeon's Journey into the Afterlife*. New York: Simon & Schuster, 2012.

Basham, Arthur Llewellyn, and Brian K. Smith. "Hinduism | Origin, History, Beliefs, Gods, & Facts." In *Encyclopaedia Britannica*. Chicago: Encyclopaedia Britannica, Inc., April 3, 2025. https://www.britannica.com/topic/Hinduism.

Biran, Avraham. *Biblical Dan*. Jerusalem: Hebrew Union College, 1994. https://www.goodreads.com/book/show/5957331.

Biden, Joe. *Promise Me, Dad: A Year of Hope, Hardship, and Purpose*. New York: Flatiron Books, 2017. https://us.macmillan.com/books/9781250171696/promisemedad/

Bostrom, Nick. "Nick Bostrom's Home Page." Nick Bostrom, 2025. https://nickbostrom.com/.

———. "The Simulation Argument." *The Philosophical Quarterly* 53, no. 211 (2003): 243–55. https://www.simulation-argument.com/.

Brown, Kathryn Selig. "Life of the Buddha." Museum educational resource / Art history essay. Timeline of Art History, October 1, 2003. https://www.metmuseum.org/toah/hd/buda/hd_buda.htm.

Burchard, Brendon. *The 6 Habits of Growth*. Original Recording Audiobook, 2022. https://www.audible.com/pd/The-6-Habits-of-Growth-Audiobook/B0BBY76WP4.

Bushman, Richard Lyman. "Joseph Smith | Biography & Facts." In *Encyclopædia Britannica*. Chicago: Encyclopædia Britannica, Inc., March 27, 2025. https://www.britannica.com/biography/Joseph-Smith-American-religious-leader-1805-1844.

———. *Joseph Smith: Rough Stone Rolling*. Illustrated, Reprint. Vintage. New York: Knopf Doubleday Publishing Group, 2005.

Capra, Fritjof. *The Tao of Physics: An Exploration of the Parallels between Modern Physics and Eastern Mysticism*. Reprint. Boston: Shambhala, 2010.

Church of Jesus Christ of Latter-day Saints. "Section 119, The Law of Tithing." *Doctrine and Covenants Student Manual*, July 8, 1838.

Cole, W. Owen, and Piara Singh Sambhi. *The Sikhs: Their Religious Beliefs and Practices*. 2nd Revised. The Sussex Library of Religious Beliefs & Practice. Liverpool: Liverpool University Press, 1998.

Dalai Lama. *The Dalai Lama's Little Book of Buddhism*. Newburyport, MA: Red Wheel Weiser, 2015.

Deepak Chopra LLC. "Deepak Chopra- Official Website," 2025. https://www.deepakchopra.com/.

Dehejia, Vidya. *Indian Art*. Paperback. London / New York: Phaidon Press, 1997.

DeWoskin, Kenneth J. *Doctors, Diviners, and Magicians of Ancient China: Biographies of Fang-Shih*. Illustrated. Columbia Asian Studies Series: Translations from the Oriental Classics. New York: Columbia University Press, 1983. https://archive.org/details/isbn_023105596x.

Diniejko, Andrzej. "Sir Arthur Conan Doyle and Victorian Spiritualism." The Victorian Web, 2013. https://victorianweb.org/authors/doyle/spiritualism.html.

Division of Perceptual Studies. "Study of Reincarnation." UVA School of Medicine – Division of Perceptual Studies, 2025. https://med.virginia.edu/perceptual-studies/publications/books/study-of-reincarnation/.

Does God Exist? William Lane Craig vs. Christopher Hitchens - Full Debate [HD], 2014. https://www.youtube.com/watch?v=0tYm41hb48o.

Does Neil deGrasse Tyson Believe in the Multiverse? Video. YouTube, 2022. https://www.youtube.com/watch?v=B5jel0q2Ygk.

Doniger, Wendy. "Veda | Definition, Scriptures, Books, & Facts." In *Encyclopaedia Britannica*. Chicago: Encyclopaedia Britannica, Inc., March 13, 2025. https://www.britannica.com/topic/Veda.

Doty, James R. *Mind Magic: The Neuroscience of Manifestation and How It Changes Everything*. 1st ed. New York: Avery, 2024.

Douglass, Herbert E. *Messenger of the Lord: The Prophetic Ministry of Ellen G. White*. Nampa, ID: Pacific Press Publishing Association, 1998.

Doyle, Arthur Conan. "Life After Death: An Interview with Sir Arthur Conan Doyle." Arthur Conan Doyle Official Website, March 1919. https://www.arthur-conan-doyle.com/index.php?title=Life_after_Death.

Doyle, Sir Arthur Conan. *The History of Spiritualism (Vols. 1 and 2)*. United States: Curious Publications, 2021. History-Spiritualism-Vols-Arthur-Conan/dp/1735320137

Dunnett, Warwick. *Poker Wizards: Poker Strategy from the World's Top No-Limit Hold'em Players*. Cardoza, 2008. https://www.amazon.com/Poker-Wizards-strategy-No-Limit-Players/dp/1580422276.

Dunnett, Harrison Subversive. *Speak My Mind; From the Bay; Grindin*. Subvers!ve Music. https://linktr.ee/subversivemusic.

Encyclopaedia Britannica Editors. "Adhan | Words, Call to Prayer, & History." In *Encyclopaedia Britannica*. Chicago: Encyclopaedia Britannica, Inc., March 6, 2025. https://www.britannica.com/topic/adhan.

———. "Ellen Gould Harmon White | American Religious Leader & Prophetess." In *Encyclopædia Britannica*. Chicago: Encyclopædia Britannica, Inc., 2025. https://www.britannica.com/biography/Ellen-Gould-Harmon-White.

Encyclopædia Britannica Editors. "Kabbala | Definition, Beliefs, & Facts." In *Encyclopædia Britannica*. Chicago: Encyclopædia Britannica, Inc., March 25, 2025. https://www.britannica.com/topic/Kabbala.

Encyclopaedia Britannica Editors. "Paticca-Samuppada | Buddhist Doctrine of Dependent Origination." In *Encyclopaedia*

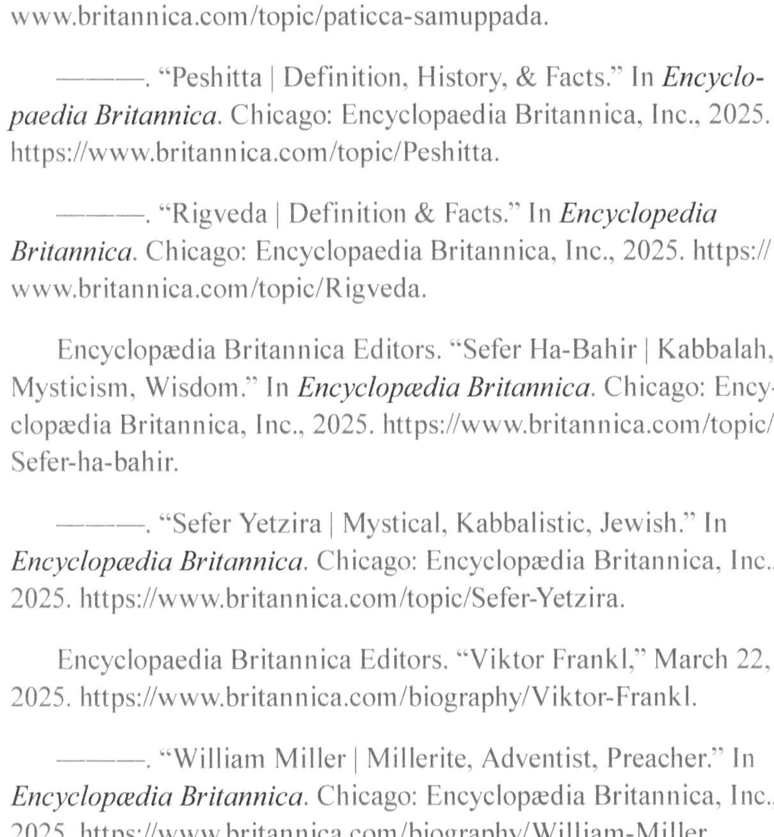

Britannica. Chicago: Encyclopaedia Britannica, Inc., 2025. https://www.britannica.com/topic/paticca-samuppada.

———. "Peshitta | Definition, History, & Facts." In *Encyclopaedia Britannica*. Chicago: Encyclopaedia Britannica, Inc., 2025. https://www.britannica.com/topic/Peshitta.

———. "Rigveda | Definition & Facts." In *Encyclopedia Britannica*. Chicago: Encyclopaedia Britannica, Inc., 2025. https://www.britannica.com/topic/Rigveda.

Encyclopædia Britannica Editors. "Sefer Ha-Bahir | Kabbalah, Mysticism, Wisdom." In *Encyclopædia Britannica*. Chicago: Encyclopædia Britannica, Inc., 2025. https://www.britannica.com/topic/Sefer-ha-bahir.

———. "Sefer Yetzira | Mystical, Kabbalistic, Jewish." In *Encyclopædia Britannica*. Chicago: Encyclopædia Britannica, Inc., 2025. https://www.britannica.com/topic/Sefer-Yetzira.

Encyclopaedia Britannica Editors. "Viktor Frankl," March 22, 2025. https://www.britannica.com/biography/Viktor-Frankl.

———. "William Miller | Millerite, Adventist, Preacher." In *Encyclopædia Britannica*. Chicago: Encyclopædia Britannica, Inc., 2025. https://www.britannica.com/biography/William-Miller.

Encyclopaedia Judaica Editors. "Sefer Ha-Bahir." In *Encyclopaedia Judaica*. Detroit: The Gale Group, 2008. https://www.jewishvirtuallibrary.org/sefer-ha-bahir.

Endowment Lecture Series Dr Alex Hankey PART 1, 2021. https://www.youtube.com/watch?v=vgfDFcriwH0.

Ep. 6: Joseph Campbell and the Power of Myth -- "Masks of Eternity." Joseph Campbell and The Power of Myth, 1988. https://billmoyers.com/content/ep-6-joseph-campbell-and-the-power-of-myth-masks-of-eternity-audio/.

Esposito, John L. *What Everyone Needs to Know About Islam*. 2nd ed. What Everyone Needs to Know®. New York: Oxford University Press, 2011. http://dx.doi.org/10.1093/wentk/9780199794133.001.0001.

Fenech, Louis E., and W. H. McLeod. *Historical Dictionary of Sikhism*. Historical Dictionaries of Religions, Philosophies, and Movements. Lanham: Rowman & Littlefield Publishers, 2014. Historical-Dictionary-Dictionaries-Religions-Philosophies/dp/1442236000.

Fenwick, Peter, and Elizabeth Fenwick. *The Art of Dying*. London: Continuum, 2008.

Finkelstein, Israel, and Neil Asher Silberman. *The Bible Unearthed: Archaeology's New Vision of Ancient Israel and the Origin of Its Sacred Texts*. Paperback. New York: Free Press, 2002.

Frankl, Viktor E. *Man's Search for Meaning*. Beacon Press, 2006. https://www.viktorfrankl.org/books_by_vf.html#English.

Fraser, Gary E. *Diet, Life Expectancy, and Chronic Disease: Studies of Seventh-Day Adventists and Other Vegetarians*. 1st ed. New York: Oxford University Press, 2003. https://global.oup.com/academic/product/diet-life-expectancy-and-chronic-disease-9780195113242?cc=pk&lang=en&.

Freeman, Aaron. "Planning Ahead Can Make a Difference in the End." All Things Considered, June 1, 2005. https://www.npr.org/transcripts/4675953.

Friedman, Richard Elliott. *Who Wrote the Bible?* Illustrated, Reprint, Revised. New York: HarperCollins, 1997.

Frontiers Media Release. "Does Our Life Flash before Our Eyes during Death?" *Scimex*, February 22, 2022. https://www.scimex.org/newsfeed/does-our-life-flash-before-our-eyes-during-death.

Gadgil, Madhav, and V. D. Vartak. "Studies on Sacred Groves along Western Ghats in Maharashtra and Goa: Role of Belief and Folklores." In *Glimpses of Indian Ethnobotany*, edited by S. K. Jain, 272–78. Bombay, India: Oxford University Press, 1981. https://portals.iucn.org/library/node/26468.

Girardot, N. J. *Myth and Meaning in Early Taoism: The Theme of Chaos (Hun-Tun)*. Illustrated, Reprint. Vol. 11. Hermeneutics Series; Hermeneutics, Studies in the History of Religions 1; 11. Berkeley, California: University of California Press, 1988. https://www.cambridge.org/core/journals/bulletin-of-the-school-of-oriental-and-african-studies/article/abs/n-j-girardot-myth-and-meaning-in-early-taoism-the-theme-of-chaos-huntun-xiii-422-pp-berkeley-los-angeles-and-london-university-of-california-press-1983/8AAF44C22EC97956314A2CBD08E43EA6.

Givens, Terryl. *By the Hand of Mormon: The American Scripture That Launched a New World Religion*. Paperback. Oxford; New York: Oxford University Press, 2002. https://archive.org/details/byhandofmormonam0000give_g9i5.

Goswami, Amit. *The Self-Aware Universe: How Consciousness Creates the Material World*. Illustrated. East Rutherford: Tarcher, 1995.

Greyson, Bruce. "Near-Death Experiences." In *Varieties of Anomalous Experience: Examining the Scientific Evidence*, edited by Etzel Cardena, Steven J. Lynn, and Stanley Krippner, 2nd ed., 333–67. Washington, DC: American Psychological Association, 2014. https://doi.org/10.1037/14258-012.

Hameroff, Stuart. "'Orch OR' Is the Most Complete, and Most Easily Falsifiable Theory of Consciousness." *Cognitive Neuroscience* 12, no. 2 (2021): 74–76. https://doi.org/10.1080/17588928.2020.1839037.

Harper, Douglas. "Islam (n.)." In *Online Etymology Dictionary*. Online Etymology Dictionary, 2025. https://www.etymonline.com/word/Islam.

Harvey, Peter. *An Introduction to Buddhism: Teachings, History and Practices*. 1st ed. Introduction to Religion. Cambridge, UK: Cambridge University Press, 1990. https://www.goodreads.com/book/show/418423.An_Introduction_to_Buddhism.

Hawking, Stephen. *Brief Answers to the Big Questions*. Reprint. New York: John Murray, 2018. https://www.goodreads.com/book/show/40277241-brief-answers-to-the-big-questions.

Holden, Janice Miner, Bruce Greyson, and Debbie James, eds. *The Handbook of Near-Death Experiences: Thirty Years of Investigation*. 2nd Printing. Santa Barbara, CA: Praeger, 2009. https://search.worldcat.org/title/The-handbook-of-near-death-experiences-:-thirty-years-of-investigation/oclc/876613447.

Huang, Yuanji. *Tao Te Ching: The Science of Life*. Translated by Thomas Cleary. Vol. 1, 2020. https://archive.org/details/tao-te-ching-huang-yuanji/page/7/mode/2up.

Jones, Jeffrey M. "U.S. Church Membership Falls Below Majority for First Time." *Gallup*, March 29, 2021. https://news.gallup.com/poll/341963/church-membership-falls-below-majority-first-time.aspx.

Kabat-Zinn, Jon. *Wherever You Go, There You Are: Mindfulness Meditation in Everyday Life*. 10th anniversary ed. New York, N.Y.: MJF Books, 2005. https://www.barnesandnoble.com/w/wherever-you-go-there-you-are-jon-kabat-zinn-phd/1102636030.

Kausiki Books. *Garuda Purana: Pretha Khanda: English Translation Only without Slokas*. Vol. 3. Kausiki Books, 2021.

Keyes, Katherine M., Charissa Pratt, Sandro Galea, Katie A. McLaughlin, Karestan C. Koenen, and M. Katherine Shear. "The Burden of Loss: Unexpected Death of a Loved One and Psychiatric Disorders across the Life Course in a National Study." *The American Journal of Psychiatry* 171, no. 8 (August 1, 2014): 864–71. https://doi.org/10.1176/appi.ajp.2014.13081132.

Knight, George R. *A Brief History of Seventh-Day Adventists*. illustrated ed. Hagerstown, MD: Review and Herald Publishing, 2000. https://adventistbookcenter.com/books/a-brief-history-of-seventh-day-adventists.html.

Kohn, Livia. *Early Chinese Mysticism: Philosophy and Soteriology in the Taoist Tradition*. 1st ed. Princeton, New Jersey: Princeton University Press, 1991. https://press.princeton.edu/books/paperback/9780691020655/early-chinese-mysticism?srsltid=AfmBOopBDMCZOo5seqjF_BUuPt-jnv57AraF2agGcxHuD09oid3j_SOK.

Kornfield, Jack. "The Ancient Heart of Forgiveness." *Greater Good Science Center*, August 23, 2011. https://greatergood.berkeley.edu/article/item/the_ancient_heart_of_forgiveness.

Krishnananda, Swami. "Chapter IV, Section 4 - Fourth Brahmana: The Soul of the Unrealised After Death." In *The Brihadaranyaka Upanishad*. Rishikesh, India: The Divine Life Society, 1983. https://www.swami-krishnananda.org/brdup/brhad_IV-04.html.

Kübler-Ross, Elisabeth, David Kessler, and Maria Shriver. *On Grief and Grieving: Finding the Meaning of Grief Through the Five Stages of Loss*. New York: Scribner, 2014.

Kübler-Ross, Elisabeth. *On Life After Death*. Berkeley: Celestial Arts, 1991.

Ladinsky, Daniel. *A Year with Hafiz: Daily Contemplations*. New York: Penguin Publishing Group, 2011.

Laozi. *Lao-Tzu: Te-Tao Ching: A New Translation Based on the Recently Discovered Ma-Wang-Tui Texts*. Translated by Robert G. Henricks. New York: Ballantine Books, 1989. https://archive.org/details/laotzutetaoching0000laoz/mode/2up.

Learn about the Many-Worlds Picture of Quantum Mechanics. Video. Encyclopaedia Britannica, 2025. https://www.britannica.com/video/Description-worlds-picture-quantum-mechanics/-204065.

Leininger, Bruce, and Andrea Leininger. *Soul Survivor: The Reincarnation of a World War II Fighter Pilot*. New York: Grand Central Publishing, 2010.

Levine, Lee I. *Jerusalem: Portrait of the City in the Second Temple Period (BCE–70 CE)*. Illustrated. Philadelphia: Jewish Publication Society, 2002.

Liverani, Mario. *Israel's History and the History of Israel*. London; Oakville, CT: Equinox, 2005. https://archive.org/details/israelshistoryhi0000live/page/n3/mode/2up.

Lommel, Pim van. "Near-Death Experiences: The Experience of the Self as Real and Not as an Illusion." *Annals of the New York Academy of Sciences* 1234, no. 1 (October 2011): 19–28. https://doi.org/10.1111/j.1749-6632.2011.06080.x.

Lonnerstrand, Sture. *I Have Lived Before: The True Story of the Reincarnation of Shanti Devi*. American ed. Huntsville, AR: Ozark Mountain Pub, 1998. https://archive.org/details/ihavelivedbefore00stur/page/n3/mode/2up.

Lopez, Donald S. "Four Noble Truths." In *Encyclopaedia Britannica*. Chicago: Encyclopaedia Britannica, Inc., February 24, 2025. https://www.britannica.com/topic/Four-Noble-Truths.

Mann, Gurinder Singh. *The Making of Sikh Scripture*. 1st ed. New York: Oxford

University Press, 2001. https://global.oup.com/academic/product/the-making-of-sikh-scripture-9780195130249?cc=pk&lang=en&.

Maisel, Eric. *A Writer's Paris: A Guided Journey for the Creative Soul.* Cincinnati: Writer's Digest Books, 2005.

Marshall, Sir John, ed. *Mohenjo-Daro and the Indus Civilization: Being an Official Account of Archæological Excavations at Mohenjo-Daro Carried Out by the Government of India Between the Years 1922 AD 1927.* Vol. 1. London: A. Probsthain, 1931. https://archive.org/details/in.ernet.dli.2015.722.

Masci, David. "How Income Varies among U.S. Religious Groups." Pew Research Center, October 11, 2016. https://www.pewresearch.org/fact-tank/2016/10/11/how-income-varies-among-u-s-religious-groups/.

May, Edwin. "Curriculum Vitae of Edwin May." Academia.edu, 2025. https://independent.academia.edu/EdwinMay/CurriculumVitae.

McLeod, William Hearst. *The Sikhs: History, Religion, and Society.* Lectures on the History of Religions 14. New York: Columbia University Press, 1989. https://search.worldcat.org/title/1025956184.

McLeod, William Hewat. "Guru Nanak | First Sikh Guru, Biography, Teachings, & Facts." In *Encyclopædia Britannica.* Chicago: Encyclopædia Britannica, Inc., April 11, 2025. https://www.britannica.com/biography/Guru-Nanak.

———. *Gurū Nānak and the Sikh Religion.* Reprint. Oxford India Paperbacks. Oxford: Clarendon Press, 1968. https://search.worldcat.org/title/1015130383.

Melton, J. Gordon. "Spiritualism | Religion, Beliefs, Practices, & History." In *Encyclopedia Britannica.* Chicago, IL:

Encyclopædia Britannica, Inc., February 22, 2025. https://www.britannica.com/topic/spiritualism-religion.

Meulenbeld, Gerrit Jan. *A History of Indian Medical Literature*. Vol. 1, part 2. 5 volumes, 3 parts (1A, 1B, 2A, 2B, 3) vols. Groningen Oriental Studies. Groningen: E. Forsten, 1999. https://archive.org/details/Meulenbeld-HIML/HIML%201A%20/.

Michaelson, Jay. "Was Obama Right about the Crusades and Islamic Extremism? (ANALYSIS)." *The Washington Post*, February 6, 2015, sec. Religion. https://www.washingtonpost.com/national/religion/was-obama-right-about-the-crusades-and-islamic-extremism-analysis/2015/02/06/3670628a-ae46-11e4-8876-460b1144cbc1_story.html.

MIT Health. "FAQ: Common Reactions to Traumatic Events." MIT Health, April 21, 2025. https://medical.mit.edu/faqs/mental-health/common-reactions-to-traumatic-events.

Mobbs, Dean, and Caroline Watt. "There Is Nothing Paranormal About Near-Death Experiences." *Trends in Cognative Science* 15, no. 10 (October 2011): 447–49. https://doi.org/10.1016/j.tics.2011.07.010.

Moffitt, Phillip. *Dancing with Life: Buddhist Insights for Finding Meaning and Joy in the Face of Suffering*. Emmaus, Pa.; Godalming: Rodale : Melia [distributor], 2012. http://www.vlebooks.com/vleweb/product/openreader?id=none&isbn=9781605298962.

———. "The Art and Practice of Forgiveness (PM3D21)." Meditation retreat presented at the Spirit Rock Retreat Program, Spirit Rock Meditation Center, November 21, 2021. https://spirit-rock.secure.retreat.guru/program/the-art-and-practice-of-forgiveness-pm3d21/.

Mukundananda, Swami. "Chapter 2: Sānkhya Yog | Verse 22-23." In *Bhagavad Gita - The Song of God*. Jagadguru Kripaluji Yog, 2014. https://www.holy-bhagavad-gita.org/chapter/2.

Mumford, Michael D, Andrew M Rose, and David A Goslin. "An Evaluation of Remote Viewing: Research and Applications." The American Institutes for Research, September 29, 1995.

Nasr, Seyyed Hossein. *The Heart of Islam: Enduring Values for Humanity*. San Francisco, California: HarperSanFrancisco, 2002. https://archive.org/details/heartofislamendu0000nasr.

Nasr, Seyyed Hossein, and Asma Afsaruddin. "Ali | Biography, History, & Facts." In *Encyclopaedia Britannica*, February 20, 2025. https://www.britannica.com/biography/Ali-Muslim-caliph.

Neusner, Jacob. *The Talmud: A Close Encounter*. Minneapolis, MN: Augsburg Fortress, 1992. https://www.abebooks.com/Talmud-Close-Encounter-Neusner-Jacob-Augsburg/31876679941/bd.

Newton, Michael. *Journey of Souls: Case Studies of Life Between Lives*. 1st ed. St. Paul, Minn: Llewellyn Publications, 1994.

Newton Institute, Michael. "Home Page." Michael Newton Institute, 2025. https://www.newtoninstitute.org.

Oakes, Sean. "Dependent Origination." Meditation center. Spirit Rock Meditation Center – Practice Guides, January 1, 2023. https://www.spiritrock.org/practice-guides/dependent-origination.

Olivelle, Patrick. "Karma | Indian Philosophy & Its Impact on Life." In *Encyclopaedia Britannica*. Chicago: Encyclopaedia Britannica, Inc., March 28, 2025. https://www.britannica.com/topic/Karma.

———. "Moksha | Salvation, Dharma & Karma." In *Encyclopaedia Britannica*. Chicago: Encyclopaedia Britannica, Inc., 2025. https://www.britannica.com/topic/moksha-Indian-religion.

OpenAI. *ChatGPT* (large language model). San Francisco: OpenAI, 2025. https://chat.openai.com

Ostaseski, Frank. "Facing Death with Courage." Presented at the Radical Compassion and Courage, 1440 Multiversity, Scotts Valley, CA, October 7, 2018. https://www.1440.org/blog/dont-wait-talking-about-radical-compassion-and-courage-with-frank-ostaseski.

———. "Frank Ostaseski Home Page." Frank Ostaseski, January 25, 2025. https://frankostaseski.com/.

———. *The Five Invitations: Discovering What Death Can Teach Us about Living Fully*. Deckle Edge (Hardcover). New York: Flatiron Books, 2017.

Patañjali. "Chapter 3: Vibhūti Pāda." In *The Yoga Sūtras of Patañjali*, translated by Edwin F. Bryant, 1st ed., 672. New York: Farrar, Straus and Giroux, 2015. https://patanjaliyogasutra.in/vibhooti-pada-3-55/.

Perry, Marsha. "Arthur Conan Doyle and Spiritualism." Conan Doyle Info, October 7, 2024. https://www.conandoyleinfo.com/life-conan-doyle/conan-doyle-and-spiritualism/.

Pew Research Center. "American Muslims' Views on Terrorism and Concerns About Extremism." Washington, D.C.: Pew Research Center, July 26, 2017. https://www.pewresearch.org/religion/2017/07/26/terrorism-and-concerns-about-extremism/.

———. "The Changing Global Religious Landscape." Research Report. Washington, D.C.: Pew Research Center, April 5, 2017. https://www.pewresearch.org/religion/2017/04/05/the-changing-global-religious-landscape/.

Pressfield, Steven. *The War of Art: Winning the Inner Creative Battle*. London: Orion, 2003. https://www.goodreads.com/book/show/24856285.

Preston, Charles, and Dylan Shulman. "Spiritism | Beliefs, Practices, & History." In *Encyclopedia Britannica*. Chicago, IL: Encyclopædia Britannica, Inc., November 20, 2024. https://www.britannica.com/topic/Spiritism.

Pruitt, Sarah. "Who Wrote the Bible?" HISTORY, July 17, 2020. https://www.history.com/news/who-wrote-the-bible.

Quran.com Team. "Quran Surah Az-Zumar [39:42] — Juz 24 / Hizb 47." Quran.com, 2025. https://quran.com/39/42?translations=18,19,20,21,22,84,95,85,101.

Radin, Dean I. *Supernormal: Science, Yoga, and the Path to Extraordinary Psychic Abilities*. Illustrated. New York, NY: Deepak Chopra, 2013.

Rao, Shikaripur Ranganatha. *Lost City of Dvaraka*. New Delhi: Aditya Prakashan, 1999.

Redford, Donald B. *Egypt, Canaan, and Israel in Ancient Times*. 1st Princeton Paperback Printing. Princeton, N.J.: Princeton University Press, 1992. https://archive.org/details/egyptcanaanisrae00redf.

ReligionFacts. "Timeline of Buddhism." ReligionFacts, March 17, 2004. https://religionfacts.com/buddhism/.

Reynolds, Frank E., and Donald S. Lopez. "Buddhism | Definition, Beliefs, Origin, Systems, & Practice." In *Encyclopaedia Britannica*. Chicago, IL: Encyclopaedia Britannica, Inc., April 7, 2025. https://www.britannica.com/topic/Buddhism.

Robert Segal. "Joseph Campbell | Biography, Books, & Facts." In *Encyclopaedia Britannica*. Encyclopaedia Britannica, Inc., March 22, 2025. https://www.britannica.com/biography/Joseph-Campbell-American-author.

Robinet, Isabelle. *Taoism: Growth of a Religion*. Translated by Phyllis Brooks. First English edition. Stanford, California: Stanford

University Press, 1997. https://www.sup.org/books/asian-studies/taoism.

Rogers, Kara. "Apophenia | Description, Forms, Gambler's Fallacy, & Intervention." In *Encyclopaedia Britannica*. Chicago: Encyclopaedia Britannica, March 13, 2025. https://www.britannica.com/topic/apophenia.

Said, Sammy. "The 10 Richest Religions in the World." *Church and State* (blog), December 8, 2013. https://churchandstate.org.uk/2016/06/the-10-richest-religions-in-the-world/.

Stockler, Asher. "Mormon Church Stockpiled $100 Billion Intended for Charities and Misled LDS Members, Whistleblower Says." *Newsweek*, December 17, 2019. https://www.newsweek.com/mormon-church-stockpiled-100-billion-intended-charities-misled-lds-members-whistleblower-says-1477809.

Seidel, Anna K., and Roger T. Ames. "Taoism | Definition, Origin, Philosophy, Beliefs, & Facts." In *Encyclopaedia Britannica*. Chicago: Encyclopaedia Britannica, Inc., April 15, 2025. https://www.britannica.com/topic/Taoism.

Seventh-day Adventist Sabbath School Net. "Death and Resurrection - Seventh-Day Adventist Fundamental Belief 26." *Sabath School Net* (blog), June 2, 2011.

Shu, Frank H. "Cosmic Microwave Background | Electromagnetic Radiation & Big Bang Theory." In *Encyclopaedia Britannica*. Chicago: Encyclopaedia Britannica, Inc., April 8, 2025. https://www.britannica.com/science/cosmic-microwave-background.

———. "Cosmology - Inflation, Expansion, Big Bang." In *Encyclopaedia Britannica*. Chicago: Encyclopaedia Britannica, Inc., March 23, 2025. https://www.britannica.com/science/cosmology-astronomy/Inflation.

Simon, Linda. "Psychical Research and the Science of the Mind." Harvard Library, 2023. https://library.harvard.edu/sites/default/files/static/onlineexhibits/james/psychical.html.

Singh, Nikky-Guninder Kaur. *The Name of My Beloved: Verses of the Sikh Gurus*. Sacred Literature. New Delhi: Penguin Books, 2003. https://www.goodreads.com/book/show/2708762-the-name-of-my-beloved.

Sorenson, John L. *An Ancient American Setting for the Book of Mormon*. Salt Lake City: Deseret Book Company, 1996.

Southerton, Simon G. *Losing a Lost Tribe: Native Americans, DNA, and the Mormon Church*. Paperback. Salt Lake City, Utah: Signature Books, 2004.

Stefon, Matt. "Bardo Thödol." In *Encyclopaedia Britannica*. Chicago: Encyclopaedia Britannica, Inc., 2025. https://www.britannica.com/topic/Bardo-Thodol.

———. "Dao | Chinese Philosophy & Religion." In *Encyclopaedia Britannica*. Chicago: Encyclopaedia Britannica, Inc., February 18, 2025. https://www.britannica.com/topic/dao.

———. "Wuwei | Daoism, Non-Action & Spontaneity." In *Encyclopaedia Britannica*. Chicago: Encyclopaedia Britannica, Inc., 2025. https://www.britannica.com/topic/wuwei-Chinese-philosophy.

———. "Yama | Ruler of Dead, Judge of Souls & Lord of Dharma." In *Encyclopaedia Britannica*. Chicago: Encyclopaedia Britannica, Inc., 2025. https://www.britannica.com/topic/Yama-Hindu-god.

Stevenson, Ian. *Twenty Cases Suggestive of Reincarnation*. 2nd ed. Charlottesville: University Press of Virginia, 1974. / Twenty-Cases-Suggestive-Reincarnation-2nd/dp/081390546X.

Templeton. "Home | Templeton World Charity Foundation, Inc." Organizational website. Templeton World Charity Foundation, Inc., 2025. https://www.templetonworldcharity.org/.

The Associated Press. "About 333,000 Children Were Abused within France's Catholic Church, a Report Finds." *NPR*, October 5, 2021. https://www.npr.org/2021/10/05/1043302348/france-catholic-church-sexual-abuse-report-children.

The Wise Apple. "Taoism." National Geographic Education, July 23, 2024. https://education.nationalgeographic.org/resource/taoism/.

Tolle, Eckhart. 2018. A New Earth: The Life-Changing Follow up to The Power of Now. "My No.1 Guru Will Always Be Eckhart Tolle." Chris Evans. London: Michael Joseph.

Tucker, Jim B. "Children's Reports of Past-Life Memories: A Review." *EXPLORE* 4, no. 4 (July 2008): 244–48. https://doi.org/10.1016/j.explore.2008.04.001.

———. *Return to Life: Extraordinary Cases of Children Who Remember Past Lives*. First St. Martin's Griffin edition. New York: St. Martin's Griffin, 2015. https://med.virginia.edu/perceptual-studies/publications/books-by-dops-faculty/study-of-reincarnation/return-to-life-extraordinary-cases-of-children-who-remember-past-lives/.

Tuszyński, Jack and Templeton Staff. "Is Consciousness a Quantum Phenomenon? Recent Findings Lend Some Support to Orch OR Theory." Organizational website. *Templeton World Charity Foundation Blog* (blog), June 19, 2023. https://www.templetonworldcharity.org/blog/interview-jack-tuszynski-aarat-kalra.

Unschuld, Paul U. *Huang Di Nei Jing Su Wen: Nature, Knowledge, Imagery in an Ancient Chinese Medical Text*. 1st ed. Berkeley: University of California Press, 2003. https://doi.org/10.1525/california/9780520233225.001.0001.

Vaidyanathan, Venkatesh. "What Is The Observer Effect In Quantum Mechanics?" ScienceABC, May 10, 2019. https://www.scienceabc.com/pure-sciences/observer-effect-quantum-mechanics.html.

Vermes, Geza. *The Complete Dead Sea Scrolls in English*. 7th ed. London, United Kingdom: Penguin Books Ltd, 2011. https://www.kennys.ie/mind-body-and-spirit/the-complete-dead-sea-scrolls-in-english-7th-edition-penguin-classics.

Vicente, Raul, Michael Rizzuto, Can Sarica, Kazuaki Yamamoto, Mohammed Sadr, Tarun Khajuria, Mostafa Fatehi, et al. "Enhanced Interplay of Neuronal Coherence and Coupling in the Dying Human Brain." *Frontiers in Aging Neuroscience* 14 (February 22, 2022): 813531. https://doi.org/10.3389/fnagi.2022.813531.

Watt, William Montgomery, and Nicolai Sinai. "Sīrat Muḥammad Rasūl Allāh." In *Encyclopaedia Britannica*. Chicago: Encyclopaedia Britannica, Inc., February 25, 2025. https://www.britannica.com/topic/Sirat-Muhammad-rasul-Allah.

Wehrstein, KM. "Shanti Devi (Reincarnation Case)." In *Psi Encyclopedia*. London: The Society for Psychical Research, September 15, 2021. https://psi-encyclopedia.spr.ac.uk/articles/shanti-devi-reincarnation-case.

Weiss, Brian. "Brian L. Weiss, M.D." Brian Weiss, 2024. https://www.brianweiss.com/.

What Really Happens When You Die: End-of-Life Phenomena. Thanatos.TV,2018. https://www.youtube.com/watch?v=78SkTuk8Zd4&feature=youtube.

White, Ellen Gould. *The Great Controversy*. Vol. 5. Conflict of the Ages. Mountain View, CA: Pacific Press Publishing Association, 1911. https://text.egwwritings.org/book/b132.

Whitfield, S. "Review of T'ai-Shang Kan-Ying P'ien: Lao-Tzu's Treatise on the Response of the Tao." *Journal of the Royal Asiatic Society* 6, no. 1 (1996): 139. https://doi.org/10.1017/S1356186300015194.

Williams, Mark, John Teasdale, Zindel Segal, and Jon Kabat-Zinn. *The Mindful Way through Depression: Freeing Yourself from Chronic Unhappiness*. New York: Guilford Press, 2007.

Wong, Eva. *The Shambhala Guide to Taoism*. Shambhala Guides. Boston: Shambhala Publications, Inc., 2011. https://www.goodreads.com/book/show/620675.The_Shambhala_Guide_to_Taoism.

Zhuangzi and Chuang-Tzu. *Chuang-Tzu: The Inner Chapters*. Translated by A. C. Graham. Reprint, Revised. Hackett Classics. Indianapolis: Hackett Publishing Company, Inc., 2001. / Chuang-Tzu-Inner-Chapters-Hackett-Classics/dp/0872205819#.

Zukav, Gary. *Dancing Wu Li Masters: An Enlightening Exploration of Quantum Physics, Eastern Philosophy, and the Interplay of Science and Spirituality*. Reprint. New York: HarperOne, 2009.

Glossary

Abrahamic
Relating to religions tracing their origins to Abraham: Judaism, Christianity, Islam.

Adhan
Islamic call to prayer announced just prior to the time of prayer, traditionally from the minaret of a mosque.

Anatta
Buddhist concept of *non-self*; no unchanging, permanent self or soul.

Atman
In Hinduism, the eternal self or soul beyond ego or body.

Bardo
In Tibetan Buddhism, the transitional state between death and rebirth.

Bhagavad Gita
Sacred Hindu scripture; dialogue between Krishna and Arjuna on the nature of duty.

Bhakti
Devotional worship directed to one supreme deity in Hinduism.

Clairvoyant
A person claiming to have the supernatural ability to perceive beyond the five senses.

Conditionality
Buddhist concept that all phenomena arise dependent on causes and conditions.

Consciousness
The state of being aware—including thoughts, feelings, and surroundings.

Deity
A god or divine being.

Existential
Relating to human existence, often questioning life's meaning or purpose.

Hajj (journey)
The Islamic pilgrimage to Mecca that is required of all Muslim men and women once in their lifetime if they are able.

Henotheistic
Belief in one primary god without denying the existence of others.

Kabbalah
Jewish mystical tradition interpreting divine nature and the universe.

Karma
Hindu and Buddhist belief that actions determine future experiences.

Ketuvin
Hebrew Bible's third section; includes writings like Psalms and Proverbs.

Khalsa
The collective body of initiated Sikhs, founded by Guru Gobind Singh.

LDS Church
Common name for The Church of Jesus Christ of Latter-day Saints.

LIDAR
Acronym for *light detection and ranging*; a technology that uses laser light to map distances and create 3D images.

Mahayana
A major Buddhist tradition emphasizing the aspiration to bring enlightenment to all beings, carried out with the help of bodhisattvas.

Microtubules
Microscopically small tubes as referenced in Orch-OR theory.

Moksa
Alternate spelling of moksha; liberation from the cycle of reincarnation in Hindu belief.

Moksha
Hindu liberation from the cycle of rebirth; union with the divine.

Monotheism
Belief in a single, all-powerful deity.

Mukti (or Mukhti)
Sikh concept of liberation from the cycle of life and death.

Multiverse
Hypothetical theory proposing the existence of multiple or infinite universes.

NDE (Near Death Experience)
Profound experiences reported by those who have undergone clinical death and returned to life.

Neuroscience
Scientific study of the nervous system, especially the brain and mind.

Nevi'im
The second section of the Hebrew Bible, containing the Prophets.

Nirvana
Buddhist state of liberation from suffering and the cycle of rebirth.

Noble Eightfold Path
Buddhist guide for ending suffering through right living and wisdom.

Nonlocal Consciousness
Theory suggesting consciousness is not confined to the brain or body.

Orch-OR Theory
A theory suggesting consciousness arises from quantum computations in brain microtubules, proposed by Dr Stuart Hameroff and British physicist Sir Roger Penrose.

Peshitta
Standard version of the Bible for churches in the Syriac tradition.

Polytheism
Belief in or worship of multiple deities.

Quantum Mechanics
Physics branch studying particles at atomic and subatomic levels.

Quran
Islam's holy scripture, believed to be the word of Allah.

Quranic
Relating to or derived from the Quran, Islam's holy book.

Reincarnation
Belief in rebirth into a new body after physical death.

Rigveda
Oldest Hindu scripture; collection of hymns in Vedic Sanskrit.

SDA (Seventh Day Adventists)
Christian denomination emphasizing Sabbath observance and Christ's second coming.

SLS (Structured Light Sensor) Camera
Device that projects light patterns to capture 3D shapes digitally.

Salah
The five daily ritual prayers in Islam.

Samsara
Cycle of birth, death, and rebirth in Hinduism and Buddhism.

Sawm (fasting)
Islamic fasting during Ramadan that takes place from dawn to sunset.

Shahada
Islamic declaration of faith: *There is no god but Allah.*

Shia
The second-largest branch of Islam; its religious leadership is descended from Prophet Muhammad's family line.

Sikhism
Indian religion founded by Guru Nanak that advocates equality and monotheism.

Simulation Theory
Hypothesis that reality is a simulated or virtual construct.

Skandhas
In Buddhism, the five aggregates that constitute human existence: form, feeling, perception, formations, consciousness.

Smriti
Traditional Hindu texts, including epics and laws, that have a known author.

Soul
Spiritual or immaterial essence believed to survive bodily death.

Spiritism
Philosophy and belief in communication with spirits through mediums.

Spiritualism
Belief that spirits of the dead can communicate with the living.

Spirituality
Personal or philosophical search for meaning, connection, or the divine.

Sruti
Hindu scriptures, including Vedas, considered to be divinely revealed.

Sunni
Largest denomination in Islam; emphasizes consensus and the prophetic tradition.

Sutras
Scriptural teachings in Hinduism, Buddhism, and Jainism; concise aphorisms.

Talmud
Central Jewish text of rabbinic law and theology.

Tao (Dao)
In Chinese philosophy, the fundamental principle underlying the universe.

The Four Noble Truths
Core Buddhist teaching on suffering, its cause, cessation, and the path to enlightenment (the end of suffering).

Theism
Belief in the existence of a god or gods.

Theravada
Oldest surviving Buddhist school focusing on personal enlightenment and monastic life.

Torah
First five books of the Hebrew Bible; core of Jewish teaching.

T'al Shang Kan Ying P'ien
Taoist text emphasizing moral cause and effect.

Upanishads
Philosophical Hindu texts exploring ultimate reality and human consciousness.

Vedanta
Hindu philosophical school based on teachings of the Upanishads.

Vedas
Ancient sacred texts forming the foundation of Hinduism.

Yama
Yama is the Hindu and Buddhist god of death and justice; *yamas* refers to ethical restraints in yoga philosophy.

Zakat
Obligatory charity in Islam; one of the Five Pillars.

Zhuangzi
Influential Taoist text containing stories that exemplify the nature of the ideal Taoist sage.

Acknowledgments

Thank you, Harrison, for giving me 20 years of brightness, laughter, and excitement. Life will never be the same or as joyous without you.

Thank you to my lovely daughter, who has given me so much love and happiness and continues to deliver.

All my thanks to the following team who helped produce this book:

Artwork and Book Cover by

Jacqueline Dunnett/Dragan Bilic

Interior Design

Dragan Bilic (*dragan74@gmail.com*)

My fantastic assistant:

Margorie Regidor

And my perceptive but always gentle editor:

Lynn Gray

About the Author

Warwick Dunnett is an Australian author of *Dance with Angels* and *Poker Wizards*, an avid poker player, a public speaker, an ex-futures trader on Wall Street, and a retired commercial pilot. He spent the last 22 years of his 45-year flying career as the Captain of Boeing 747s for an air cargo company with operations in 65 countries and substantial contracts with the US military. Sometimes, he circumnavigated the globe twice in his 17-day rotations on adventurous missions to fascinating destinations. Still, he always found his way home for two weeks each month as a devoted, full-time father to his two children, Harrison and Jacqueline.

Sadly, on December 31, 2016, his 20-year-old son passed away. Warwick believes that his son's death was the direct result of medical misconduct by a nurse practitioner, a doctor, and other staff at a rehabilitation centre, who he suggests conspired to over diagnose and over prescribe medications so as to inflate the number of charges to insurance companies. Warwick's son was wrongly medicated with nine different drugs all on the same day. One incorrect diagnosis was for a heroin addiction he did not have, and another for alcohol addiction when he had not consumed alcohol for nearly a month. Eventually the Doctor lost his license for a separate conviction of medical insurance fraud, the Rehab had its license revoked, and the nurse practitioner was found guilty of negligence in her care and treatment.

While navigating a devastating period of deep grief and recovery, Warwick discovered that others who had lost loved ones often found solace on this heartbreaking journey if they held a strong religious or scientific belief system. He chose to seek a faith that resonated with him while also exploring theories and beliefs about what happened to his son's spirit and energy. Unable to find a book that provided a comparative look at various religious and scientific beliefs about life after death, he decided to write one. That journey is chronicled in the memoir, *Dance with Angels*.

Together, Warwick and Harrison's mother, Gail, in honour of Harrison, established a charity called *The Subversive Music Foundation*, which runs camps to help children produce rap and hip-hop music with a positive message and supports other positive messaging for at-risk youth. Information about the foundation can be found at: *SubversiveFoundation.org*. The foundation also launched a second initiative at *TooMuchRx.org* to raise awareness of the overuse of prescription drugs and provide valuable resources for anyone wanting to find safer drug treatment.

Today, when not writing, Warwick enjoys the calm and camaraderie of a floating-home community just north of San Francisco. Whenever possible, he also spends a few months each year in his beloved Sydney, Australia.

Warwick Dunnett can be reached
through any of the following methods:

Websites:

WarwickDunnett.com

Subversivefoundation.org

LighthouseLaneBooks.com

Email:

Support@LightHouseLaneBooks.com

Published Books:

Poker Wizards

Dance with Angels

Upcoming Books releases planned for 2026:

Dance with Angels ~ A Personal Belief Workbook

To obtain a free **weekly newsletter of insights**,
check out our website:

LightHouseLaneBooks.com

www.ingramcontent.com/pod-product-compliance
Lightning Source LLC
Chambersburg PA
CBHW030054110726
47973CB00002B/18